THE CONCISE GUIDE TO WINE AND BLIND TASTING

VOLUME 1

NEEL BURTON

ACHERON PRESS

Chi più conosce
più ama
più amando
più gusta.

Who knows more
loves more
and loving more
tastes/enjoys more.

—Santa Caterina da Siena

THE CONCISE GUIDE TO WINE AND BLIND TASTING

CONTENTS

PREFACE

James Flewellen and I wrote the first edition of this book for varsity blind tasting, to pass down the theory of blind tasting to successive generations of students—rather than having to repeat it orally every October. In the event, the book found a much broader audience, and has even made it into Chinese.

Aside from numerous amendments, revisions, and elaborations, this fourth edition contains new sections on Crete, Lebanon, Sardinia, Tenerife, Sétubal (Portugal), China, and Japan. Despite the concision of the writing (the title is not a misnomer), the book is now over 500 pages long, so that I felt it best to divide it into two volumes. This division makes the book more convenient for wine students: easier to read and annotate, more portable, and more economical for those who wish only for a particular section. It also makes it much more manageable on an e-reader.

The other big change is that I have moved the title to print-on-demand, the quality of which has greatly improved in recent years. Print-on-demand is much greener, since stock no longer has to be shipped all around the world. It is also much niftier, enabling me to make updates and corrections whenever the need arises (although I can't promise to always keep on top of everything).

The one downside of print-on-demand is that the cost of colour printing remains prohibitive. To keep the price down for wine students, the maps in the print edition have returned to black and white. But, should you wish for them, the colour maps are still available here, along with a number of downloadable blind tasting resources: https://neelburton.com/blind-wine-tasting-resources/

Differences of opinion are inevitable in a work such as this, and I may have made a few errors or significant omissions. Do let me know if you spot any, and I will do my best to address them.

Happy tasting, and may this book assist you on this very worthwhile journey.

Neel Burton
Email: neel@neelburton.com
Twitter: @blindtasters

ACKNOWLEDGMENTS

I am very grateful to Dr James Flewellen for his contributions to the first edition of this title. I am also deeply indebted to Dr Hanneke Wilson, the Oxford University blind tasting coach, for all her help throughout the years.

PART I: FOUNDATIONS AND BLIND TASTING

1

THE PHILOSOPHY OF WINE

*W*ine lovers know that wine is so much more than a drink, but how to explain the love of wine to those who do not already share it?

When you uncork a bottle of mature fine wine, what you are drinking is the product of a particular culture and tradition, a particular soil and exposure, a particular climate, the weather in that year, and the love and labour and life of people who may since have died. If you know how to read it, the wine, like a book, will speak to you of all those things and more.

The wine is still changing, still evolving, so much so that no two bottles can ever be quite the same. By now, the stuff has become incredibly complex, almost ethereal. Without seeking to blaspheme, it has become something like the smell and taste of God. This moving mirror, this trans-dimensional distillate, will send shivers down your spine. It will make you burst into laughter. It will knock you right out of yourself, release you from the abstract and self-absorbed prison of the mind and redeliver you into the magic and mystery of the world as though you had just been reborn. Remarkably, every wine that can do this does it in its own way, so that there can be no end to your journey.

To get the most out of wine, you will need to sharpen your senses, and you will need to deepen your knowledge. By wine, we become more aware of our senses, and we begin to develop them, especially the neglected, almost vestigial, senses of smell and taste. By awakening our faculties, we begin to experience the world more intensely. We also begin to experience it in a different way, almost as though we were a different kind of animal. Through wine, I have learnt a great deal about geography, geology, meteorology, biology, agriculture, chemistry, gastronomy, art, history, languages, literature, psychology, philosophy, religion, even sales and marketing. By wine, I have communed with, and actually visited, many parts of the world—and should add that wine regions, with their gardened slopes and goldilocks climates, make for the most agreeable destinations. Blind tasting has accelerated my development. It has also taught me about the methods of the mind, and, in the process, made me less bigoted, less dogmatic. On so many levels, wine offers a medium and motivation to apprehend the world. It is, ultimately, a kind of homecoming, a way of feeling at home in the world.

Wine is also an ideal vehicle for alcoholic intoxication, serving to loosen the mind and dissolve the ego. Wine brings people together, helps them be together, and be inventive together, as in the Greek *symposia* and Roman *convivia*, in which measured drinking could lead to expansive elation and creative conversation and the voicing of disruptive ideas and perspectives. Wine played a central role in the secret rites of Greek mystery cults such as the Dionysian Mysteries and the Cult of Cybele, which aimed above all at ecstatic union with the divine—an idea that has survived to this day in the sacramental blood of Christ. Dionysus, who, like Jesus, died and was reborn, was the god of wine, regeneration, fertility, theatre, and religious ecstasy. He was an important god—no doubt, in certain periods and places, the most important—and most fervently celebrated around the time of the vernal equinox.

Let me paint you a picture of a Dionysian orgy. The procession begins at sunset, led by torchbearers and followed by wine and fruit bearers, musicians, and a throng of revellers wearing masks and, well, not much else. Closing the parade is a giant phallus representing the resurrection of the twice-born god. Everyone is pushing and shoving, singing and dancing, and shouting the name of the god stirred in with ribaldry and obscenity. Arriving at a clearing in the woods, the crowd goes wild with drinking, dancing, and every imaginable manner of sex. The god is in the wine, and to imbibe it is to be possessed by his spirit—although in the bull's horn the booze has been interlaced with several other mind-expanding substances, or entheogens (substances that 'generate the divine from within'). Animals, which stand in for the god, are hunted down, torn apart with bare hands, and consumed raw with the blood still warm and dripping.

The Dionysian cult spread through the Greek colonies to Rome. In 186 BCE, the Senate restricted it by the *Senatus consultum de Bacchanalibus* ['Senatorial decree concerning the Bacchanalia']. According to the historian Livy, the decree led to more executions than imprisonments, with many choosing instead to commit suicide. Illicit Bacchanalia persisted but gradually folded into the much tamer Liberalia in honour of Liber Pater ('Free Father'), the Roman god of wine and fertility who so resembled Bacchus/Dionysus as, eventually, to merge into him. The fourth century reign of Constantius II marked the beginning of the formal persecution of paganism by the Christian Roman Empire. But the springtime fertility orgy survived through the centuries, albeit in attenuated forms. At last, unable to suppress it, the Church integrated it into its calendar as Carnival.

The Dionysian impulse for irrationality and chaos can be understood as a natural inversion of, and release from, the habitual Apollonian order and restraint imposed by the state and state religion—and blind tasting, with its emphasis on reason and deduction, as an attempt to marry the Apollonian and the Dionysian and attain to the ever receding dream of civilization. In the *Birth of Tragedy* (1872), Nietzsche recognizes the Dionysian impulse as a primal and universal force:

> Either through the influence of narcotic drink, of which all primitive men and peoples speak, or through the powerful coming on of spring, which drives joyfully through all of nature, that Dionysian excitement

arises. As its power increases, the subjective fades into complete forget-
fulness of self. In the German Middle Ages under the same power of
Dionysus constantly growing hordes waltzed from place to place,
singing and dancing. In that St. John's and St. Vitus's dancing we recognize the Bacchic chorus of the Greeks once again, and its precursors in
Asia Minor, right back to Babylon and the orgiastic Sacaea.

By diverting the Dionysian impulse into special rites on special days,
the orgy kept it under control, preventing it from surfacing in more
insidious and perfidious ways. More than that, it transformed it into an
invigorating and liberating—and, in that much, profoundly religious—
celebration of life and the life force. It permitted people to escape from
their artificial and restricted social roles and regress into a more
authentic state of nature, which modern psychologists have associated
with the Freudian id or unconscious. It appealed most to marginal
groups, since it set aside the usual hierarchies of man over woman,
master over slave, patrician over commoner, rich over poor, and citizen
over foreigner. In short, it gave people a much-needed break—like
modern holidays, but cheaper and more effective.

'Ecstasy' literally means 'to be or stand outside oneself'. It is a trance-
like state in which consciousness of an object is so heightened that the
subject dissolves or merges into the object. Einstein called it the 'mystic
emotion' and spoke of it as 'the finest emotion of which we are capable',
'the germ of all art and true science', and 'the core of the true religious
sentiment'. More than ever before, modern society emphasizes the
sovereign supremacy of the ego and the ultimate separateness and
responsibility of each and every one of us. From a young age, we are
taught to remain in tight control of our ego or persona with the aim of
projecting it as far out as possible. As a result, we have lost the art of
letting go—and, indeed, no longer even recognize the possibility—
leading to a poverty or monotony of conscious experience. Letting go
can threaten the life that we have built and even the person that we
have become, but it can also free us from our modern narrowness and
neediness, and deliver, or re-deliver, us into a bigger and brighter world.

Man, said Balzac, dies in despair, while the spirit dies in ecstasy.

2

THE HISTORY OF WINE

*E*arly foragers and farmers made wine from wild grapes or other fruits. According to archaeological evidence, by 6000 BCE grape wine was being made in the Caucasus, and by 3200 BCE domesticated grapes had become abundant throughout the Near East. In Mesopotamia, wine was imported from the cooler northern regions, and so came to be known as 'liquor of the mountains'. In Egypt as in Mesopotamia, wine was for nobles and priests, and mostly reserved for religious or medicinal purposes. The Egyptians fermented grape juice in amphorae covered with cloth or leather lids and sealed with Nilotic mud.

By biblical times, wine had acquired some less exalted uses. According to the Old Testament, Noah planted a vineyard, and 'drank of the wine, and was drunken; and he was uncovered within his tent' (Genesis 9:21). Skip to the New Testament and here is Jesus moonlighting as a wine consultant: 'And no man putteth new wine into old wineskins: else the wine bursts the skins, and the wine is lost as well as the skins: but new wine must be put into new skins' (Mark 2:22).

Many of the grape varieties found in Greece are identical or similar to those that thrived there in ancient times. Wine played a central role in Ancient Greek culture, and the vine was widely cultivated. The

Minoans, who flourished on Crete from c. 2700 BCE to c. 1450 BCE, exported and imported different wines, which they poured out for recreational as well as religious and ritual purposes. Wine played a similarly important role for the later Mycenæans, who flourished on mainland Greece from c. 1600 BCE to c. 1100 BCE. In fact, wine was so important to the Greeks as to be incarnated in a major deity, Dionysus or Bacchus, who was celebrated and worshipped in a number of annual festivals. One such festival was the three-day Anthesteria, which, held in February each year, celebrated the opening of the wine jars to test the new wine. Active in the eighth century BCE, Homer often sang of wine, famously alluding to the Aegean as the 'wine dark sea'. In the *Odyssey*, he says that, 'wine can of their wits the wise beguile/ Make the sage frolic, and the serious smile.' In the *Works and Days*, Hesiod, who lived in the eighth or seventh century BCE, speaks of pruning vines and drying grapes. The Greeks plainly understood that no two wines are the same, and held the wines of Thassos, Lesbos, Chios, and Mende in especially high regard. Theophrastus, a contemporary and close friend of Aristotle, even evinced some very clear notions of terroir.

In Ancient Greece, vines were supported on forked props or trained up trees. The wine was neither racked nor fined, and so it was not uncommon for the drinker to pass it through a sieve or strainer. Aromatic herbs, spices, honey, or seawater were often added to improve and preserve the wine, which could also be concentrated by boiling. Finished wine was stored in amphorae lined with resin or pitch, which imparted some additional flavour. Generally speaking, wine was sweeter than it is today, reflecting contemporary tastes, the use of natural yeasts in fermentation, and the lack of temperature control during fermentation (Chapter 4). It did, however, come in a variety of styles, some of which were markedly dry and austere. To drink wine undiluted was considered a bad and barbarian practice, almost as bad as drinking beer like those Babylonian or Egyptian peasants. Instead, wine was diluted with two or three parts of water to produce a beverage with an alcoholic strength of around three-to-five per cent. According to the comedian Hermippus, who flourished during the golden age of Athens, the finest vintage wines smelt of violets, roses, and hyacinths.

Together with the sea-faring Phoenicians, the Greeks disseminated the vine throughout the Mediterranean, and even named southern Italy *Oenotria*, or 'Land of Staked Vines'. If wine was important to the Greeks, it became even more so to the Romans, who looked upon it as a daily staple and democratized its drinking. It is no coincidence that, on all four sides, in all four corners, the borders of the Roman Empire stopped where wine could no longer be made. The Romans established a great number of Europe's most notable wine producing regions, including Burgundy, Bordeaux, the Loire, and the Mosel, both to supply their soldiers and colonists and to trade with native tribes and convert them to their cause. Following Virgil's precept that *Bacchus amat colles* ['Bacchus loves hillsides'], they favoured inclined terrain, typically near a river and an urban centre. The trade of Hispanic wines soon surpassed that of Italian wines, with Hispanic amphorae unearthed as far north as Britannia and the *Limes Germanicus* [German frontier]. In his *Geographica* of 7 BCE, Strabo says that the vineyards of Hispania Beatica, which roughly corresponds to modern Andalucia, were famous for their great beauty. The area of Pompeii also produced a great deal of wine, much of it destined for Rome; and the eruption of Vesuvius in 79 CE led to a dramatic penury. The people of Rome panicked, uprooting food crops to plant vineyards. The result was a wine glut and food shortage, which in 92 compelled the emperor Domitian to issue an edict that banned the planting of vineyards in Italy and ordered the uprooting of half the vineyards in the provinces.

Roman agricultural treatises provide us with detailed insights into the viticulture and winemaking of the age. Cato the Elder's *De agri cultura*, which emphasizes vineyard care, ripeness of fruit, and cellar hygiene, served for several centuries as the standard manual of winemaking. In *De re rustica*, Columella surveys the main grape varieties, which he divides into three main groups: noble varieties for great Italian wines, high yielding varieties that can nonetheless produce ageworthy wines, and prolific varieties for ordinary table wine. Pliny the Elder, who also surveys the main grape varieties, feels sure that 'classic wines can only be produced from vines grown on trees', and it is true that the greatest wines of Campania, such as Cæcuban or Falernian, nearly all came from vines trained up elms and poplars. Both Cæcuban and Falernian were white and sweet, although there was also a dry style of Falernian. Falernian was deemed best at fifteen-to-twenty years old, and another classed growth called Surrentine at more than twenty-five years old. The Opimian vintage of 121 BCE, named for one of the consuls in that year, Lucius Opimius, acquired legendary fame, with some examples still being enjoyed more than one hundred years later.

The best wines were made from the highly prized free-run juice obtained from the initial treading of the grapes. At the other end of the spectrum were *posca*, a mixture of water and sour wine that had not yet turned to vinegar, and *lora*, a thin drink, or *piquette*, obtained from a third pressing of the berries (or, by now, skins). Following the Greek invention of the screw, screw presses became commonplace on Roman villas. Grape juice was fermented in large clay vessels, or *dolia*, with white wine often left to age on its lees. The wine was then racked into amphorae for storing and shipping. Barrels invented by the Gauls and, later still, glass bottles invented by the Syrians vied as alternatives to amphorae. As in Greece, additives were common: chalk or marble to neutralize excess acidity; and boiled must, herbs, spice, honey, resin, or seawater to improve and preserve thin offerings. Maderization was common and sought after; even so, rooms destined for wine storage were often built to face north and away from the sun.

Following the decline and fall of the Western Roman Empire, the Church perpetuated the knowledge of viticulture and winemaking, first and foremost to furnish the blood of Christ for the Eucharist.

NB. Histories of individual wine regions are subsumed under their respective chapters.

3

PRINCIPLES OF VITICULTURE

To blind taste proficiently, it is necessary to have at least some basic notions of viticulture and winemaking. Long gone is the era in which wine was flavoured with herbs and spices, or diluted with fresh or salt water. For our purposes, wine is made from grapes and grapes alone: although wine may be described in terms of fruits, flowers, and so on, for the most part these aromas and flavours derive from the grapes themselves. Other aromas and flavours arise from processes in winemaking and maturation, including maturation vessels and especially oak barrels.

Vines

Today, almost all wine is made from the fruit of the Eurasian grape vine, *Vitis vinifera*, or 'Wine-making vine'. Over thousands of years, human beings domesticated the dioecious [with male and female reproductive organs on different plants] forest creeper *V. vinifera silvestris* into the hermaphroditic crop-bearing *V. vinifera sativa*. The success of *V. vinifera* owes to its adaptability, its readiness to self-propagate, and, of course, its heavy crop of flavoursome fruit with high levels of sugar that can readily be fermented into alcohol.

Today, over one thousand identifiable varieties of *V. **vinifera*** are commercially cultivated to make wine. Some of these varieties are ancient, others much less so, often the products of modern cultivation and crossing techniques, although not (yet) of genetic modification. A single variety can have several **clones**, which, although closely related, are genetically distinct, each with differing properties such as better disease resistance, higher yield, earlier ripening, deeper colour, or a more complex aroma and flavour. Whether a plant is counted as a clone or a separate variety can be a matter of debate, especially among us blind tasters!

Other species of *Vitis* include *V. labrusca*, *V. berlandieri*, *V. riparia*, and *V. rupestris*, which are indigenous to North America, and *V. amurensis*, which is indigenous to the Far East. Early settlers to North America cultivated **V. *labrusca***, and *labrusca* varieties such as Concord are still entertained on the Eastern seaboard of the United States. **Hybrid crosses** of *vinifera* and non-*vinifera* vines such as Seyval Blanc, Vidal Blanc, and De Chaunac are more commonly found in North America than in Europe, not least because the European Union prohibits their use in quality wine. By far the most important contribution of non-*vinifera* vines to modern viticulture has been to provide phylloxera- and nematode-resistant rootstocks on which to graft *vinifera* scions (see later).

Grapes

It has become a cliché that 'good wine is made in the vineyard'. While one can make bad wine from good grapes, one cannot make good wine from bad grapes: a balanced wine can only be made from balanced grapes.

As they ripen, grapes concentrate sugars that can be partly or wholly fermented into alcohol. The amount of sugar in the grapes, or **sugar ripeness**, corresponds to the potential alcohol of the wine. **Phenolic ripeness** on the other hand refers to the maturity of flavour in the grapes, as ascertained by examining and sampling (tasting) them. With increasing phenolic ripeness, the skin, pips, and stems change colour, the skin and pulp become softer, and the tannins in the skin and pips become less bitter.

Although sugar ripeness and phenolic ripeness are related, they do not necessarily go hand in hand. In overly hot conditions, grapes can reach sugar ripeness before they arrive at phenolic ripeness. The grower is then caught between a rock and a hard place: either pick early to make a wine with astringent tannins and a green streak; or wait to make a full-bodied, alcoholic wine that is flat and flabby and lacking in acidity. Conversely, in overly cool conditions, grapes can struggle to accumulate sugars, and turn into wines that are unpleasantly thin and acidic.

Grape ripening is a function of sunlight and heat, which can vary markedly from one region to another and even from one vineyard to the next. One of the challenges for the grower is to arrive at ripe-tasting fruit with optimal levels of sugars and acids. This balancing act calls upon a finely honed understanding or appreciation of the vine's inter-action with elements of its environment, from climate, topography, and geology down to the life cycles of local plants and insects and the feeding patterns of birds, bats, boars, and baboons. These all are aspects of *terroir*, a French concept that denotes the entire ecosystem of a vine and vineyard. At its broadest, terroir also encompasses local customs and traditions honed over decades and centuries, including methods of planting, training, harvesting, and even wine-making and ageing. The Romans also had a concept of terroir, which they called *genius loci*—the spirit or genius of the place.

Climate and geography

A vine with an ample supply of water and nutrients tends to expend its energy on foliage rather than fruit. For it to focus on fruit, it must come under sufficient stress that it feels the need to propagate its genetic material. The quality of fruit produced depends to a large extent on the climate, which in turn depends on a number of geographical factors such as latitude, altitude, proximity to the sea or ocean, and exposure to prevailing winds.

Whereas **weather** refers to short term or exceptional events such as rains, frosts, hailstorms, flooding, and drought, **climate** refers rather to long-term underlying patterns measured in terms of sunshine hours, mean temperature, diurnal temperature range, rainfall, humidity, and such like. Broadly, **macroclimate** describes the climate of a particular region, **mesoclimate** the climate of a particular sub-region or vineyard site, and **microclimate** the specific conditions in a small part of the vineyard or even within the canopy of a single vine.

Grapes require a certain amount of warmth and sunshine to arrive at sugar and phenolic ripeness. But too much heat can impede ripening, and too much sunshine can burn the grapes. Optimal results are obtained in temperate climates with a growing season that extends over 180 or more consecutive frost-free days, with, during the growing season, average temperatures of 13–21°C and in excess of 1,250 sunshine hours. The judicious exploitation of mesoclimates, varieties, rootstocks, trellising methods, canopy management techniques, irrigation, harvest times… can mitigate adverse or marginal macroclimatic conditions. Outside the growing season, vines are able to tolerate frost, but sustained double-digit negative temperatures can lead to damage or death. In Cahors, the Great Frost of February 1956 killed off all but 1% of the vines.

The world's most successful wine regions lie within latitudes 30–50° North and South. Within these diverse temperate zones, some grape varieties such as Riesling, Pinot Noir, and Sauvignon Blanc do best in cooler, more marginal climates. Others, such as Grenache, Nero d'Avola, and Touriga Nacional call for much hotter conditions. Cabernet Sauvignon insists on a moderate but sunny climate, whereas Chardonnay is adaptable, yielding lean and mineral wines in cool Chablis but blousy and buttery wines in hotter parts of South Australia. Generally speaking, white varieties need less heat than black varieties, and so predominate in the coolest, most marginal regions such as Ontario, Southern England, Muscadet, Champagne, and the Mosel. Wines from such marginal regions may be softened or made more palatable by double fermentation, arrested fermentation (to retain residual sugar), the addition of sugar, or ageing on the lees.

In practice, the geographical distribution of a grape variety is a function not only of climate but also of cultural, economic, and even legal factors. Stellenbosch may enjoy a Mediterranean climate, but plantings of Italian or Spanish varieties are nonetheless rare.

Regions that are in the interior of a large landmass or sheltered from the sea by mountains (or both, as with Alsace, Ribera del Duero, and Alto Adige) are described as **continental**, with cold winters and hot, relatively dry summers. In contrast, coastal regions such as Bordeaux or the Mornington Peninsula with direct exposure to the sea are described as **maritime**, with warmer winters and milder, wetter summers. Some regions such as Châteauneuf-du-Pape and Chianti are best described as **Mediterranean**, with mild winters and very warm and dry summers. A similar 'Mediterranean' climate can also be found in parts of California, Western and South Australia, central coastal Chile, and the Western Cape in South Africa.

Altitude can make it possible to produce quality wine in hotter regions such as Alto Maipo in Chile, Cederberg in South Africa, Mount Etna in Sicily, Mount Teide in Tenerife, and Mount Canobolas in New South Wales. As a general rule, for every 100m (328ft) of ascent, the mean temperature drops by 0.5–0.6°C. Higher altitudes are also associated with cooler nights and greater diurnal temperature variation, which enable grapes to ripen and concentrate flavour while preserving natural acidity.

In more marginal regions such as the Rheingau or Côte de Nuits, vines are more often planted on steep **slopes**. At higher latitudes, slopes, depending on their exposure, can receive much more incident sunlight than flatlands, especially during the critical autumn ripening period. Slopes also offer thinner topsoil, better drainage, and increased air circulation from convection currents. In the northern hemisphere, many vineyards are planted on south-facing slopes to capture as much sunlight as possible, and vice versa in the southern hemisphere. Conversely, in hot climates, north-facing slopes can be exploited for their cooler conditions. In the northern hemisphere, the most favoured slopes are generally those that face south-east or south-south-east because they receive the first sun and warm up and dry out more quickly. In many regions, they are also sheltered from the prevailing winds. Steep slopes do have some disadvantages: they are prone to erosion and the vines can be expensive and dangerous to access. In the Mosel, some of the slopes are steeper than 45°, with the steepest, Bremmer Calmont, at 65°.

Water bodies such as oceans, rivers, and lakes also exert an important influence on climate. Maritime air blown off the Antarctic Benguela current makes Hemel-en-Aarde in South Africa much cooler than more sheltered, inland regions such as Stellenbosch, Paarl, and Swartland. With average summer highs of just 25°C, on a par with Burgundy, Hemel-en-Aarde is reputed for its fine Chardonnay and Pinot Noir. The River Loire moderates temperatures, as does the River Mosel, making viticulture possible at such high latitudes. Rivers also reflect sunlight, increase air circulation, and provide water and transportation. Sea mists that form off the Californian coast penetrate far inland into regions such as Mendocino Valley, exercising an important cooling influence; and mists from the River Ciron in Sauternes or Lake Neusiedl in Burgenland create ideal conditions for the development of noble rot (see later).

Even **trees and other plants** have a role to play. The *Forêt des Landes* shields Bordeaux from strong and salty winds. On a more modest scale, trees and hedges shelter a vineyard from gales and storms and stabilize steeper slopes. As well as looking good, ground cover crops protect the soil from erosion and runoff, improve soil structure and fertility, provide a habitat for beneficial predators, and promote biodiversity. A monoculture of vines on a flat and featureless expanse of land treated with synthetic fertilizers, herbicides, fungicides, and pesticides enables the farmer to machine harvest a heavy and consistent crop, but does nothing for the quality of the grapes or the long-term health of the soil and environment. More and more, growers are learning to work with, rather than against, nature.

Soils

Soils are complex, layered systems, with the visible topsoil of critical importance only to very young vines. As a vine ages and develops, its roots dig deep into the subsoil in search of water and nutrients. A vine must come under some strain to produce high quality fruit, and most vineyards are planted on thinner, poorer soils that stress the vine and promote deep rooting into the mineral-rich subsoil. Happily, the best vineyards are seldom suited to other forms of exploitation, which, in regions such as Burgundy, the Rhône, and the Douro, has ensured their survival into the modern day.

A soil that is heavy in **clay** (particles up to 2μm in diameter) behaves like a sponge, expanding and contracting in function of its water content. It is compact and hard to penetrate, and in a dry spell can crack and damage the roots of the vine. A clay-based soil is only suitable for viticulture if it contains substantial proportions of larger particles such as **silt** (2μm-0.05mm) and **sand** (0.05mm-2mm), which lend it a lighter, loamier texture. **Gravel** (>2mm) is the lightest and most free-draining of all soil types, with the added advantage of retaining solar heat. Some varieties do best on gravelly soils, while others prefer clay-based soils. Thus, in Bordeaux, Cabernet Sauvignon prevails on the gravelly Left Bank, while the clayey Right Bank is mostly given to Merlot. A sandy soil, if not too sandy and dry, can offer good drainage and high heat retention and discourage pests and disease. Sandier soils, as in the Graves, Roero, and Swartland, are held to produce softer, lighter wines with greater perfume and lighter acidity and tannin.

Sedimentary soils such as limestone and chalk that developed from fossilized seashells have been favoured for centuries. Although free-draining, they are able to retain moisture through dry spells. They also facilitate deep rooting and preserve the acidity of the grapes. Calcareous soils underlie the success of such diverse regions as Saint-Emilion, Coonawarra, Châteauneuf-du-Pape, Piedmont, Chianti, Rioja, Jerez, and the South of England, which lies on the Kimmeridgian Ridge, an ancient seabed of limestone clay that also runs through the vineyards of Champagne, Chablis, and Sancerre.

Soils of volcanic origin are a feature of Napa Valley, Willamette Valley, Mount Etna, Santorini, and Kaiserstuhl, among others. Volcanic soils are very diverse in composition and decomposition, and may contain various combinations of basalts, tuffs, pumices, and sand. Owing to their porosity and relative fertility, they tend to yield riper, richer wines with greater acidity, minerality, and longevity, although some of these properties may derive at least in part from confounding factors such as slope and altitude.

Other important soil types are **alluvium**, a river deposit composed of clay, silt, sand, and gravel; **marl**, a friable deposit composed of clay and lime (limestone can be considered as a purer, lithified form of marl); **tufa**, a porous rock composed of silica and calcium carbonate that is precipitated from a source of water such as a spring or lake; **granite**, a hard and coarse-grained igneous rock composed of feldspars, quartz, and other minerals; and **schist**, a coarse-grained metamorphic rock with a foliated, often flaky, structure composed of mica and other minerals. Schist, slate, and gneiss are foliated metamorphic rocks that originate from shale, which itself originates from the consolidation of clay. Whereas schist is a medium-grade metamorphic rock, slate is low-grade and gneiss high-grade.

Pests and diseases

The **phylloxera** louse, *Daktulosphaira vitifoliae*, is the most devastating of vineyard pests. It is indigenous to North America, so that American vines are resistant to it, but not the European vine. The louse arrived in France in the early 1860s and set about ravaging the vineyards of Europe. The life cycle of the louse is complex: in short, the damage is inflicted by the crawling form of the insect, which disrupts the root system of the vine and exposes it to secondary infection. The discovery that resistance can be conferred by grafting European vines onto American rootstocks led to replanting on an unprecedented scale, often, as in Bordeaux, Jerez, or South Africa, leading to important changes in the distribution and diversity of grape varieties. To this day, phylloxera continues to pose a near universal threat, and almost all

European vines are grafted onto American rootstocks. Geographical isolation and strict quarantine measures have so far preserved South Australia and much of Chile and Argentina from the pest, but it can only be a matter of time before it rears its ugly head. Some areas seem immune to phylloxera, for example, in Europe, the Mosel, Santorini, and Tenerife.

Most **other vineyard pests** are insects such as flies, mites, moths, beetles, caterpillars, and locusts, although larger animals such as birds, rabbits, boars, monkeys, baboons, kangaroos, and snakes can also destroy crops and damage vines as well as imperil vineyard workers. Some insects can be controlled with sulphur or chemical pesticides, although 'integrated pest management' (IPM, 'sustainable viticulture', *lutte raisonnée, culture raisonnée*) often presents a more effective and less damaging alternative.

With IPM, synthetic chemicals can be used, but only in small amounts and as a last resort once non-chemical interventions have been exhausted. Such interventions may include selecting disease-resistant varieties and rootstocks, improving soil structure, planting cover crops, and introducing or encouraging natural predators. IPM can be close to **organic viticulture**, which seeks to achieve a natural balance in the vineyard by using nothing more than certain natural preparations. **Biodynamic viticulture**, which derives from the 1924 lectures of Austrian philosopher Rudolf Steiner, goes one step further by looking upon the farm as an ecosystem, starting with the soil, which is treated as a living organism. In addition, biodynamic practitioners seek to connect the farm with natural rhythms by aligning operations with lunar and other cycles.

Before phylloxera, the vineyards of Europe had been battling with **powdery mildew or oidium** (*Uncinula necator*), a fungal disease which, like phylloxera, had come from America. Unlike most fungi, oidium prefers dry conditions. The first symptoms of infection are whitish powdery patches on the undersurfaces of basal leaves, although canes, flowers, and fruit can also be affected. Diseased berries fail to thrive and may split open. The original solution of spraying or dusting the vines with sulphur is still practised, often assisted by canopy management techniques aimed at increasing air and light penetration.

Vines are also susceptible to a number of **other fungal diseases** such as downy mildew and grey rot, which, like noble rot (see later), owes to *Botrytis cinerea*. Many of these diseases can be prevented by canopy management techniques and copper-containing sprays such as Bordeaux mixture, although harsher treatments can be required. Some fungal diseases, notably oak-root fungus, attack the roots of the vine and are difficult to detect let alone treat. Eutypa dieback is a fungal infection of the trunk and branches that may be introduced through grafts and transmitted on infected shears at the time of pruning. The damage is often confined to one arm of the vine, whence the byname 'dead arm'. There is no treatment, but other parts of the plant remain largely unaffected. When life gives you lemons, make lemonade: d'Arenberg makes a premium wine called *Dead Arm Shiraz* from old Eutypa-infected vines in McLaren Vale. Historically, rose bushes planted at the edge of vineyards alerted vineyard workers to fungal diseases such as powdery mildew and downy mildew, with the delicate rose bushes developing signs of disease in advance of the vines.

Prevention is by far the most effective measure against **bacterial and viral infections**. It involves disinfecting the soil prior to planting; observing the strictest standards of hygiene in grafting, pruning, and other operations; and, where possible, controlling vectors of disease. For instance, Fanleaf virus is transmitted by nematodes in the root system, and can be controlled by grafting vines onto nematode-resistant American rootstocks.

Lifecycle of the vine

Vines are generally propagated through cuttings which preserve the genetic makeup of the particular grape variety or clone. This can be achieved either by taking and planting **cuttings**, or, less commonly, by burying a branch of an existing plant, so- called **layering**, which is still practised in some phylloxera-free vineyards. Layering preserves the identity and genetic diversity of a vineyard, but another and better method of propagation is '**massal selection**', which involves taking cuttings from the most outstanding vines in the vineyard or nearby vineyards. In most places, *vinifera* cuttings must be taken to a nursery and grafted onto American rootstocks to protect them from phylloxera. **Grafting** onto American rootstocks can also protect against other pests and diseases and supply a root system that is better suited to the climate and soil type. Young vines are typically planted in rows to facilitate vineyard operations, but can also be planted pell-mell, or *en foule*. Densely planted, that is, closely spaced, vines compete with one another for nutrients and water, which can help to stress the vine into producing higher quality fruit.

Old vines generally make for better wine, because they have deeper roots and lower yields. This, however, should not be overstated: the Great Frost of February 1956 required large scale replanting in Saint-Emilion and Pomerol, but the youth of the vines did not prevent the 1961 vintage from achieving cult status. In fact, very young vines, being, like old vines, less vigorous, can also produce superior fruit.

Training

After planting, vines need about three years to establish themselves and start bearing quality fruit. In these early years, they are especially vulnerable to harsh sunlight, droughts, frosts, insects, and so on. Being natural creepers, they require some form of support on which to spread and fruit. Trellises range from a simple stake in the ground to elaborate overhead pergola systems. A simple structure, while cheap, may render vineyard operations more difficult and costly. The choice of trellis is also contingent upon other factors such as the chosen grape variety, the vigour of the vine, the aspect of the vineyard, and the potential for hazards such as storms and frosts. In practice, vines are often trained along one or more horizontal wires to optimize the microclimate and ease vineyard operations.

A common training system, especially in cooler climates, is the single or double **Guyot system.** With single Guyot, each vine has one cane held back to support the following season's fruiting canes, and one spur which gives rise to the following year's replacement cane. With double

Guyot, there are two canes and two spurs, with the canes trained in opposite directions.

The Guyot system originated in the nineteenth century, when most vines were trained in a bush (*gobelet*), with the spurs arranged on short arms in an approximate circle at the top of a short trunk (hence *gobelet* or 'cup'). This ancestral system, which does not require supporting wires, is still favoured in some regions with a dry climate and infertile soils, notably Châteauneuf-du-Pape, where it offers greater resistance against drought and wind.

Cordon training is not dissimilar to gobelet, with a short trunk and spur pruning. But instead of head training, one or two spur-bearing permanent branches, or cordons, are trained along a wire. Unilateral cordon training, with a single permanent branch, is sometimes referred to as *cordon de Royat*.

The modern Scott Henry training system for overly vigorous vines is similar to double Guyot, but with two canes running out to either side. On either side, the fruiting canes on the upper cane are trained upwards, and those on the lower cane are trained downwards. The Smart Dyson training system is a variation on the Scott Henry with cordons instead of canes.

Other common training systems include the Geneva double curtain (GDC), which reduces shade from a dense canopy by splitting it into two; and the lyre which is similar to the GDC but with the fruiting canes trained upward rather than being left to hang down.

More localised, and distinctive, training systems include the basket (*kouloura*) of Santorini and the braided cord (*cordón trenzado*) of Tenerife.

Pruning

Traditionally, pruning to remove old wood kicked off on 22 January, the Feast of Saint Vincent of Saragossa, patron saint of winemakers (the patron saint of vines is Pope Saint Urban). By and large, the functions of pruning are to: optimize the balance between vegetative growth and fruit production by controlling the size and shape of the vine; remove dead, broken, or diseased tissue; and regulate bud break.

Essentially, there are just two pruning methods, short (cordon/spur pruning) and long (cane pruning, traditionally used with the Guyot system among others). Spur pruning is easier, at least while the cordons remain healthy, but cane pruning is more flexible and offers better frost protection (because there is less wood on the vine).

With **spur pruning**, the gnarly main branch or cordon is left intact. Spur positions on the cordon typically support two or more one-year old canes. The weaker or more distal canes are completely taken out including about 5mm of the old wood. The remaining cane is pruned short, typically to two buds and just a few inches. This short cane is called a spur.

With **cane pruning**, the two-year-old cane carrying most of the previous season's growth is completely taken out. One or more well-formed one-year-old canes are then selected and pruned to about six-to-ten buds and one-to-two feet long, before being tied down in early spring. Replacement (or renewal) spurs, which have been cut back to two or three buds, are also left behind to provide the next season's one-year-old canes.

On the road to harvest

The vine jumps to life in mid-spring: buds appear and tiny leaves and embryonic tendrils emerge from the buds. The vine is now susceptible to **spring frosts**, and a single frosty night can destroy the entire harvest. Pruning late delays bud burst and can help to protect against spring frosts, as can sprinklers, smoke-belching smudge pots, wind machines, and helicopters, among others.

Shoots grow rapidly over the coming months and need to be positioned according to the trellising system and pruned back to restrict vegetative growth. As it develops, the foliage begins to affect the microclimate surrounding the flowers and fruit, and may need to be thinned or adjusted to optimize the ripeness and quality of the crop. **Canopy management**, a term coined in the 1980s by viticulturalist Richard

Smart, can usefully restrict vegetative growth, increase or decrease sun exposure, promote air circulation, and protect against vine diseases. Growers of Marlborough Sauvignon Blanc may cut back the leaves so as to uncover only one half of the fruit. This leads to a wine with both ripeness of fruit and a fresh grassy note.

By early summer, bunches of proto-grapes—caps of fused petals—have formed. **Flowering** begins when these caps fall off and the tiny stamens are exposed for fertilization. This is another critical juncture in the vine's development: adverse conditions at flowering, which takes place over one or two weeks, can lead to various degrees of *coulure* (failure of grape development) and *millerandage* (uneven grape development). Crop potential is a function not only of the current season's weather conditions, but also of the previous season's, when the current season's fruiting buds were forming.

Berries develop over the summer months, accumulating water, sugars, acids, and other flavour compounds. In late summer, the berries change from mid-green to black, red, or pale green. This colour change, called *véraison*, marks the beginning of the ripening period during which sugars accumulate more rapidly, the harsh acids soften, and the tannins, anthocyanins, and other phenolic flavour compounds develop and mature. **Green harvesting** around *véraison* to remove immature bunches of grapes can improve the rest of the crop, especially if the vines are vigorous or the yields are high.

In recent years, Burgundy and Bordeaux in particular have fallen victim to violent summer **hailstorms**, with both grapes and vines suffering significant damage. Netting is common in hail-prone Mendoza and has been authorised in France since 2018 after tests carried out in Burgundy showed a 90% reduction in damage with negligible effects on wine character. But netting is expensive and labour intensive, and limited in range. An alternative is to detect potential hail clouds by radar and then seed them with nuclei to increase the number of hailstones, and thereby reduce their size. Suitable substances for seeding include silver iodide, potassium iodide, calcium chloride, or dry ice, lifted into the hail clouds by ground-sited generators, helium balloons, aeroplanes, or rockets. Traditionally, church bells were pealed at the approach of hail clouds, and, today, some estates use hail cannons in the hope of disrupting hail formation with shock waves. But this, it seems, is much less effective than either netting or seeding.

In the autumn, the grapes reach optimal sugar and phenolic ripeness (ideally at the same time) and are ready for harvest. The grapes are harvested by hand or machine, and whisked away to the winery where the fermentation process can begin. Meanwhile, the vine stores complex carbohydrates in its canes, trunk, and roots to sustain it over the winter. The leaves are shed, shoots lignify, and the plant falls into dormancy.

For **sweet wines**, the grapes need to be left on the vine for longer, and, often, call for several pickings. Luscious botrytized wines are made from late harvest grapes infected by *Botrytis cinerea*. Unless the infection is carefully managed, it can lead to grey rot rather than noble rot. For noble rot to develop, the berries must have ripened to a potential alcohol of at least 7%, beyond which the fungus can feed on the berry without splitting or otherwise damaging it. The fungus punctures the skin, gradually shrivelling the berry and concentrating its sugars and aromatics. Mesoclimates suited to the development of noble rot such as Tokaji, Sauternes, and Coteaux du Layon feature autumn mists that dissipate in mid-morning to make place for dry and sunny afternoons. In other cases, grapes are left to dry on the vine and then harvested, or else harvested and then dried, traditionally on straw mats, to make so-called straw wines. Grapes can also be left on the vine until partially frozen by a deep winter frost. They are then harvested in the dead of night and pressed to extrude the ice crystals, leaving behind small quantities of super-concentrated ice wine (*Eiswein*), which is a specialty of parts of Germany, Austria, and Canada.

4

PRINCIPLES OF WINEMAKING

*I*deally, harvesting begins once the grapes have reached optimal phenolic and sugar ripeness. If it is not operationally possible to harvest all the grapes at optimal ripeness, then it is a matter of compromising. Grapes that are harvested too early can introduce unripe, 'green' notes into the wine, while grapes that are harvested too late can make for a flabby or jammy wine. Many wines are made from a blend of fruit from multiple vineyards, in which case the grapes may be harvested at the best time (or close to the best time) for each individual site. The grower must also take weather conditions into account: for instance, if a storm is brewing, it may be judicious to bring in the grapes even if they are still slightly under-ripe.

In many cases, large harvesters are driven through the vineyards. These machines beat the vines with rubber sticks, shaking off the grapes onto a conveyor belt that transfers them into a holding bin. Harvesters enable grapes to be harvested quickly, day and night, without the costly and sometimes unobtainable labour associated with hand harvesting. Some modern harvesters can even be controlled remotely through computers and GPS tracking systems. On the other hand, harvesters are expensive, can only operate on flat or gently sloping land, and place restrictions on planting and trellising. They can also damage the grapes, colouring the juice and exposing it to oxygen. Ambitious producers invariably opt for **hand harvesting**, which is gentler and more selective. Pickers can be trained to recognize and discard rotten or under-ripe bunches and even, for botrytised wines, to select individual berries. They can also pick whole bunches, which may be desirable, as in Champagne, or necessary, as in much of Beaujolais.

After harvesting, the grapes must be transported to the winery as fast as possible to minimize **oxidative damage**, and some large estates operate a number of pressing stations in or near the vineyards. Otherwise, grapes can be protected from oxidation by a blanket of carbon dioxide or a dusting of antioxidant powder, typically potassium metabisulphite (sulphur dioxide). Once the grapes have been pressed and turned into juice, it becomes much easier to protect them from oxidation. In warmer climates and conditions, and with aromatic white wines, it is especially important to keep the picked grapes cool to limit biochemical degradation. Grapes are often harvested at night or first thing in the morning and may be refrigerated, especially if long transports are necessary.

Crushing and pressing

Upon arrival at the winery, the grapes are spread onto a sorting table fitted with a conveyor belt and any undesirable material is discarded, either by hand or by an automated process. This includes under-ripe and rotten grapes, leaves, twigs, large insects, and the like. If the grapes have been hand harvested, a decision has to be made as to whether to remove the stems. Although they add to bulk, **stems** create drainage channels that increase the efficiency of the pressing process. If ripe, they can also contribute good tannins and flavour; but if not, they can introduce bitter tannins and vegetal notes. Stems can also absorb colour and alcohol. Increasingly, winemakers who know their grapes and know their stems are experimenting with various degrees of whole bunch fermentation to bring extra elegance and expression to their wines. The process of de-stemming involves feeding bunches through a rotating drum perforated with grape-sized holes. The naked stems are sometimes collected and added back at a later stage, either to reduce cap compaction or contribute extra tannins and flavour.

Next, the juice has to be extracted from the grapes by crushing and/or pressing. Less commonly, the grapes are left intact to ferment. In **crushing**, the grapes are passed through a pair of rollers and the grape skins are ripped open. The rollers mimic traditional crushing by the human foot, which is still occasionally practised in places such as Georgia and the Douro. The crusher is calibrated to avoid damaging pips and stems and releasing bitter tannins and vegetal notes into the free-run juice.

The lightest and most delicate **white wines** are made exclusively from the free-run juice obtained by crushing, which contains none of the colour and tannin of the grape skins, pips, and stems. However, many white wines benefit from a small degree of 'skin contact', with the free-run juice left on the skins for a short period. If the period of skin contact is extended throughout fermentation, the result is a more astringent amber, or orange, wine. **Rosés** are made in a similar fashion, but on the skins of black grapes—especially in the European Union, which, with the notable exception of champagne, forbids the blending of white and red wine. Depth of colour varies according to duration of **skin contact**, which for rosé typically lasts one-to-three days. As the juice of almost all grape varieties is clear, red wines depend for their colour, and indeed most of their tannins, on contact with skins, pips, and sometimes also stems, which are said to be 'macerating' in the juice. 'Must' is the collective term for the juice and solid matter.

For most white wines, the free-run juice is augmented by juice extracted by pressing the grapes. In fact, some economy-conscious winemakers entirely forgo crushing in favour of pressing alone. **Pressing** releases juice from the cells on the inner surface of the grape skins, along with aroma, flavour, and polyphenols. A traditional wine press consists of a slatted basket with gaps between the slats and a lid that is screwed down to press the grapes. Pressing inevitably involves the release of bitter polyphenols, and the winemaker must strike a balance between volume and quality. Nowadays, most winemakers use more gentle and efficient presses such as the Willmes pneumatic press. With the Willmes, grapes are loaded into a horizontal, perforated cylinder with a rubber bladder running through the centre. The bladder is then inflated like a balloon so as to exert gentle pressure onto the grapes. For red wines, the grapes are pressed *after* fermentation: during fermentation, the skins macerate in the juice, releasing colour and tannin.

Crushing and pressing ought to be carried out efficiently, with minimal exposure to oxygen. The addition of **sulphur dioxide** to the must can protect against oxidation but can also impede fermentation (which can be desirable if the must is to be clarified prior to fermentation, a process that can take several days). The high polyphenols in red wines offer some protection against oxidation. Even so, some sulphur dioxide may be added to assist in polyphenol extraction. The use of sulphur dioxide can be minimized by refrigerating the must, although this too can impede fermentation. True anaerobic pressing can be achieved with a tank press, which is essentially a Willmes enclosed in a tank flushed with inert nitrogen. However, it is possible to take protection from oxidation too far, resulting in a foul smelling 'reductive' wine (Chapter 5).

Prior to fermentation, the must can be adjusted to suit the winemaker's purposes. Especially in marginal climates, the must might be enriched with sugar ('chaptalized') to increase potential alcohol. Cane or beet sugar is commonly used. The must might also be de-acidified by the addition of a carbonate or bicarbonate compound. Conversely, in hotter climates, wines may be acidified by by the addition of tartaric acid. Acidification can bring balance to a wine, but poorly or overly acidified wines can come across as bitter, poorly integrated, and 'doctored'. By the same token, chaptalized wines can seem boozy and out of balance.

Fermentation

In essence, wine results from the fermentation by yeast cells of sugar into ethyl alcohol, or ethanol. The chemical formula for this reaction is:

$$C_6H_{12}O_6 \rightarrow 2C_2H_5OH + 2CO_2$$
Sugar (glucose:fructose = ~50:50) $\rightarrow$ ethanol + carbon dioxide

There are many different species of yeast, and, for each species, several genetically distinct strains. However, the most important yeast in winemaking is *Saccharomyces cerevisiae*, which is efficient at fermenting sugars into ethanol and able to survive high levels of its ethanol waste product.

The winemaker pumps the must into a fermentation vessel, which can range from an airtight stainless steel tank to an open-air concrete pool to an oak barrel. He or she can either inoculate the must with a commercially produced yeast culture, or rely on the yeast cells on the grape skins and winery equipment to start a 'natural' fermentation. With **natural fermentation**, the winemaker is unable to select the best-suited strain of yeast for the wine that he or she is seeking to make; however, many winemakers maintain that natural fermentation, which typically involves several species of yeast, results in more complex flavours and aromas. Various yeast species can start the fermentation but it is invariably *Saccharomyces cerevisiae* that completes it, as it is (almost) the only yeast capable of metabolizing sugar in the presence of high levels of ethanol.

Throughout fermentation, carbon dioxide is being produced and protects the fermenting must from oxidation. This carbon dioxide needs to be let out of the fermentation vessel—and, because it can lead to suffocation, the winery as well. Another by-product of fermentation is heat, and the temperature of the must may need controlling to keep it within the optimal range for the desired yeast or yeasts to function. Temperature of fermentation also has a bearing on aroma and flavour: in particular, the esters that make a wine (especially a white wine) seem fruity and floral will be lost at higher temperatures.

In most cases, the fermentation comes to an end when the yeasts run out of nutrients, typically after one-to-two weeks. The wine has then been fermented 'to dryness', meaning that there is very little sugar left in it. In some cases, the initial sugar levels are so high that the alcohol produced kills off all the yeasts, resulting in a wine with substantial residual sugar. This is one way of making an off- dry or sweet wine. Alternatively, the fermentation can be artificially terminated by filtering out the yeasts or killing them, for example, by pasteurization or the addition of sulphur dioxide or alcohol (fortification). Unless the wine is being fortified, artificial termination of fermentation generally results in a wine with low alcohol and high residual sugar.

While conversion of sugars to ethanol is the predominant reaction, it is only one of potentially thousands of biochemical reactions taking place during fermentation. As a result, wine contains trace amounts of a large number of organic acids, esters, sugars, alcohols, and other molecules. Wine is, in fact, one of the most complex of all beverages: the fruit of a soil, climate, and vintage, digested by fungi through a process guided by the culture, vision, and skill of an individual man or woman.

White wines

There are almost as many approaches to fermentation as there are wine-makers. This section covers the most common techniques for white wines, red wines, and rosés. Sparkling wines and fortified wines are covered in Chapters 12 and 24–25, respectively.

For white wines, the must is usually fermented in the absence of solid matter. Skin contact for the extraction of polyphenols, if any, occurs prior to the onset of fermentation. For a fresh, fruity, vibrant style, fermentation is carried out in sealed, inert vats, usually made from stainless steel, with active temperature control to keep the must from becoming too warm. For a more complex style rich in secondary aromas and flavours, a more traditional vinification is preferred. Large vats and small barrels made of oak have found particular favour, and can be used for both fermentation and maturation. The wood allows for a small amount of air exchange, which facilitates the development of more complex aroma and flavour compounds. Alternatives to oak include vats of concrete or clay, including the concrete egg, which harks back to the Roman amphora or Georgian kvevri. **Concrete eggs** promote circulation with the lees continuously in movement, which adds depth and structure to the wine without the need for lees stirring (see later). They also minimize evaporation, stabilize fermentation temperatures, and allow the wine to breathe as in oak—but without imparting oak aromas and flavours. On the other hand, concrete eggs are initially costly and difficult to transport, and need protection against acid corrosion. But above all they can lead to a wine that is too round or soft, which is why their use is often limited to a fraction (e.g. 20%) of the cuvée.

Red wines and rosés

Red wines rely on contact with the grape skins, pips, and sometimes also stems for their colour, phenolics, and tannins. Rosés and light red wines may undergo no more than cold maceration before the juice is drained off for fermentation. However, most red wines are fermented together with the solid matter, or pomace [*marc*], for at least part if not all of the process. Fermentation temperatures are higher than with white wines, 20–30°C versus ≤15°C, to enhance extraction of colour and polyphenols. The carbon dioxide released from fermentation forces the pomace to the top of the vat, where it is pressed into a solid cap [*chapeau de marc*].

The cap needs to be broken down at frequent intervals to return the solid material to the fermenting juice. This can be achieved by one or more of: punching down, pumping over, and racking and returning—which, according to their application, become methods of controlling colour extraction and quantity and quality of tannins. Of the three, **punching down** [*pigeage*] is the most simple and ancient, and involves depressing the cap to the bottom of the vessel, traditionally with a flat disc attached to a pole. It is a gentle process that minimizes the release of bitter tannins from the outermost cells of the grape skins. **Pumping over** [*remontage*] involves extracting the juice from the bottom of the vat and pumping it onto the cap so as to re-submerge it. This can be achieved with anything from manually operated hoses to automated fermentation vats with nozzles that spray the juice onto the cap. **Racking and returning** [*délestage*] involves draining all the juice from the fermentation vat into a second vessel and then returning it to the original vat by spraying it over the cap. Racking can also be used at other stages of the winemaking process to separate the juice or wine from the solid matter that has accrued at the bottom of the vat. Cos d'Estournel in Bordeaux and Vega Sicilia in Ribera del Duero go so far as to carry up the juice in 'elevator tanks' to avoid stressing it with pumps and pipes! At any point, the wine can be pumped off the solid matter to continue fermenting in a separate vessel, which is another method of making rosé.

Carbonic maceration

In carbonic maceration, bunches of intact grapes are placed in a closed vat and smothered in carbon dioxide. The gas inhibits conventional fermentation; instead, fermentation occurs through an intracellular process driven by natural enzymes within the grape. This process releases further carbon dioxide that bursts the skins open. After one-to-two weeks, the semi-liquid must arrives at an alcoholic strength of around 2-3%, after which it is pressed and transferred to another vat for a conventional yeast fermentation. Wines made by carbonic maceration are almost invariably red, and noted for their pink to purple hue, vibrant estery aromas (bubblegum, strawberry, banana...), softer acidity, and lower tannins. The archetype is Beaujolais Nouveau, which is so approachable as to be ready for market within a few weeks of harvest. Sometimes, only part of a wine is made by carbonic maceration and blended in for a subtle more estery effect. It is unusual to make a white wine by carbonic maceration, since the wine would be coloured by the process (white wines are usually pressed off the skins immediately) and also lose in freshness and definition.

A variant of carbonic maceration is **semi-carbonic maceration**, in which bunches of intact grapes are placed into a vat. The berries at the bottom of the vat are crushed by the weight above them and undergo yeast fermentation. This releases carbon dioxide onto the berries higher up, which in turn undergo intracellular fermentation.

Malolactic (secondary) fermentation

After the alcoholic, or primary, fermentation, the wine may remain in the fermentation vat to undergo a secondary fermentation. The most common type of secondary fermentation is malolactic fermentation, or, more properly, malolactic *conversion*, which principally involves the decarboxylation of malic acid to form lactic acid and carbon dioxide. Although often inoculated, lactic acid bacteria such as *Oenococcus oeni* are naturally present in the must (assuming that the must has not been sterilized) and spontaneously begin the malolactic conversion once the alcoholic fermentation has been completed, or even before. Compared to malic acid, lactic acid is softer and richer on the palate. Lactic acid is found in high concentrations in soured milk products, and white wines that have undergone malolactic conversion can display a yogurt or dairy note.

Almost all red wines undergo malolactic conversion, sometimes over several weeks. As well as reducing acidity and adding texture and complexity, malolactic conversion stabilizes the wine, preventing a later malolactic conversion in the bottle, which could make for a turbid, slightly carbonated product smelling of sauerkraut. With white wines such as Riesling, Gewurztraminer, and Sauvignon Blanc, the wine-maker typically suppresses the malolactic conversion, often by adding sulphur dioxide, to retain the sharpness of the malic acid and the fruity and floral aromas and flavours. Chardonnay on the other hand commonly benefits from malolactic conversion, developing a fuller texture and notes of butter or butter popcorn (diacetyl). Champagne houses usually encourage malolactic conversion, although some, most notably Lanson, Gosset, and Alfred Gratien, prefer to eschew it.

Maturation

Most wines benefit from a period of post-fermentation maturation. White wines might be kept in contact with the lees, which consist primarily of dead yeast cells, for some time after fermentation. **Lees ageing** adds to the texture and complexity of the wine and imparts notes of yeast, bread, brioche, and biscuit. Champagne undergoes lees ageing after the second, bottle fermentation, and much quality Muscadet is left *sur lie* for several months before being bottled. The lees may be stirred through the wine at regular intervals in a process called *bâtonnage*, which increases lees contact and encourages oxygen to percolate to the lees. In the relative absence of oxygen, the reactions involved in the enzymatic decomposition of the lees can lead to an accumulation of foul-smelling hydrogen sulphide. Through increased lees extraction, *bâtonnage* can lead to a fuller wine. But it can also 'tire' the wine, possibly promoting premature oxidation ('premox').

The Romans adopted the Gaulish custom of storing beer and other liquids in oak barrels to facilitate the transportation of wine throughout their extensive empire. Compared to many other woods, oak was soft, pliable, and tight-grained, as well as abundant. Today, wine is commonly matured in oak barrels, which, although watertight, allow small amounts of oxygen to percolate into the wine. Too much oxygen can damage a wine, but a small amount, so-called natural micro-oxygenation, has a number of beneficial effects, including enhancing colour stability and intensity, dispelling reductive and vegetative notes, and, above all, polymerizing and thereby 'softening' astringent tannin compounds.

In the main, three species of oak are used: American oak (*Quercus alba*) and two species of French oak. Of the two French species, the sessile oak (*Quercus petraea/sessiflora*) is tighter grained than the pendunculate oak (*Quercus robur/pedunculata*). Oaks are themselves influenced by terroir, and oak from particular forests such as Allier, Tronçais, and Nevers may be particularly sought-after for their flavour profiles. Until supplies were interrupted in the early twentieth century, many French winemakers favoured oak from Eastern Europe, especially the smaller and slower growing sessile oak from Hungary's Zemplén Mountains, which is said to be 'more French than French'. American oak barrels are less expensive because American oak has a tighter structure which allows it to be sawn, whereas French oak has to be split along the grain of the wood if it is to remain watertight. **American oak** is low in tannins and high in aromatics, imparting notes of coconut and vanilla to the wine. **French oak** imparts more subtle notes of vanilla, toast, caramel, spice, cedar, and smoke. French oak is also high in tannins and can add appreciably to the structure of a wine.

To make top quality barrels, staves of wood are seasoned outdoors for up to three years to leach out the bitterest compounds. The wood is then toasted over a brazier to bend the staves into shape. This charring process brings out certain flavour compounds, and the degree of toasting is another important determinant of a barrel's flavour profile. Some winemakers source barrels from different regions and cooperages with different degrees of toasting to enhance the complexity of their wines.

The most common barrel sizes are the Bordeaux *barrique* of 225l and the shorter, fatter Burgundy barrel of 228l. Didier Dagueneau of Pouilly-Fumé in the Loire experimented with a longer, narrower 'cigar barrel' of 265l that aims to maximize lees contact. A barrel's surface area to volume ratio has an important bearing both on the micro-oxygenation effect and on the transfer of flavour compounds. Maximum flavour is imparted from the barrel in the first year of use, when it is referred to as 'new oak'.

A winemaker may mature a variable proportion of a wine in new oak and the remainder in old oak or a neutral vessel and then blend the two together. Commonly, the winemaker renews a certain fraction of the barrels every year. If, for example, he or she renews a quarter of the barrels every year, the wine will be aged in 25% new oak, 25% two-year-old oak, 25% three-year-old oak, and 25% four-year-old oak. Old barrels can be sanded and re-toasted, but this undermines their structural integrity and is not best practice. Some wines, for example, Bordeaux blends and Rioja, are well suited to a high proportion of new oak; whereas others, for example, Pinot Noir, Rhône reds, and many Italian reds, are better suited to a high proportion of old oak. Yet other wines, especially aromatic white wines such as Riesling or Sauvignon Blanc, are not generally suited to oak ageing, which would detract from their qualities. There are of course important exceptions to these principles, such as Grand Cru Burgundy and Sauvignon Blanc from Graves in Bordeaux, which are commonly aged in a high proportion of new oak.

A number of techniques aim to replicate some of the properties of oak ageing at a small fraction of the cost. These include adding 'oak flavour' powder or inserting oak staves or a giant 'teabag' of oak chips into the wine. Unfortunately, the resulting oak influence usually comes across as coarse and clumsy. To mimic the micro-oxygenation effect of oak ageing, some winemakers introduce small amounts of oxygen through a ceramic diffuser at the bottom of the vat, often with good results.

Clarification and stabilization

After vinification and maturation, which may last anything from a few months to several years, the wine is readied for bottling. In some cases, the wine may be blended from a number of base wines with the aim of improving quality, complexity, and consistency. These base wines may consist of different grape varieties or fruit from different vineyards, vinification vats, or maturation vessels.

The wine may need to be clarified to remove suspended solids, and stabilized to prevent degradation. A wine can be clarified by racking it off its lees in what can be a long and laborious process. Many winemakers prefer to use one of several techniques, most commonly fining or filtration. **Fining** involves the addition of a clarifying substance, traditionally egg white, which leads particles to precipitate, and which is subsequently removed along with the particles. Fining, although often thought of solely in terms of clarification, can also be directed at removing excessive colour, off-flavours and odours, and bitterness or astringency.

Some white wines are susceptible to the gradual accretion of harmless **tartrate crystals** (potassium bitartrate, aka cream of tartar), which can form precipitously if the wine is exposed to colder temperatures. Aficionados look upon these 'wine crystals' or 'wine diamonds' as a mark that the wine has not been overly processed, but less experienced consumers are liable to mistake them for shards of glass. So as not to have bottles returned, the winemaker may decide to bring the wine to near freezing point to precipitate the crystals and then remove them. Unfortunately, this 'cold stabilization' adds nothing to the wine, and may even subtract from it.

Any potentially damaging microorganisms that still remain in the wine ought to be removed or killed to guard against spoilage, including malolactic conversion or a second fermentation on residual sugar. The winemaker may add sulphur dioxide to the wine or filter it to remove the microorganisms, in which case the bottles and bottling equipment have to be kept sterile. Alternatively, he or she may first bottle the wine and then pasteurize it.

A wine crafted with skill and patience is naturally clarified and free from damaging microorganisms, and might be bottled without suffering any of the above interventions. Many quality-conscious wine-makers minimize clarification and stabilization to avoid removing from the colour, aroma, flavour, texture, or ageing potential of their wine.

Some winemakers go further still to produce a 'natural' wine. A **natural wine** is a wine made from handpicked grapes from a biodynamic or organic farm, with minimal manipulation in the cellar. Criteria accepted by most natural wine producers and organizations include: no foreign yeasts, no added sugars, no acidity adjustments, no or minimal contact with new oak, no or minimal fining or filtration, and no or minimal sulphites. Natural wine can be regarded as a reaction to doctored, engineered, or 'industrial' wines, and entails the extension of organic and biodynamic principles into the cellar. It is, of course, a risky business, but the most successful examples are wines of great vivacity, with a broad yet harmonious spectrum of flavours, silky texture, and strong sense of place.

Bottles

Most wines are bottled in what has become a standard 750ml glass bottle. It is sometimes said that the *barrique* is 225l because that is the largest size a man could carry, and that the bottle is 750ml because that is the largest size a glassblower could blow. Other bottle sizes, or *formats,* include piccolo (equivalent to 1/4 of a standard bottle), demi (1/2), magnum (2), jeroboam or double-magnum (4), methuselah (8), salmanazar (12), balthazar (16), and nebuchadnezzar (20). Why these Biblical names, nobody knows. Sweet wines often come in a 500ml jennie, and Vin Jaune from the Jura in a 620cl *clavelin.*

As well as different sizes, wine bottles also come in different shapes, which, in many cases, have become enshrined in EU law. The three most common shapes are the Bordeaux bottle, which is straight-sided and high-shouldered with a pronounced punt [the indentation in the base of the bottle]; the Burgundy and Rhône bottle, which is tall with sloping shoulders and a smaller punt; and the Mosel and Alsace or hock bottle, which is narrow and tall with little or no punt. The punt may be a vestigial remnant from a time when bottles were blown with a blowpipe and pontil. Other possible accounts of the punt include: catching sediment; strengthening or stabilizing the bottle; making the bottle easier to handle, store, or transport; and impressing/deceiving the customer by making the bottle seem more capacitous. Alternatives to glass bottles include plastic bottles, cardboard bricks, and metallic-plastic bags set in cardboard boxes, none of which outperform glass bottles for long-term storage, or romance.

Closures

Cork, the traditional closure, is harvested from the cork oak tree, *Quercus suber.* It is elastic and watertight, but allows a tiny amount of air exchange which assists maturation and guards against the development of reductive odours.

Problems with cork hygiene from the 1960s, when the wine industry was booming, led to an increase in the frequency of 'cork taint' (Chapter 5). This prompted a search for alternative closures such as stoppers made from reconstituted cork or synthetic materials, aluminium screw caps lined with plastic, and glass stoppers fitted with a plastic washer seal. Some of these closures have been engineered to 'breathe', and can boast a more consistent rate of oxygen ingress than genuine corks.

Many producers of aromatic white wines, especially in Australia and New Zealand, prefer screw caps on the grounds that they preserve volatile aromas.

Debate and research into the 'best' closure is ongoing. Some of the world's top producers are carrying out longitudinal studies with a single wine under multiple closures. As the finest wines can take decades to mature, a definitive answer may yet have to wait. Meanwhile, the quality of cork is improving and instances of cork taint are now much less common than they used to be. It has even become possible to test each individual cork by a simple albeit time consuming process known as 'dry soak sensory screening'. Other factors for the winemaker to consider in selecting a closure include cost, renewability, and durability.

Today, the most common type of corkscrew is the waiter's friend or wine key, with a helix and two-step lever, which, when folded up, is no larger than a penknife. The device was patented in 1882 by the German inventor Karl Wienke. But the English couldn't pronounce Wienke, so took to calling it a 'wine key'. For fragile corks, it is better to use a two-pronged butler's friend, so-called because it enables the butler, or sommelier, to secrete some wine and replace the cork unbeknownst. For old vintage port, nothing beats the traditional pair of red-hot tongs to cut the neck off the bottle.

For many purists, the aesthetics of the customs, movements, and sounds associated with uncorking a bottle, not to mention the secret pride and pleasure in calling out a corked bottle, outweigh the risk of cork taint or a dried-out, crumbling cork. Today more than ever, a genuine cork is an indication of a quality wine that is expected to improve with age.

Bottle ageing

If correctly stored at a constant temperature of about 10–15°C and out of direct sunlight, a fine wine continues to evolve through a plethora of complex chemical reactions—the overall effect of which is to lend the wine 'tertiary' notes that complement the primary fruit profile and secondary notes from the winemaking. Over time, often several years, the primary fruit recedes and tertiary notes such as earth, mushroom, and truffle come to the fore. The oak flavours become more integrated, and the tannins polymerize and 'soften'. The larger the bottle size, the more gradual and graceful these changes, such that, in time, a wine matured in a standard 750ml bottle can taste quite different to the same wine matured in a magnum or jeroboam. But what a disaster if the jeroboam is corked!

In the course of ageing, a wine may slip into a dumb phase [*age ingrat*] with muted aromas and flavours. The **drinking window** of a wine is perhaps best described as the period during which all its elements come into harmony. This is partly a matter of taste: for instance, the Bordelais prefer to drink their wines at about five-to-seven years old, whereas the British look upon this as infanticide. According to Coates's Law of Maturity, a wine will remain within its drinking window for as long as it took to reach it. For instance, if a wine took five years to reach its drinking window, it will remain within that window for another five years. But nothing lasts forever, and the process of maturation is also one of decay: wait too long, and you'll be pouring yourself something that looks and tastes like death.

One of the saddest things about ageing is that, as you get older, old wines will seem less old.

The EU and French classification systems

The French *Appellation d'Origine Protég*ée (AOP, formerly AOC) system, governed by the *Institut national des appellations d'origine* (INAO), dates back to 1935. It has inspired or influenced many other national systems and, ultimately, the European Union (EU) wine laws.

The European Union

EU law requires that wines produced within the EU be divided into two quality categories, Protected Geographical Indication (PGI) and Protected Designation of Origin (PDO), each with different rules for winemaking practices and labelling. Some member states have more than two levels of classification, but each level fits into either PGI or PDO.

Some winemaking practices, such as deacidification and chaptalization, are governed by where the grapes are grown rather than PGI or PDO rules. Thus, every EU wine growing region belongs to one of six wine growing zones, with Zone A the coolest and Zone C III b the warmest.

France

French law divides wine into three categories:

• *Vin de France* (formerly *Vin de Table*). The label specifies the producer and that the wine is from France. Unlike with *Vin de Table*, grape variety (or varieties) and vintage can also be indicated on the label.

• *Indication Géographique Protégée* (IGP, formerly *Vin de Pays*). The label specifies a particular French region, *département*, or delimited area, for example, IGP Pays de l'Hérault or IGP Pays d'Oc. The wine has to be made from certain grape varieties or blends, and has to be submitted for analysis and tasting. Maximum or minimum limits are placed on yields, alcohol, pH, and sulphur dioxide. There are currently 75 IGPs, with most concentrated in the southern third of the country, especially Languedoc-Roussillon. Significantly, the designation enables French producers to make non-traditional blends and varietal wines to compete with those from the New World. A IGP varietal wine must contain at least 85% of the stated grape variety.

• *Appellation d'Origine Protégée* (AOP, formerly *Appellation d'Origine Controlée*). Specifies a delimited terroir together with a number of rules and restrictions governing such factors as grape varieties, blends, training systems, yields, and winemaking methods. The focus is on style and tradition, as well as geographical origin. There are over 300 wine AOPs. Some, such as Romanée-Conti AOP in Burgundy, are the size of a vineyard; others, such as Alsace AOP, are more expansive and correspondingly less restrictive. Smaller AOPs are typically nested in one or more larger AOPs, which are, in turn, nested in an IGP.

Vin de France and IGP fit into the EU's PGI category, and AOP into the PDO category.

Other classification systems, such as the US one, are discussed in the country chapters.

Top wine producing countries

Country	Wine production (Unit: mhl) 2020 Provisional	Wine production (Unit: mhl) 2021 Forecast
Italy	49.1	44.5
France	46.7	34.2
Spain	40.7	35.0
USA	22.8	24.1
Australia	10.9	14.2
Argentina	10.8	12.5
South Africa	10.4	10.6
Chile	10.3	13.4
Germany	8.4	8.8
China	6.6	NA
Portugal	6.4	6.5
Russia	4.4	4.5
Romania	3.8	5.3
New Zealand	3.3	2.7
Hungary	2.9	3.1
Brazil	2.3	3.6
Greece	2.3	1.7
World total	262	250

Source: OIV – World Wine Production Outlook, 4 November 2021.
(mhl, million hectolitres)
NB. In 2021, production levels were very low across much of Europe.

Top wine exporting countries

According to the OIV, in 2020, the leading wine exporting countries by volume were Italy (20.8mhl), Spain (20.2), France (13.6), Chile (8.5), Australia (7.5), and Argentina (4.0). Italy and Spain each accounted for almost a fifth of total world wine exports by volume. The leading wine exporting countries *by value* were France (€8736m), Italy (6233), Spain

(2626), Australia (1787), Chile (1596), and the USA (1147). France accounted for almost a third of total world wine exports by value. When, in 2016, Italian Prime Minister Matteo Renzi lightheartedly told French President François Hollande that Italy makes the better wines, Hollande is said to have retorted, "You may be making and selling more wine, but I think ours are more expensive."

5

THE ART AND SCIENCE OF BLIND TASTING

*W*ine is a complex combination of acids, alcohols, sugars, polyphenols, and other biochemicals suspended in an aqueous solution. These biochemicals may be experienced as colour, aromas and flavours, structure or mouthfeel, and by their effects—either pleasant or unpleasant, depending upon the amount consumed—on mind and body. Parameters such as grape variety, soil, climate, winemaking, and ageing express themselves through the ever-changing makeup of the liquid in the glass, which can be analysed and inter-preted (sometimes almost divined) by the experienced or attentive taster.

Unfortunately, unconscious bias and suggestion are all too readily introduced into this process of identification and appreciation. Ideally, a wine ought to be evaluated objectively, with only an afterthought for such factors as price or prestige, the reputation of the region or producer, the shape of the bottle, the type of closure used, and the design on the label. Even our past experiences ("I once had a lovely picnic in this vineyard", "I hate Sauvignon Blanc") and the context and conditions of the tasting ("This room is freezing", "This Empire style château is amazing") can influence our appraisal of the wine. While all these factors may play a part in our personal enjoyment of a wine, they can lead us to prejudice one grape variety, region, producer, vintage, etc. over another, and, ultimately, one wine over another. By holding us back from tasting different wines and thinking about wine, they limit our understanding, and so our enjoyment, of those wines and wine in general.

By far the best way to control for biases is to be blinded to everything but the liquid itself, which is served naked in a standard wine glass, preferably in a more or less neutral setting and without flourish or fanfare. The wine may be tasted either on its own or in a flight, in which case it may be usefully compared and contrasted with the other wines in the flight. The wines within a flight may or may not have certain things in common, for instance, grape variety, country or region of origin, and/or vintage. If these commonalities are revealed prior to the tasting, the tasting is said to be 'semi-blind'. The precise identity of a wine is only revealed once it has been thoroughly assessed and, for more advanced tasters, an attempt at identification has been made.

Aside from setting a standard of objectivity, there is much pleasure to be taken from this process, in:

- Focusing on nothing else but the wines in our glasses.
- Testing, stretching, and developing our senses.
- Applying our judgement.
- Relying upon and recalling old memories.
- Comparing our analysis and interpretations with those of our peers.
- Getting it completely right, more or less right, or 'wrong for the right reasons'.
- Discussing the wine and learning about it, and about wine in general.
- Imbibing the wine with the respect and consideration that it deserves.

In refining their senses and aesthetic judgement, blind tasters become much more conscious of the richness not only of wine but also of other potentially complex beverages such as tea, coffee, and spirits, and, by extension, the aromas and flavours in food, the scents in the air, and the play of light in the world. For life is consciousness, and consciousness is life.

In philosophy, phenomenology is the study of the structures of human consciousness and experience. Wine blind tasting is a phenomenology in its purest form, returning us from our heads into the world, and, at the same time, illuminating the methods of the mind.

The more down-to-earth among you may rest assured that blind tasting also has some more immediately practical purposes: winemakers need to taste a wine as they are making it; wine buyers before adding it to their stocks; journalists, critics, and sommeliers before recommending it to their readers and patrons; and imbibers before sharing it with their friends. Especially as a student, you can enter into a growing number of local, national, and international blind tasting competitions. You can also pursue more formal qualifications and give yourself the option of entering into the wine trade, which is less soul destroying than most other lines of work.

How to organize a blind tasting

Materials

- Six to twelve different wines.
- Standardized unmarked bottles or receptacles in which to decant the wines (or bottle sleeves with which to mask the original wine bottles).
- A corkscrew.
- ISO wine tasting glasses or similar, one per wine in each flight.
- Spittoons (these need not be more elaborate than cups or jugs).
- Tasting sheets, which can be downloaded from https:// neelburton.com/blind-wine-tasting-resources/

Optional materials

- A foil cutter to remove any foil capsules.

- A funnel.
- Metal foil wine pourers to minimize dripping.
- Some spare pens.
- Crib sheets, which can be downloaded from https://neelburton.com/blind-wine-tasting-resources/

Method

Broadly, a blind tasting can be horizontal, vertical, or a combination of horizontal and vertical. A horizontal tasting involves different wines (sometimes although not necessarily from the same vintage), while a vertical tasting involves the same wine in different vintages. Horizontal tastings in which grape varieties and regions and terroirs are compared are, if only for logistical purposes, far more common than vertical tastings.

A typical blind tasting consists of between six and twelve white or red wines, sometimes with a focus or theme such as 'Chardonnay', 'South Africa', 'The Rhône', 'Left Bank Bordeaux', or 'Oak'. If there are twelve different wines, they may be presented in two flights of six, typically a flight of white wines followed by a flight of red wines. This has a number of advantages, including dividing up the evening and limiting the number of glasses required to just six per person, while still enabling the white wines to be compared with one another, and the same for the reds. If there are six wines, they can be presented as a flight of six or two flights of three, and so on. Obviously, if the theme is 'Chardonnay', then only white wines can be served, so maybe choose a theme such as 'Chardonnay and Pinot Noir'.

The wines ought to be decanted into standardized unmarked bottles or receptacles. Bottle sleeves or socks, which are available commercially, may be adequate for beginners' classes or if there is no variation in shape or type of closure among the selected bottles. In the absence of unmarked receptacles or bottle sleeves, the guests need to leave the room while the wine is being poured into their glasses, which is quite a palaver.

The best **glasses** for tasting are long-stemmed and tulip-shaped. The long stem ensures that the wine does not warm up through contact with the hand, and also keeps the smells of the hand at a distance from the aromas emanating from the wine. Above all, it helps to direct the wine into the front of the mouth, which facilitates tasting. The tulip-shape concentrates volatile compounds inside the glass. As the bowl is wider than the rim, the wine can be swirled around without fear of spillage, and the glass and its contents can be tilted to near horizontal for a thorough inspection of colour. The ideal shape of the tulip varies according to the wine style, hence the Bordeaux glass, the red Burgundy glass, and so on. But when blind tasting, it is best to use the same type of glass for all the wines so that like is being compared with like. The style of glass that is used in most blind tasting societies and blind tasting competitions is the International Standards Organization (ISO) glass, which is cheap, sturdy, portable, not inelegant, and adequate for most purposes.

It is important to pour the right amount of wine into the glass: too little and it is difficult to smell and taste all the components; too much and the wine cannot breathe in the glass. With the ISO glass, a finger-breadth is a good rule of thumb (no pun intended). At most, a bottle of wine can serve 18–20 portions, equivalent to about 40cl per portion.

The **temperature** of a wine influences the perception of its aromas and structure. At higher temperatures, there is more energy in the wine, such that more and larger molecules can escape the surface of the liquid. On the other hand, if the temperature is too high, much of the aromatic subtlety is lost and the wine becomes much less enjoyable. Higher temperatures also decrease sensitivity to acidity and tannin, which is why overly cool red wines can come across as 'hard'. Broadly, the fuller the body of a wine, the warmer it has to be to yield its volatile compounds. In practical terms, this means that most white, rosé, and sparkling wines ought to be served at around 8–10°C, sometimes referred to as 'fridge door temperature'. Highly aromatic sweet wines such as Sauternes are best served slightly cooler, while full-bodied, oaky white wines such as Meursault are best served slightly warmer. Red wines ought to be served at around 14–18°C. Pinot Noir and other light-bodied red wines with delicate bouquets are best served slightly cooler, while full-bodied red wines such as Australian Shiraz are best served at the warmer end of the quoted range. Eventually, one develops a feel for the temperature of a wine and the temperature at which it ought to be served. If in doubt, err on the side of cool, as the wine will warm up in the glass and can be warmed further or faster by cupping the glass in one's hands. If the wine is still in the bottle, it can be cooled or kept cool with a thermic bag, frozen sleeve, or ice bucket (water around the bottle leads it to cool much faster). Depending on the weather, it might be possible to keep the wine on an outer windowsill or even in a river or stream.

Each wine calls for five to ten minutes of analysis and ten minutes of discussion. So if there are, for example, six wines presented in two flights of three, allocate thirty minutes for assessing the first flight, thirty minutes for discussing the first flight, thirty minutes for assessing the second flight, and thirty minutes for discussing the second flight. Remind guests that they need not progress systematically from the first to the last wine in the flight; encourage them instead to start with the lightest wine in the flight and work their way up to the heaviest or sweetest wine, which, if attempted first, could interfere with their ability to taste the more delicate wines. The general principles of **tasting order** are: white before red, dry before sweet, young before old, and modest before fine. 'White before red' merely reflects that white wines are generally lighter in body, but one may prefer to taste a delicate Pinot Noir ahead of a rich Chardonnay.

Wine is also about bringing people together, so remember to make time for guests to socialize. If possible, sit everyone around a single table: this is more convivial and also facilitates the discussion of the wines. Sit beginners next to more experienced tasters who can encourage them and guide them through the tasting process. Some people prefer to assess the wines in silence, but complete silence can be intimidating to beginners and restricting to more gregarious types.

Do not be too rigid about time allocation: if everyone has stopped sniffing and scribbling, move on to discussing the wines. Upon discussing a wine, it is customary to call for one or two tasting notes before taking guesses and opening up the table to a general discussion of the wine. Once the discussion has been exhausted, the identity of the wine can be revealed. In some cases, particularly if there is a common theme to the flight, it may be more politic to delay the guessing and/or revealing until all the wines in the flight have been discussed. Wine used to be prescribed by doctors, among others, as an orexigenic, or appetite stimulant. With the tasting at a close, consider asking the guests to dinner with whatever remains of the wines.

In an informal and intimate setting such as a dinner party, every guest can be requested to bring a bottle to blind taste, which makes the event much more entertaining for the organizer and also spreads the cost around. Guests naturally compete with one another to bring the finest or most interesting wine, which can make for a jolly good evening!

Tasting conditions

Most amateur blind tastings are conducted in the evening. However, our senses are at their sharpest earlier in the day, which is why many critics prefer to taste mid-morning. When tasting, it generally helps to be relaxed, alert, concentrated, well-hydrated, and slightly hungry. The best light is bright natural daylight, although the open outdoors with its draughts and smells should be avoided. Indoors, cut flowers and fragrant foods should be removed to another room, as should anyone wearing scent or aftershave! Whether outdoors or indoors, weather conditions can influence our ability to taste. In particular, wine is less enjoyable at lower atmospheric pressures. In aeroplanes, tasting is impeded by low cabin pressure, dry air, and engine background noise, with wines seeming less fruity, more acidic, and more tannic. Even music can alter our perception of wine. According to research from the Crossmodal Research Laboratory at the University of Oxford, people associate higher notes, flutes, and tinkling piano with sweetness; and deeper, more resonant notes with bitterness.

Food and wine pairing

Food and wine can have a synergistic relationship, such that the wine improves the food and the food the wine, unleashing the full taste potential of both. In many European wine regions, the wine styles and culinary traditions developed reciprocally such that the wines naturally pair with the regional fare. Many of these so-called 'food wines' can seem overly tart or tannic if drunk independently, but come into their own once paired with food, and, in particular, those dishes that they co-evolved with. If you respect these time-honoured pairings, you are unlikely to go wrong.

Otherwise, you need to choose what to put into focus: the food or the wine. For instance, if it is the wine that you wish to emphasize, pick a dish that is slightly lighter and complements rather than competes with it. Take care not to pick a dish that is too light or it will be overwhelmed by the wine: although you want the wine to lead, you want the dish to follow closely behind. If it is the food that you wish to emphasize, you are effectively using the wine as a sauce or spice. In all instances, the wine and the food should interact synergistically, with the wine bringing out the best in the food, and the food the best in the wine. This is certainly the case with such classic pairings as Muscadet and oysters, Claret and lamb, and Sauternes and Roquefort.

Taste, however, is subjective, and there cannot and should not be rigid rules for pairing foods and wines. Indeed, part of the pleasure of the wine lover is in experimenting with combinations and, in so doing, multiplying the flavours, textures, and sensations of everyday life. That said, you do need to be versed in the principles that you may, or may not, decide to break.

First, identify the dominant component of your dish. For example, the dominant component of fish served in a creamy sauce is more likely to be the sauce than the fish itself. Then pick out a wine that either complements or contrasts with the dominant component. Examples of complementary pairings are: a citrusy Sauvignon Blanc with sole in a lemon sauce, an earthy Pinot Noir with a mushroom tart, a peppery

Syrah with a steak in peppercorn sauce, a robust Madiran with a duck confit, and a nutty Vin Jaune with Comté cheese.

Four important elements to bear in mind are weight, acidity, tannins, and sweetness. The **weight and texture** of a wine is determined by such factors as alcohol level, amount of extract and tannin, and winemaking processes such as extended maceration, lees ageing, and oaking. In general, lighter wines pair with lighter foods, whereas heavier, more robust wines pair with heavier, more rustic foods. Good examples of pairings by weight are Chardonnay and lobster or Chardonnay and roast chicken.

Acidity whets the appetite and cuts through heaviness, accounting for the success of such contrasting pairings as Sancerre and goat cheese, Alsatian Riesling and pork belly, and Tokaj and foie gras. In all cases, the wine must be at least as acidic as the dish, and preferably more so: if not, the wine is going to seem thin or insipid.

Tannins can lend chalkiness or grittiness to a wine, and also bitter astringency. Tannins are 'softened' when they bind to and react with proteins in food. While tannic wines go hand in hand with red meats and cheeses, they pair poorly with spicy or sweet dishes, which can accentuate their bitterness and astringency, and also with fish oils, which can make them taste 'metallic'.

A sweet dish requires a wine that is just as sweet or sweeter if the wine is not to be overpowered. **Sweetness** balances heat and spiciness, and also contrasts with saltiness, as, for example, with port and blue cheese. Conversely, alcohol accentuates the heat in spicy food—and spicy food the heat in alcohol. So much explains why Mosel Riesling, which is both high in residual sugar and low in alcohol, is often an excellent choice for spicy food. However, very spicy food will overwhelm almost any wine, so pair with some other beverage such as water, tea, beer, or lassi. Some foods are difficult to pair with wine, most notably eggs, most oily fish, artichokes, asparagus, Brussels sprouts and other cabbages, chili peppers, fresh tomatoes, and chocolate.

Finally, remember also to match your wine to the occasion, your companions, the season, the weather, the time of day or night, and your mood and tastes. If you are serving more than one wine, think about your line up and make it as varied or interesting or educational as possible.

And of course—even if the tasting conditions are far from ideal—serve the wines blind!

The components of wine

Wine is estimated to contain over one thousand different aroma and flavour compounds, half of which are produced by yeasts during fermentation. Some of these compounds leap out of the glass, while others with a lower relative volatility need to be coaxed out by warming and swirling. Over time, some compounds polymerize and might precipitate out of solution to form tartrate crystals or a tannin sediment.

Alcohol

Aside from water, the most important component in most wines is ethyl alcohol, or ethanol, which is formed by the fermentation of sugars by yeast cells. Although pure ethanol is tasteless and odourless, it does provide body to the wine, and also alters the perception of other compounds. A wine with a lower alcohol can come across as more savoury than a similar wine with a higher alcohol, while very high or excessive alcohol can obscure fruit aromas and flavours. When alcohol is in balance with the other components of the wine, it is perceived as unobstrusive or 'integrated'.

Acids

Next come organic acids. In the main, grapes contain malic acid, tartaric acid, and much smaller amounts of citric acid. **Malic acid** [Lat. *malum*, apple] gives green apples their characteristic, biting taste. During winemaking, malic acid is commonly converted to **lactic acid** through a decarboxylation reaction variously referred to as secondary fermentation, malolactic fermentation, or, more properly, malolactic conversion. This reaction can occur naturally, but is often initiated by an inoculation of desirable lactic acid bacteria, usually *Oenococcus oeni* (Chapter 4). Lactic acid is also found in soured milk products, whence the name, and is softer than malic acid, lending the wine a rounder and richer texture. With some fruity and floral white grape varieties such as Riesling or Sauvignon Blanc, the malolactic conversion is likely to be suppressed to retain fruity and floral aromas and a crisp acidity. Of all fruits, grapes contain the highest concentrations of **tartaric acid**, which might help explain why wine made from grapes is so much better than wine made from any other fruit. Tartaric acid stabilizes the finished wine, but some of it may precipitate out of solution to form tartrate crystals resembling shards of glass ('wine crystals', 'wine diamonds'). In the kitchen, potassium bitartrate is called cream of tartar, and used to stabilize eggs whites and whipped cream.

Other acids in wine include succinic acid, which is a by-product of fermentation, acetic acid (vinegar), and butyric acid. Excessive amounts of acetic acid or butyric acid (which smells like spoiled milk or rancid butter) are bacteria-induced wine faults.

Aside from preserving it, the acids in a wine contribute to its freshness and depth of contrast; balance alcohol, sugars, and other components; and help to cleanse and refresh the palate by dissolving fats from accompanying food. The wine writer Michael Broadbent has described acidity as 'the nervous system of a wine', and I also like to think of it as a coat hanger or climbing frame. A wine that lacks in acidity can come across as flat, dull, and uninteresting.

Sugars

Grapes contain near equal amounts of glucose and fructose sugars, which are converted to ethanol during the fermentation process. In some cases, the fermentation process is arrested so that the wine is left with a certain amount of 'residual' sugar. During fermentation, yeasts preferentially feed on glucose, meaning that most residual sugar is the sweeter tasting fructose. Dry wines have a residual sugar of 4g/l or less, which is undetectable on the palate, or only indirectly detectable as offset acidity or a slightly fuller body. At the other end of the scale, some sweet wines can contain more than 100g/l of residual sugar and Tokaji Eszencia in excess of 800g/l! The sweetness of a wine can be masked by acidity, and, to a lesser extent, tannins.

Polyphenols

Polyphenols are a broad group of biochemicals that are principally found in the grape skins. They account for much of the taste of a wine, and, over time, interact with other biochemicals in the wine to form a vast array of secondary and tertiary compounds.

Anthocyanins are a class of red, blue, and purple polyphenols that leach into wine through skin contact during fermentation. They are unstable and, in the presence of oxygen, react with tannins to form larger compounds that precipitate out of the wine, leading to some colour loss. At the same time, anthocyanins are antioxidants that preserve the wine and possibly also the drinker.

Tannins are a group of polymerized polyphenols found in grape skins, pips, and stems. The tannin levels of a wine are related to, among others, the grape variety or varieties and the degree and duration of contact with the skins and other solid matter. Although tannins are generally associated with red wines, some white wines may be left on the skins for a short period for additional texture and astringency. Oak barrels can represent another source of tannins for both red and white wines. Tannins are experienced as a textural or structural element together with a certain astringency (a physical sensation) and bitterness (a taste). They are surfactants that interact with salivary proteins to form large compounds that prevent the saliva from lubricating the mouth, leading to a drying, puckering sensation (astringency). They also interact with proteins and fats in foods, which is why tannic wines seem less bitter and astringent when imbibed with meat or cheese. Lastly, they enhance our enjoyment of food and wine by stripping the film of fat that coats the mouth and re-exposing the taste buds. With increasing bottle age, tannins come across as softer, sometimes almost silky or velvety. The process by which this occurs is poorly understood, and part of the magic of wine.

Volatile compounds

The aroma and most of the flavour of a wine is experienced not in the mouth but in the nose, produced by volatile compounds escaping from the surface of the liquid and stimulating the olfactory bulb. These volatile compounds arise either from the grape itself or as by-products of biochemical reactions during fermentation and maturation.

Aromas in wine often remind us of other aromas, such as gooseberry, pepper, or vanilla, by which we can describe the wine. With increasing experience, we may begin to associate some of these aromas with a particular volatile compound or class of volatile compounds, including esters, terpenes, rotundone, pyrazines, thiols, lactones, aldehydes, and fusel oils.

Esters give rise to fruity and floral aromas. They are formed when an acid reacts with an alcohol, typically during fermentation, malolactic conversion, or maturation. The particular yeast strain as well as the temperature of fermentation are important determinants of the range of esters produced.

Terpenes are found in conifer resin and the essential oils of various plants and flowers. Unlike many wine aromatics, they derive primarily from the grape itself, and contribute to the floral and fragrant aspect of numerous white grape varieties, including Muscats, Gewurztraminer, Pinot Gris, Riesling, Albariño, Torrontés, and Viognier. In wine, the most important terpenes are geraniol (rose), linalol (rose, coriander), nerol (rose), citronellol (citronella), α-terpineol (lily of the valley), and hotrienol (linden or lime tree). 1,8-cineole is behind the eucalyptus note in many an Australian wine. The petrol note associated with mature Riesling has been linked to trimethyldihydronaphthalene (TDN), which can be classed as a terpene.

Rotundone is a recently identified aromatic sesquiterpene found in the essential oils of peppercorns, marjoram, oregano, rosemary, thyme, basil, and geranium. In grapes, it is most present in Syrah/Shiraz, giving rise to a characteristic peppery note. It is also part of the signature of Mourvèdre, Durif, and Grüner Veltliner, among others. Rotundone originates in the grape itself, with higher levels in cooler sites and vintages. Although it has a very low sensory threshold, about 20% of people seem unable to detect it.

Pyrazines are responsible for the green, herbaceous, or vegetative notes in the Bordeaux varieties Sauvignon Blanc, Cabernet Sauvignon, Cabernet Franc, Merlot, and Carmenère. They are linked with notes of bell pepper, grass, leaves, herbs, and earth, which are appreciated in Sauvignon Blanc but much less so in red wines. The ripeness of the grapes at harvest is inversely correlated with the intensity of the pyrazine note. The most important pyrazine in wine is isobutyl-methoxypyrazine, which is present in concentrations of just 5–30ng/L.

Whereas pyrazines are heterocyclic compounds derived from grapes, **thiols** are sulphur-containing alcohol analogues formed during fermentation. Thiols are most prevalent in Sauvignon Blanc, especially New Zealand Sauvignon Blanc, but are also found in other varieties including Riesling, Semillon, Cabernet Sauvignon, and Merlot. Like terpenes, they can be pungent, and are linked with notes of gooseberry, grapefruit, passion fruit, guava, blackcurrant, cat's pee, and sweat.

Lactones are cyclic esters that can derive from grapes, fermentation, maturation, botrytization, flor, and, most of all, contact with oak. **Oak lactones**, which contribute notes of coconut and vanilla, are the most important oak-derived volatiles in wine. American oak is richer in lactones than French oak, which is however higher in tannins. Other oak-derived volatiles include guaiacols, associated with smoke; furfurals, associated with caramel and butterscotch; and the phenolic aldehyde vanillin. The lactone sotolon, associated with nuts and curry, is a key volatile in flor wines such as sherry (Chapter 25) and *vin jaune* (Chapter 11).

Aldehydes are dehydrogenated alcohols, whence their name. They are formed as a byproduct of fermentation or by the subsequent oxidation of alcohol. The most important aldehyde is **acetaldehyde**, which, in many wines, accounts for over 90% of aldehydes. Acetaldehyde is linked with notes of bruised apple, straw, and nuts, and is the key impact aroma compound in sherry and other flor wines. But in many other wines, much lower levels are regarded as a detracting fault. Aside from contributing aroma and flavour, aldehydes help to stabilize colour and polymerize tannins. Indeed, it is through the production of acetaldehyde that the micro-oxygenation of red wine leads to tannin polymerization. Acetaldehyde binds to sulphur dioxide so strongly that a wine cannot contain free sulphur dioxide unless all the acetaldehyde has been tied up, and vice versa, with major implications for winemaking.

Fusel oils are higher alcohols produced during fermentation. They can contribute to the complexity of a wine, but are found in much higher concentrations in distillates in which they are of much greater importance.

Wine faults

A discussion of volatile compounds naturally leads on to the subject of wine faults and their detection. Wine faults commonly owe to a lack of care in the winery or bottling plant.

Sulphur compounds

In ancient times, winemakers burnt sulphur candles in amphorae to help preserve their wines. Ever since, the use of **sulphites/sulphur dioxide** has been an almost constant feature of winemaking. Generally speaking, sulphite levels are higher in white than in red wines, and highest in sweet wines. Sulphites inhibit the growth of microorganisms and bind with acetaldehyde and other oxidizing agents to conserve aroma and flavour. However, higher levels of sulphur dioxide can produce a note of struck match and irritation or stinging of the nasal passages. High levels of sulphur dioxide have also been associated with potentially fatal allergic reactions and other health problems, including veisalgia (alcoholic hangover).

If sulphites can be thought of as oxidized sulphur, **hydrogen sulphide** can be thought of as reduced sulphur. Hydrogen sulphide, which is associated with reductive taint, suppresses fruit aromas and, at higher levels, produces an odour of rotten eggs, boiled cabbage, or drains. It can result, among others, from: added sulphur dioxide; reduction by yeast enzymes of elemental sulphur (from sulphur sprays) on grape skins; and nutrient deficiency in yeast, with the yeast degrading sulphur-containing amino acids.

Like hydrogen sulphide, **mercaptans** are sulphur compounds derived from the degradation of amino acids. Mercaptans and thiols (see above) are in fact the same type of molecule: thiols are the desirable ones, mercaptans the undesirable. Methyl mercaptan is associated with notes of cabbage, garlic, onion, and rubber. Levels of hydrogen sulphide and mercaptan can be reduced by copper fining—which might explain why the Ancients often drank from goblets of copper and lead.

Oxidation and reduction

Oxidation is probably the most common wine fault, although consumers often attribute its musty note to cork taint. In both red and white wines, excess exposure to oxygen leads to a browner colour. The wine loses its fruit character, and develops a musty, dusty, 'flat' note redolent of beef stock, often with a bitter, drying finish. Oxidation may result from careless winemaking or an inadequately sealed bottle. Corks degrade over time, especially if the bottles are stored upright and they are left to dry out, which is why most cellaring companies offer a re-corking service for older bottles.

Of course, some wines, such as sherry, madeira, or tawny port, are made in a deliberately oxidative style that is part of their character and appeal. Table wines that spend prolonged periods in oak such as Rioja bear oxidative notes such as nuts, dried fruits, beeswax, and honey that contribute to their complexity without detracting from their other qualities.

Reduction is the opposite chemical reaction to oxidation and occurs when a wine is deprived of oxygen. This lack of oxygen, or anoxia, encourages the conversion of sulphur dioxide to hydrogen sulphide (see above). Reductive taint is most common in bottles sealed with an airtight screw cap. Mild reductive taint ought to dissipate as the wine is swirled around in the glass. Severe reductive taint can be treated with a copper coin, which serves to precipitate sulphide ions.

Cork taint

True cork taint owes to 2,4,6-trichloroanisole (TCA), formed when certain phenolic compounds react with chlorine-containing compounds, especially the disinfectant trichlorophenol. Cork taint need not result from the cork itself, as TCA can also be found on barrels and other winery equipment. In bad cases of cork taint, the wine smells like wet cardboard and falls flat on the palate. Some people are highly sensitive to cork taint, others much less so. Cork and cork taint are also discussed in Chapter 4.

Brettanomyces

Brettanomyces in wine is cause for controversy. The yeast is encouraged by a lack of hygiene in the winery. Some claim that it lends added complexity to a wine in the form of horsey or farmyard notes; others that it is a taint that overlies the natural fruit character of the wine with 'unclean' notes of sweaty saddle, sticking plaster, and rancid cheese. Some of the world's finest wines, most notably older vintages of Château de Beaucastel in Châteauneuf-du-Pape, contain traces of 'Brett'. Whether this is a benefit or a fault is ultimately a matter of personal preference: the least that can be said is that no wine should be drowning in Brett.

Other microorganisms

If active yeasts and fermentable sugars remain in a wine, it will continue to ferment in bottle. This **second fermentation** and the carbon dioxide released is exactly what is wanted in traditional method sparkling wine, but not, of course, in other wines which will become inappropriately cloudy and fizzy. In severe cases, the bottle may even burst. Off-dry and semi-sweet wines are particularly susceptible to a second fermentation, and great care must be taken to remove or kill all the yeasts before bottling.

Bacteria within the bottle can make a wine go off. **Lactic acid bacteria** in a finished wine can be associated with a smell of mouse droppings or cracker biscuit. The taint is experienced not on the nose but late on the palate, and can linger in the mouth.

In the presence of oxygen, **acetic acid bacteria** convert ethanol to acetic acid, the acid ingredient in vinegars. The acetic acid then reacts with ethanol to form ethyl acetate, which smells of glue or nail varnish remover. A miniscule amount of this so-called **volatile acidity** can be desirable. Some Italian red wines and some Châteauneufs tend to volatility, as does the highly regarded Château Musar in Lebanon. Volatile acidity is also common in botrytized wines. The botrytis fungus splits the grape skin, promoting co-infection with bacteria and yeasts and so the formation of acetic acid and ethyl acetate.

Geosmin

Geosmin [Greek, 'smell of the earth'] is produced by microorganisms in the soil, particularly *Streptomyces*, and can also form on rotting grapes through the action of *Botrytis cinerea* and other microorganisms. Geosmin smells of moist or freshly ploughed soil, and is a key impact aroma in beetroot. It can find its way into water supplies, freshwater fish, and, of course, wine, potentially lending them an unpleasant earthy, musty, or muddy taste. Camels are highly sensitive to geosmin, which they use to locate oases.

A note on minerality in wine

Certain volatile sulphur compounds, especially in more modest concentrations, may be partly responsible for 'minerality', an elusive but desirable descriptor that means different things to different people. Some people find minerality on the nose, others on the palate, and yet others on both nose and palate. On the nose, 'minerality' can refer to, among others, a matchstick or struck flint note on a Chardonnay, chalk or flint on a Chablis, or slate on a Mosel Riesling. On the palate, it can mean a chalky texture, a certain 'stony' minerality, or the energy or vibrancy associated with high acidity. Minerality can also be found on red wines, including, archetypically, Priorat, Bierzo, and Cahors. As yet, there is no hard evidence that minerality derives from direct mineral transfer from soil to wine, still less from 'dissolved rocks'. To my mind, minerality is a reflection of complexity in a cool climate wine with high acidity and a relative lack of aromatic compounds such as esters and terpenes. A mineral wine is typically grown on an infertile soil (helping to explain the complexity) and made reductively.

The perception of wine

Our sense of taste arises from specialized sensory cells in taste buds on the tongue, palate, soft palate, and pharynx. There are around five thousand taste buds in the mouth, each with fifty to one hundred of these sensory cells, or chemoreceptors. Each chemoreceptor is sensitive to one of five groups of chemicals, with each chemical within a group interpreted as one of the five basic or fundamental tastes: alkaloids as bitterness, sugars as sweetness, ionic salts as saltiness, acids as sourness, and amino acids as umami or savouriness. Although some parts of the tongue are more sensitive to certain tastes than others, the 'tongue map' that divides the tongue into discrete tasting areas very much overstates the case.

Chemical sense of taste is supported by the physical and chemical sensation of the liquid in the mouth, or **mouthfeel**. The physical sense of touch, which is responsive to dissolved particles as small as three microns, transmits the temperature and texture of the wine. The prickle of dissolved carbon dioxide is transmitted by chemesthesis, the same sense or sensibility by which chemical irritants such as chilli or mustard register their fieriness.

Sense of smell, or **olfaction**, is triggered by airborne chemicals acting on olfactory receptors on the tiny hair-like cilia of olfactory receptor neurons in the nasal epithelium. The axons of these olfactory receptor neurons converge onto the olfactory bulb of the brain, travelling up through the sieve-like cribriform plate of the skull and merging into the olfactory nerve (cranial nerve I). There are around five hundred types of olfactory receptor, which, through a form of combinatorial processing, are capable of discerning several thousand aromas. Sensitivity to aromas can differ significantly, both from one aroma to another and from one individual to the next, with some aromas detectable in concentrations one hundred million times smaller than others. The olfactory apparatus can be stimulated orthonasally, through the nostrils and nose, or retronasally, from within the mouth and pharynx. Much 'tasting' actually takes place retronasally, which is why a runny or blocked nose can leave our food tasting of cardboard.

The 'flavour' of a wine is an integrated interpretation by the brain of all the various sensory stimuli detailed above. Upon tasting the wine, the brain experiences something of an overload, whence the difficulty in picking out individual aromas and flavours. To facilitate its task, the brain relies heavily on preconceptions (including injurious ones, or prejudices), context, and memory to inform its interpretation of the sensory stimuli. For example, if a white wine with an aroma of lemons and apples is dyed red with food colourings, most people will describe red berry aromas; and if an ordinary table wine is served in a bottle labelled 'Grand Cru', most people will praise it as 'balanced', 'complex', and such-like. The olfactory bulb is part of the **limbic system**, an area of the brain closely associated with emotions and memories. Smells and tastes can trigger strong emotions and vivid memories that bias our perception of the wine. Conversely, our emotional state affects our appreciation of sensory stimuli, which explains, for example, why wine tastes better in good company or why champagne has it easy. Blind tasting can help us overcome these biases, first, by removing a certain number of their sources, and, second, by encouraging us to hyper-focus on sensory stimuli.

In engaging intellectually with a wine, blind tasters activate not only the limbic system, but also areas of the brain responsible for cognition, which is a conscious, higher-order function. This process can be assisted and developed by writing **tasting notes** that seek to accurately describe the sensations produced by the wine. Given the limitations of language in accurately describing our sensations, this, like writing poetry, is no mean feat. Nonetheless, language is by far the best tool at our disposal for communicating our experiences to others and, indeed, to ourselves. The practice of consciously describing the sensations produced by wine alters the makeup of our brain, forging neural connections which, over time, make it much easier to taste and think about taste. As Wittgenstein famously remarked, 'The limits of my language are the limits of my world.'

Is there such a thing as a 'super-taster'? Although some people do have a higher density of taste buds, this does not make them super-tasters. To use a computing analogy, tasting is not so much a function of the hardware (the nose and palate) as it is of the software (the mind or brain). Regardless of the sensitivity of their tasting apparatus, untutored tasters struggle to 'get their head round' more complex wines, and, as a result, derive greater enjoyment from simpler, more accessible wines. To them, it can seem as though the more experienced tasters are talking mumbo-jumbo and hocus-pocus. But with enough experience and training, almost anyone can turn into a wine expert.

An approach to blind tasting

As a blind taster gathers increasing experience, he or she develops a memory bank of wine styles that makes identification more reliable, fast, and intuitive. Even so, the blind taster requires a framework to fall back upon to confirm an initial impression or come to grips with an unfamiliar style. Even the most experienced among us can stumble upon *terra incognita*, and the sheer variety and diversity of wines, even from within a single region (different producers, vineyards, vintages...), is one of the many fascinations of blind tasting. Each time I taste a grape variety or region through a wine, I only do so from a particular angle, through a particular lens, without ever beholding the thing itself, the archetype, which, like the Platonic form of justice or love, only exists in my mind, pieced together from each and every one of my tasting experiences.

Assessing the wine: in the glass

Immediately after the wine has been poured, inspect it for any bubbles or 'spritz'. Spritz is carbon dioxide that is coming out of solution, and is indicative of reductive wine making. Sparkling wines release a stream of carbon dioxide bubbles, the volume and rate, and even the sound, of which can be suggestive of the method of winemaking (Chapter 12).

Gently tilt the glass to an angle of 45° away from you and examine the wine against a white background such as a sheet of paper, tablecloth, or sleeve. Almost all modern wines are clear and limpid. Nonetheless, be sure to exclude dullness, haziness, or cloudiness, which could indicate an unfiltered or faulty wine. Adjust your focus to the surface of the wine and note its brightness. Young, light-bodied and acidic white wines such as Mosel Riesling or champagne are often star-bright or brilliant. Brightness is related to clarity. Red wines reflect less light than white wines, and therefore seem less bright.

Next, examine the colour of the wine. Look at the wine from above to assess the depth (degree, intensity, or saturation) of colour, which can be gauged from the visibility of the stem of the glass. Depth of colour can range from watery to opaque. When comparing one wine to another, ensure that you have a similar volume in each glass. Return the glass to an angle of 45° and inspect the liquid to confirm its colour, or hue. Especially with red wines, the colour at the centre or 'core' may differ from that at the edge or 'rim'.

White wines range in colour from watery-white through to green, lemon, straw, golden, and even coppery-orange in the case of certain dessert wines. Wines at the greener end of the spectrum are often pale and vice versa. Red wines range in colour from orange-red through to brick-red, ruby, violet, and indigo, and even 'black' for the inkiest wines. However pale or opaque, red wines almost invariably start off as 'red' or 'purple': with age, their colour softens, leading to more orange hues. Rosés are typically described in terms of orange, salmon, or pink.

Finally, inspect the base of the bowl for any tartrate crystals (in a white wine) or tannin sediment (in a red wine). Some wine glasses have an indentation in the base of the bowl, called an epicure, which can assist with colour assessment.

Some people like to swirl the wine to generate **legs or tears** on the side of the glass. The size, velocity, and colour, or staining, of these tears reflect the density or viscosity of the wine, which in turn reflects levels of sugar, alcohol, and extract. However, these three parameters are more readily and accurately assessed on the palate.

Assessing the wine: on the nose

The next step is to take in the aromas or bouquet of the wine. Gently tilt the glass to an angle of 45° towards you. As you approach the glass to your face, bend your neck forward so that your nostrils come to rest directly above the wine. Close your eyes and gently inhale. This first impression is often the most revealing, since your sense of smell will quickly adapt to the wine and 'cancel it out' (it is by this cancelling process that we cannot, in general, smell ourself). You can refresh or reset your acuity for a particular wine by coming back to it after one or more wines, by which time it may also have opened up. Similarly, comparing and contrasting two or more wines can throw the wines into relief—although it can also distort your overall evaluation, for instance, leading you to underestimate the aromatic intensity of the shier wine. I sometimes find myself sniffing in fast bursts, or 'odour sampling', like scent-reliant animals.

Now swirl the wine and repeat. **Swirling** transmits kinetic energy to the wine and enables it to coat a much larger surface area of the glass, amplifying the nose and bringing out heavier volatile compounds. It can also rouse the wine and shake out any passing smells, both from the wine and from the glass.

The terms 'aromas' and 'bouquet' can be more or less synonymous, although, strictly speaking, 'bouquet' refers more specifically to the tertiary aromas on a mature fine wine. The first thing to note is the intensity of the aromas. In other words, how easy or difficult is it to smell the wine? Certain styles such as New Zealand Sauvignon Blanc and Alsatian Gewurztraminer leap out of the glass; others, such as Chablis or Muscadet, are much more restrained. Some wines are closed to begin with, but gradually open up in the glass. Consider also the complexity of the wine. If you cannot quickly come to grips with a wine, this may be a sign of complexity.

It can be hard to find adequate **descriptors** with which to express and convey your experience of a wine. The descriptors that you choose are metaphors that aim to evoke your impressions of the wine. An original descriptor, such as 'autumnal fruit compote' or 'crushed skulls' (once offered up by an archaeologist) can be a thing of great glory. At the same time, there is already an established lexicon of 'wine words' that are repeatedly used and that have come to be associated with, and therefore to connote, certain more or less distinct notions. For instance, to the trained taster, 'apples' or 'lemons' suggest a cooler climate, 'vanilla' or 'butterscotch' suggests French oak, 'coconut' American oak, 'cedar wood' Cabernet Sauvignon, 'pencil shavings' Cabernet Franc, and 'undergrowth' or 'old books' a mature fine wine. This 'language of wine' is deeply rooted in European culture and experiences, which can make it seem all the more arcane to people from other backgrounds. The language of wine makes it much easier to taste and think and talk about wine, but also promotes an overly analytical approach at the expense of a more global or sensual appreciation—as does language more generally with life. Compared to experienced tasters (although not experts), novices are often better at picking up on subtle or unusual notes, and at describing them in original and evocative terms.

Having ascertained the intensity and complexity of the aromas, you now need to unpick them. Start by identifying the **fruit aromas**. Most fruit aromas are 'primary' aromas in that they originate in the grape itself. For white wines, there is an aroma spectrum that ranges from cool climate fruits such as apple, pear, lemon, and grapefruit to tropical fruits such as passion fruit, pineapple, mango, and papaya, reflecting the ripeness of the grapes at harvest and, to a lesser extent, the grape variety. For red wines, the aromas can, very broadly, be grouped into red fruits such as strawberries, raspberries, and redcurrants, and black fruits such as blackberries, black plums, and blackcurrants. With red wines the ripeness of the grapes is reflected more in the *quality* of the fruit, be it juicy, jammy, stewed, or dried.

Many other, non-fruit aromas originate in the grape itself. However, most other aromas in a wine are an expression of winemaking processes ('secondary aromas') or bottle maturation ('tertiary aromas'). **Non-fruit aromas** can fall into one of several groups: floral (e.g. lily, elderflower, rose, violet); vegetal (asparagus, grass, green pepper, tobacco leaf); mineral (slate, earth, petrichor); animal (meat, wool, leather, manure); spice (pepper, cinnamon, clove, vanilla); nutty (almond, hazelnut, walnut, coconut); autolytic (yeast, bread, brioche, biscuit); lactic (milk, yoghurt, cream), and 'other' (coffee, chocolate, honey, resin, rubber). Some quaint or quirky non-fruit descriptors include 'wet dog', suggesting aged Loire Chenin Blanc; 'cat's pee on a gooseberry bush', suggesting Loire Sauvignon Blanc; and 'sweaty saddle', suggesting traces of the yeast *Brettanomyces*. Do bear in mind that producers of Loire Chenin do not look kindly upon 'wet dog', preferring instead 'old cognac'.

Assessing the wine: on the palate

Tasting the wine enables you to confirm the aromas of the nose and examine the wine's structural elements. Do not drink the wine as you would mere water or milk. Instead, hold it in your mouth and allow it to warm up and express itself. Take a sip large enough to coat all areas of the mouth, but small enough that it can be swished around with the tongue. Now hold the wine in the front of the mouth and draw in a little air through pursed lips, as though slurping spaghetti. Gurgle the air across the wine and exhale it through the nose. Swish the wine around the mouth as if chewing upon it. If need be, repeat the spaghetti-slurping 'reverse whistle'. Spit or swallow the wine and exhale through the nose. Focus on any lingering flavours, and note their character, intensity, and duration. Although it has no bearing on tasting, some people treat spitting, or 'expectoration', as a high art or competitive sport—not merely a matter of barfing into a bucket. You can practise it in the shower, with shower water.

With the wine in the mouth, assess the intensity of flavours. Individual flavours, which are 'tasted' more by the nose than in the mouth, ought to be very similar to the aromas that you identified upon nosing the wine. However, some aromas and flavours might be more forthcoming on the palate, which can be helpful in confirming, developing, or rejecting some of your initial impressions.

Having ascertained the flavours of the wine, consider its **structural elements**, of which there are seven: acidity, alcohol, residual sugar, body, tannin, oak, and finish. Man is not a calibrated scientific machine and cannot accurately assess structural elements such as acidity and alcohol content. A wine may be high in acidity or alcohol, but not seem so, for example, if acidity or alcohol are masked by high residual sugar, or if all the structural elements are in balance. Describing structural elements such as acidity and alcohol on a three-point scale of 'high', 'medium', and 'low' (or five-point scale if you add in 'medium-minus' and 'medium-plus') may seem crude and illiterate, but suffices for most purposes. More fluent and evocative terms for describing acidity include 'flat', 'refreshing', 'bright', 'lively', 'crisp', 'tart', 'nervy', 'electric', and 'steely'. **Acidity** is primarily experienced as a tingling on the sides of the tongue, with high acidity also accompanied by a sharp taste. High residual sugar or a full body can mask acidity, such that luscious dessert wines are invariably much more acidic than they seem. Acid stimulates the secretion of saliva from the parotid and other salivary glands, so, for a more objective assessment of acidity, try to gauge your salivary response. After spitting or swallowing the wine, tilt your head forward and pay attention to the flow of saliva into the front of your mouth.

Assess the level of **alcohol** by holding a small amount of wine in the mouth and gently breathing in through the lips. The degree of heat or 'burn' at the back of the throat is roughly proportional to the alcohol level. If alcohol level is very high, a similar burning sensation is produced in the nose upon sniffing the wine. Overly alcoholic wines tend to lack flavour intensity. Even when bone dry, they can produce a sensation of sweetness on the tongue. On the other hand, wines that are lacking in alcohol may come across as thin or insipid, unless, as with Mosel Riesling, the low alcohol is balanced by high flavour intensity and residual sugar.

Sweeter wines range from off-dry to medium-dry, medium-sweet, and sweet. Some wine styles, most notably champagne, have prescribed terms for defined levels of **residual sugar** (Chapter 12). Assessing sugar levels can be quite challenging, especially with sweeter wines, which saturate sweetness receptors in the taste buds. Wines with high sugar levels call for high acidity to flush the sweetness receptors and balance the cloying sweetness with a sensation of freshness. But this freshness can make the wine seem much less sweet than it is. In such cases, the wine's body provides a clue as to its true sugar content. For example, Mullineux's straw wine contains over 300g/l of residual sugar, but we would never suspect this were it not so unctuous. Although it is possible to play that game, an accurate assessment of residual sugar in grams per litre is quite unnecessary: focus instead on whether the sugar is in balance with the other components of the wine, and, in particular, with acidity. Assessing sugar and alcohol in tandem can provide some indication of the ripeness of the grapes at the time of harvest, and also the method of winemaking. Fortunately, most wines are dry! Remember that sugar cannot be smelt: a wine that smells 'sweet' is probably one with fruity notes, high alcohol, and/or oak vanillin.

Body refers to the overall feel of the liquid in the mouth. It is in large part a measure of density or viscosity, and related to levels of alcohol, sugar, and extract in the wine. A light-bodied wine may feel like water in the mouth, whereas a full-bodied wine feels more like full fat milk from a Jersey cow. Full-bodied wines require higher levels of acidity to offset their weight. Conversely, light-bodied wines with excessive acidity can come across as unpleasantly sharp. In a white wine, a sort of creaminess to the body may suggest lees ageing, particularly when accompanied by a bready or floral aroma.

Much more than old oak, new oak leeches flavour compounds into the wine. Depending on such factors as the provenance of the **oak**, the age of the barrel, and the time spent in barrel, oak ageing can contribute notes of vanilla, butter, toast, coffee, chocolate, caramel, roasted nuts, nutmeg, clove, cedar, tobacco, and smoke. American oak is 'sweeter' than French oak, and less subtle, with dominant notes of coconut and vanilla. Oak ageing promotes tannin polymerization, which translates into a 'softening' of the wine. At the same time, heavily toasted barrels can introduce harsh and astringent tannins to the wine.

Discussion of **tannins** is usually restricted to red wines. However, there are some white wines that are fermented or matured in oak, or that undergo significant skin contact, that contain discernible tannins. Tannins are usually experienced as a certain textural mouthfeel and astringency which manifests as a drying or puckering sensation on the gums and inner surfaces of the cheeks and lips. In assessing a red wine, you ought to consider both the quantity and the quality of the tannins. Tannins can be described in terms of texture (silky, fine-grained, sandy, firm, sinewy, coarse) and flavour (ripe, bitter, green). Determining the quantity of tannins can be tricky: coarse tannins soon overwhelm the palate, leading to a false impression of high tannins, while ripe, silky tannins are only fully revealed in the delayed tannic 'grip' of the wine.

The **finish** of a wine describes the sensations that linger after the wine has been spat or swallowed. Fine wines can keep on giving for several minutes after disappearing down the gullet or bucket. Flavour compounds titillate the taste receptors in the throat, and volatile compounds rise up to brush with the olfactory bulb. Finish is, however, not merely a matter of duration, but also of character and quality, and, above all, of harmony with what went before. Finish might be described as clean, long, tapered, rounded, bitter, savoury, salty... and also according to its dominant notes, for example, 'a rounded, bitter almond finish' or 'a long finish on parma violets'.

Interpreting your findings

Having analyzed every aspect of the wine, the next step is to interpret your findings and make an educated guess as to the grape variety or blend; the country, region, and appellation of origin; the vintage; and the quality and approximate price. In competitions and exams, most (and sometimes all) available marks are for interpretation rather than tasting per se, although you can still score very highly for getting it 'wrong for the right reasons', particularly if the judges or examiners (who also taste the wines blind) happen to have shared in your reasoning.

One of the lasting appeals of blind tasting is that it is fiendishly difficult and deceptive. Upon being asked over a vinous dinner if he had ever mistaken Burgundy for Bordeaux, the great connoisseur Harry Waugh replied, 'Not since lunch-time!' If I am lucky, my first impression of, say, a Mosel Riesling matches my idea or concept of Mosel Riesling, and I am immediately and confidently able to identify it as Mosel Riesling and perhaps even as Wehlener Sonnenuhr 2006 from Dr Loosen. This sort of unconscious and effortless identification is more likely if I have multiple or vivid memories of tasting Mosel Riesling, or if I have a trigger for Mosel Riesling. A **trigger**, such as 'lemon sherbet', is any note that, *to me*, is typical of a particular style, and also more or less specific to that style. Sometimes, I can jog my memory by visualizing a map of the world, or a map of Europe, and then 'flashing' through the major wine regions.

Despite the different levels of ripeness (Kabinett, Auslese, etc.), Mosel Riesling is a style that is both fairly distinctive and fairly consistent, and, therefore, like other 'bankers' (wines with which you bank points), relatively easy to identify by intuition. With, say, a middle-of-the-road Chardonnay, my first impression may not concord with any of my concepts and memories. In this instance, I have no choice but to engage in a deductive process which, being conscious, is more laborious, more protracted, and, on the whole, less dependable than intuitive recognition.

The deductive approach rests on **three pillars**: first, an accurate analysis of the parameters of the wine under consideration; second, knowledge and experience of the most important grape varieties and wine styles; and third, the linking of the two to arrive at a best guess. In experts, it is this linking that is the weakest of the three pillars.

Unlike intuitive recognition, the **deductive process** is mostly one of elimination. For instance, I often begin by identifying the most likely grape variety or style, which enables me to eliminate all the countries and regions where that grape variety or style is uncommon. I then re-taste the wine with the possible regions in mind. If the wine does not concord with any of these regions, I rethink the grape variety or style and try again. Thus, the deductive approach is iterative, involving a back-and-forth process of forming hypotheses and seeking at each stage to verify or falsify them. 'In solving a problem of this sort,' said Sherlock Holmes, 'the grand thing is to be able to reason backward.'

Blind tasting is not unlike crime solving, and there is much that we might learn from **Sherlock Holmes**. First, approach every new case with a blank mind: 'Just simply observe and draw inferences from your observations.' Next, gather as much data as you possibly can: 'Data! Data! Data! ... I can't make bricks without clay.' As you do this, pay close attention to every little detail: 'You know my method. It is founded upon the observation of trifles.' Guard against forming theories before having obtained all the data, for 'insensibly one begins to twist facts to suit theories, instead of theories to suit facts.' When considering the data, remember that 'what is out of the common is usually a guide rather than a hindrance'. In other words, if something seems out of keeping, don't simply discount it. Consider all possible alternatives and provide against them. For instance, if you believe that you are dealing with a Pinot Noir, try to exclude other varieties that you sometimes confuse with Pinot Noir. My personal list includes Gamay (blue tinge, estery notes, lower acidity, lower alcohol, lower tannins, rarely oaked), Grenache (spicier, higher alcohol, lower acidity), Tempranillo (brick-red, less finely etched fruit, lower acidity, often oaked with American oak), and Nebbiolo (rust-red tinge, fuller body, much higher tannins). Finally, balance probabilities and plump for the most likely: 'It is the scientific use of the imagination.'

Appearance

The first thing you might notice just after the wine is poured is **spritz** or a slight effervescence, which should open your mind to Vinho Verde, Muscadet, Riesling, Sauvignon Blanc, or any white wine that has been reductively made to emphasize freshness and fruitiness. With the exception of Beaujolais Nouveau, spritz is much less common in red wine, and may indicate re-fermentation in bottle.

In a **white wine**, lighter, paler colours suggest reductive winemaking, youthfulness, or a cooler climate. A cooler climate is generally confirmed on the nose and palate by a fresher aroma profile, higher acidity, and lower alcohol. Conversely, darker, deeper colours suggest fermentation or maturation in oak, significant bottle age, or a warmer climate. On the nose and palate, a warmer climate is generally confirmed by a riper aroma profile, higher extract and alcohol, and lower acidity. Styles that can be particularly light in colour include Mosel Riesling, Clare Valley Riesling, Muscadet, Sancerre, Chablis, Pinot Grigio, and Hunter Valley Semillon. A pink tinge is associated with Alsatian Pinot Gris and Gewurztraminer, and a green tinge with youthful Riesling, Sauvignon Blanc, Grüner Veltliner, Albariño, Chablis, and Jurançon.

In a **red wine**, lighter and paler colours are associated with thin-skinned grape varieties such as Pinot Noir, Gamay, and Tempranillo, a cooler climate, unripeness, younger vines, higher yields, a rainy harvest, maturation in oak, and significant bottle age. Darker, deeper colours are associated with thick-skinned grape varieties such as Tannat, Malbec, and Corvina, a warmer or sunnier climate, higher extract or extraction, and youthfulness. A bluish tinge could suggest Gamay, Pinotage, or youthfulness. Warmth and sunshine are important determinants of colour: Pinot Noir from Central Otago is typically darker than red Burgundy, Bordeaux-style blends from Napa are typically darker than their Bordeaux counterparts, and, whereas Malbec from Cahors is deep purple, Malbec from Mendoza is inky black.

White wines that are fermented or matured in oak are often darker in colour than those fermented in inert vessels. In contrast, red wines fermented or matured in oak tend to be paler or softer in colour, and more red than deep purple. As they **age**, white wines become darker and red wines paler. Indeed, with increasing age, both white and red wines tend toward the same deathly shade of orange-brown. With red wines, a pronounced gradient from core to rim (typically red and darker in the core, and bronze and lighter at the rim) suggests significant bottle age. Note that young Tempranillo and Nebbiolo can also feature a bronze, brick-, or rust-red rim. But in this case, the gradations are not so subtle and there is less rim variation. Nebbiolo is also unusual in that it is thick-skinned and tannic yet light in colour.

Nose

Some grape varieties are more **aromatic** than others and seem to leap right out of the glass. Red wines, which derive much of their aromatic content from prolonged skin contact, are invariably aromatic. White wines, which are made with little or no skin contact, vary more markedly in aromatic intensity. Some of the most aromatic white grape varieties include Sauvignon Blanc, Riesling, Gewurztraminer, Muscat, Albariño, Torrontés, and Viognier. More restrained varieties include Melon de Bourgogne, Pinot Blanc, Semillon, Trebbiano, and the protean Chardonnay in its cooler climate expressions. In overly hot conditions, the vine starts to shut down, inhibiting the development of aromatic compounds in the grapes—and wines from excessively hot regions or vintages may for this reason be more restrained.

The **primary aromas** on the nose provide the biggest clues as to grape variety or varieties. Varieties and styles with very distinctive aromatic profiles include Gamay, Pinot Noir, Cabernet Sauvignon, Sauvignon Blanc, Mosel Riesling, Gewurztraminer, and Viognier. More middle-of-the-road varieties and styles can pose a much greater challenge, but at least you know what they are (probably) not. Blends too can complicate matters, although some classic blends, such as Sauvignon Blanc and Semillon from Bordeaux, or Châteauneuf-du-Pape, are relatively easy to recognize.

Primary aromas are also indicative of growing conditions. Cool climate white wines tend towards citrus and white fruits such as lemon, lime, apple, and pear, whereas warmer climate white wines tend towards stone fruits such as peach and apricot and, at the warmer end of the spectrum, tropical fruits such as passion fruit, pineapple, mango, and papaya. Cool climate red wines tend towards fresh fruit, while warmer climate red wines tend towards baked, stewed, or jammy fruit, and, at the warmer end of the spectrum, dried fruit and raisins. Notes of dried fruit and raisins may also indicate that the wine has been made from dried grapes, as, for example, Amarone (Chapter 18). Herbaceous notes, which, if subtle, can be pleasant, are all too often a sign of unripeness, and therefore of a cool climate or vintage.

Botrytis, or noble rot, lends a wine a characteristic aroma of honey, honeysuckle, beeswax, and ginger, sometimes with a faint antiseptic or musty note—notes which are more or less intense according to the degree of botrytization. Botrytized wines are invariably white wines such as Sauternes from Bordeaux, Coteaux du Layon from the Loire, and Tokaji Aszu from Hungary.

Primary aromas originating from the grape itself may be masked by **secondary aromas** from the winemaking or tertiary aromas from bottle maturation. Autolytic notes such as yeast, rising bread dough, brioche, and biscuit, especially when accompanied by a sort of creaminess on the palate, suggest that the wine has been aged on its lees. Because they are masked by skin contact, autolytic notes are much more prominent in white wines.

Evidence of oak on the nose (and, later, on the palate) speaks volumes about the wine, and more particularly the winemaking, grape variety (since some varieties are never or rarely oaked), and origin. To further complicate matters, oak can be French or American (or Eastern European); and old, new, or a combination of old and new. Varieties that are never or seldom oaked include Riesling, Gewurztraminer, Pinot Gris and Pinot Grigio, Garganega, Albariño, and Zweigelt. Châteauneuf- du-Pape, Bandol, Chianti, and Brunello are usually aged in old oak, and Rioja in American oak. A wine with significant new French oak, which costs twice as much as American oak, suggests a youthful wine of some quality or pretension. New oak often dominates a youthful wine, making identification more difficult, but tends to soften and integrate with passing years.

Tertiary aromas such as mushroom, truffle, wet leaves, leather, coffee, and butterscotch are associated with prolonged bottle age. Together, they form the bouquet of the wine—although most wines are not substantial enough to ever develop a bouquet. The Alsatian winemaker Pierre Gassmann once uncorked two old vintages in front of me, saying, 'This one is white truffles, this one black truffles.' A mature fine wine dominated by tertiary aromas but still retaining a core of ripe and juicy fruit is one of the wonders of the world.

Palate

The nose prefigures the palate, which in turn bears witness to the nose. Part of the pleasure of drinking fine wine is to take one's time over it and let the nose whet the palate. A disjunction between nose and palate may reflect poor winemaking or over-maturation.

The palate also allows for an assessment of the **structural components** of the wine. Acidity is an indicator of climate. Grapes grown in cooler climates tend to higher acidity. That said, early harvesting also results in a more acidic profile, and some varieties such as Riesling, Sauvignon Blanc, Chenin Blanc, Furmint, Pinot Noir, and Sangiovese are naturally high in acidity. In white wines, notes of green apples suggest high levels of malic acid and, by extension, suppression of malolactic fermentation. On the other hand, notes of dairy or yoghurt suggest higher levels of lactic acid, which is softer and richer than malic acid. A wine that has been acidified with tartaric acid, which is hard and angular, can feel poorly integrated or dominated by the alien acid.

Alcohol too is an indicator of ripeness at harvest, and so of climate. Alcohol considered alongside residual sugar provides an indication of the total pre-fermentation sugar level in the grapes. A dry wine with high alcohol and a sweet wine with low alcohol could, in theory, have been made from the same crop of grapes. In dry wines, much of the body is in fact alcohol, such that riper, higher alcohol wines are also more full-bodied. Remember that sweetness, or the impression of sweetness, is produced not only by residual sugar but also by other compounds including but not limited to alcohol, glycerol (an important by-product of fermentation), fruity esters, and oak vanillin.

In red wines, tannin levels are related to the thickness of the grape skins and so the grape variety. One is often tempted to correlate depth of colour with tannin levels. However, colour can be extracted from the skins, for instance, by cold maceration, without much tannin transfer. Moreover, some varieties, most notably Nebbiolo, are relatively light in colour but heavy in tannins. The character or quality of the tannins reflects on the variety, growing conditions, and winemaking. For instance, harsh tannins suggest a crude, mechanized method of tannin extraction that damages pips and encourages bitter compounds to leach into the wine.

Wine identification ought to be guided by an intimate knowledge of regional terroirs and varieties. The Mosel sees some of the coolest average temperatures of any renowned wine region; however, the long and dry autumn days combined with late harvesting enable the grapes to accumulate high levels of sugar. In contrast, the Hunter Valley in Australia, while very warm, is frequently clouded over: the heat promotes phenolic ripeness, but the lack of sunshine restricts sugar accumulation, leading to wines with fairly low alcohol. Some varieties, such as Semillon and Merlot, accumulate sugars rapidly, whereas others, such as Riesling, Cabernet Franc, and Nebbiolo, are slower to ripen. It is becoming increasingly difficult to distinguish between Old World and New World wines. Historically, the New World style has been bolder and more fruit-driven, whereas the Old World style is more minerally or earthy, often with higher acidity.

This Eurocentric distinction between Old World and New is more and more contentious. I, for one, am not entirely clear what the Old World refers to: Europe, the Roman Empire (including North Africa and the Levant), the Known World in antiquity, any place with a long wine-making tradition... When I put the question out to Twitter, the itinerant winemaker Nayan Gowda commented, 'Anywhere that started making wine post 1500s is New World. Tongue slightly in cheek there, but they've been making wine here in Bolivia since the sixteenth century; that's pretty old.' The wine columnist Peter Pharos remarked that 'Old/New World are anglocentric terms (and useful shorthands). Old World is anything that would be found in sizeable quantities in an English vintner in the 1950s ... New World is the primarily Anglophone former colonies that [later] came to prominence...'

Quality assessment

Wine professionals are usually more interested in assessing a wine's quality than in identifying it for sport or art, correlating price and quality in search of value. Of course, quality is largely subjective, even if most wine amateurs end up with an affinity for more complex and refined wines. Owing to their growing knowledge and tasting skills, this need not mean ever more expensive labels. In fact, I now spend much less on wine than when I first started out. Price is not only a reflection of quality, but also of demand and supply. Top wines from unfashionable regions and appellations (or countries with a deflated currency) usually offer much more 'bang for your buck', and even fashionable regions are sure to hide some great bargains for those in the know. It is still possible to enjoy great wine for around £10/$15 a bottle.

There are four-and-a-half criteria by which the quality of a wine ought to be judged: **balance**, length, intensity, and complexity, and typicity (often remembered as BLIC or BLIC-T). If the wine is balanced or harmonious or integrated, the flavours complement one another like the parts of an orchestra, the palate bears witness to the nose, and none of the structural elements obtrude.

Length refers to the procession and progression of flavours as the wine crosses the palate, triggering taste buds on the tongue, palate, soft palate, and pharynx. In the best of cases, the flavours and structure of the wine linger long after the wine has been spat or swallowed.

Intensity refers to the apparent concentration of flavour and impact of the wine in the mouth: the iron fist in the velvet glove. Intensity is related to length insofar as there cannot be length without intensity. Intensity and length are highly sought after in balanced wines, but in unbalanced wines simply serve to prolong the torture.

Complexity refers to the number of elements in the orchestra, or strands in the music. As with other markers of quality, complexity begins—and some might add, also ends—with quality grapes, often from low-yielding vines such as old vines. Above all, the task of the winemaker is to conserve what nature has given her by shepherding the grapes from vineyard to bottle in the best possible conditions. In the process, she may or may not impart additional complexity to the wine through one or several of: malolactic fermentation, lees ageing, oaking, blending, and ageing. Some styles are complex mostly for having been made from dried or botrytized grapes.

A wine ought to be a faithful representation of the kind of wine that it is, most obviously by reflecting its terroir, that is, the soil, climate, and viticultural and winemaking traditions of its provenance. This concept of **typicity**, which in Europe can be very tightly regulated, is being adopted by an increasing number of New World producers bent on quality and authenticity. Unlike the other four criteria, typicity is not an essential ingredient for greatness. There are many iconic wines, such as the original Super Tuscans (Chapter 20), that defy the traditions of their region, and, in time, even come to redefine them. As Churchill once said, 'Without tradition, art is a flock of sheep without a shepherd. Without innovation, it is a corpse.'

Worked examples

Wine 1: Recent vintage of Mosel Riesling

Tasting note

- *Star-bright. Pale straw in colour.*
- *Highly aromatic with notes of fresh lime, green apple, sherbet, slate, and hints of pineapple and honeysuckle.*
- *Fresh fruit flavours on the palate: apple and lime dominate.*
- *No evidence of new oak.*
- *High in acidity with markedly low alcohol and medium residual sugar.*
- *Creamy in texture though still light in body.*
- *Moderate in length, with an elegant and tapered mineral finish.*
- *Well balanced, with the high acidity and low alcohol compensated for by the sugar, intensity of fruit, and creamy texture.*

Analysis

The pale colour suggests that the wine is young and has spent little or no time in oak, initial impressions that are confirmed by the dominant fresh fruit aromas. The hints of pineapple and honeysuckle on the nose imply ripeness, as does the medium residual sugar. Taken together, the residual sugar and alcohol are indicative of high sugar levels at harvest and arrested fermentation. At the same time, the high acidity is a marker of an overall cool climate. Thus, the wine is likely to come from a cool climate with a long and dry autumn. The creamy texture suggests some lees ageing. The balance and elegant finish are markers of high quality.

The aroma profile, acidity, residual sugar, and lack of new oak point to Riesling as the grape variety. The pale colour, fruit-driven aroma profile, and lack of tertiary aromas such as butterscotch, toffee, smoke, and kerosene betray a very young wine, no older than one or two years. The aroma profile, in particular the sherbet, slate, and mineral, suggests that this is Riesling from the Mosel. This hypothesis is supported by the combination of high acidity, low alcohol, and medium residual sugar. It remains possible that the wine is in fact a New World imitation of Mosel Riesling, but these are rare, and the character and complexity of the nose and creamy elegance of the palate are highly in favour of Germany. The wine could also be from the nearby Rheingau or Nahe, but these styles tend to be rounder and fuller with higher alcohol levels and rather less mineral character.

Wine 2: Californian Cabernet Sauvignon with eight years of bottle age

Tasting note

- *In colour, medium-to-deep purple in the centre and brick-red at the rim.*
- *Moderately aromatic with jammy blackcurrant and mulberry fruit, meaty notes, and hints of menthol, coconut, and sweet spice.*
- *On the palate, intense jammy black fruit flavours with coconut and milk chocolate, suggesting American oak.*
- *Dry and full-bodied with high alcohol and low acidity.*
- *Tannins moderate in quantity, with a soft and velvety quality.*
- *Moderate length with a finish dominated by fruit flavours and alcohol.*
- *Overall, a complex wine with clear development, but let down by low acidity relative to full body and high alcohol.*

Analysis

The colour gradient and brick-red rim indicate significant bottle age, as later confirmed by the meaty notes. The medium depth of colour goes against overly thin- or thick-skinned grape varieties. The jammy fruit and other aspects of the aroma profile reflect a hot climate. Hints of coconut and sweet spice suggest American oak, which is corroborated on the palate. The wine, though complex, is let down by its alcoholic flabbiness and overall lack of balance.

The menthol note is suggestive of Cabernet Sauvignon. This grape variety is often marked out by blackcurrant and green pepper; however, the 'green' note can take a number of forms, including, especially in California, menthol. Taken together, the notes of menthol and jammy fruit, the high alcohol, and the American oak make California an obvious choice. Other possibilities include Australia or South Africa, which are similarly hot. Australian Cabernets capable of a similar degree of complexity are typically grown on chalky soils, such as those of Coonawarra, that preserve acidity. Moreover, the 'green' note is usually expressed as eucalyptus rather than menthol. South African Cabernets, although variable in style, tend to be more earthy and mineral, and are often matured in French oak.

Wine 3: 30-year-old Pinot Gris SGN (Sélection de Grains Nobles) from Alsace

Tasting note

- *Deep gold in colour.*
- *Dense, concentrated nose with a complex bouquet of mushroom, leather, honey, butterscotch, confected pear, peach, nutmeg, and white pepper.*
- *Intensely sweet on the palate with notes of peach, fig, dates, and butterscotch. Full-bodied with moderate alcohol and moderate-to-low acidity.*
- *High residual sugar.*
- *Very long and tapered savoury finish that echoes the earlier aromas and flavours.*

- *A wonderfully complex sweet wine. The sweetness gradually fades into a dry, savoury finish. The one slight damper is that the moderate-to-low acidity does not quite cut through the high residual sugar.*

Analysis

The deep golden colour and tertiary notes indicate significant maturity. The complexity of the nose and palate and long finish are hallmarks of the highest quality. The sweetness and honeyed notes, together with the complexity, mean that this is very likely a botrytized dessert wine.

This leaves only a few options: Auslese or Beerenauslese Riesling from Germany, sweet Chenin from the Loire (Coteaux du Layon or Vouvray), Sauternes from Bordeaux, Tokaji from Hungary, or a SGN from Alsace. The wine could not possibly hail from the New World because New World producers were not making this style and quality of wine twenty or thirty years ago. The wine is too low in acidity to be Riesling, Chenin Blanc, Tokaji, or Sauternes. While SGN from Alsace could be made from Riesling or Gewurztraminer, it is more commonly made from Pinot Gris. Notes of pear and spice rather than vanilla custard (Sauternes), apricot (Tokaji), petrol (Riesling), or Turkish delight (Gewurztraminer) support the conclusion that the wine is indeed an Alsatian Pinot Gris.

It can be difficult to pin an age on a very old wine, particularly a sweet one, but any guess that makes it 'very old' ought to garner full marks.

Nick Jackson's approach to blind tasting

In *Beyond Flavour* (2020), Nick Jackson MW emphasizes the importance of structure for blind tasting: acid structure in white wines and tannin structure in red wines. According to Nick, 'the structure of a variety does not change, whatever the winemaker or climate does.'

For white wines, we should pay attention not only to the level of the acidity, but also to its type and shape. For example, Chenin Blanc and Riesling both have high acidity, but that of Chenin is 'bracing' whereas that of Riesling is 'steely'. Moreover, Chenin Blanc has a crescendo-shaped acid structure, whereas Riesling has a vertical acid structure, like a stake, or a steel pole that glints in the light. Sauvignon Blanc also has high acidity, but in this case the acidity is spiky or jagged and is perceived distinctly and separately from the body of the wine— although this, says Nick, slightly undermining the strong form of his thesis, is not true of top examples from the Loire.

For red wines, we should note not only the level of the tannins, but also their type and location. For example, Pinot Noir has supple tannins that are primarily felt on the tongue and roof of the mouth. Sangiovese, in contrast, has sandy tannins that are primarily felt on the gums. Syrah tannins are a touch chalky or powdery in the Old World but velvety in the New, and especially felt on the tongue.

Although qualitative descriptions of acidity and tannins are nothing new, they have until now been rather *ad hoc*, and Nick is surely right to draw our attention to these structural components and invite us to think more rigorously and systematically about them.

Blind tasting for exams and competitions

When it comes to blind tasting, there can be no substitute for practice and experience. Do not merely fall back on your strengths, however impressive they may be. The best way to improve is to work at your weaknesses. Attending as many tastings as possible can really help to bring things together, as can visiting wineries and wine regions, talking to wine people, and reading the wine press and literature. But the single most important thing is to find or form a dedicated study group. Aside from the purely social aspects, the benefits of a study group include: imposing structure and discipline, sharing knowledge and experiences, shaping and strengthening indistinct impressions, uncovering blind spots, and, last but not least, dividing expenses.

Also key is familiarity with timing, as time pressure in exams and competitions is often intense. Put yourself through timed practices that mirror the format of the real McCoy. When you blind taste, say, a

Pomerol, you taste it with everything that you know about Merlot and Right Bank Bordeaux, indeed, everything that you know about wine. Last minute cramming is not going to turn you into an overnight super-taster, and might even serve to confuse or tire you. Better to spend the run-up to the exam or competition relaxing and sharpening your mind and senses.

In the hours leading up to the event, it can be helpful to taste a bench-mark such as a Rheingau Riesling to calibrate your palate. If your palate is poorly calibrated for a particular variable such as acidity, alcohol, or quality (more likely if you are ill, stressed, hungry, or dehydrated), you will be losing marks right across the board.

For competitions, if tasting in a communicating team (in which members can confer with one another), the top taster should take the lead. If there is no clear top taster, one of the stronger tasters should be designated as captain to streamline decision-making. If at any point it becomes apparent that the captain is having an off day, he or she should immediately yield the captaincy to another strong taster. If tasting in a non-communicating team as in the Oxford and Cambridge varsity match, the team is only as strong as the sum of its parts, and gains most from the stronger tasters training up the novices.

For exams, be sure to read the questions carefully and to answer them directly and comprehensively (although not necessarily exhaustively). If short of time, choose breadth over depth, as marks are likely to be distributed across a number of domains, for instance, across several aroma groups. Elaborate only if it seems appropriate, or if you are specifically asked. If you get stuck on a particular wine, come back to it later if you can.

For many exams, it is very important to use the prescribed tasting method, including the tasting format, lexicon, and grading scales. Committing the prescribed method to memory increases your speed while decreasing your chances of missing out key elements such as tannins or oak.

If there are, say, six marks allocated to 'nose', be sure to write down at least six items about the nose, across all the principal domains. In particular, do not omit to comment on a defining element such as notes of honey and honeysuckle in a botrytized wine, or notes of vanilla and toast in a wine with reams of new French oak. Conversely, be careful not to imply something that is not there. For instance, 'coconut' is so closely associated with American oak as to connote it, even if American oak is not what you intended to imply.

When writing descriptions, use only very specific descriptors: instead of 'citrus fruits', prefer 'lemon', 'lime', 'grapefruit', 'clementine', or 'orange'. Other cluster headings that can be elaborated upon include 'red fruits', 'black fruits', 'green fruits', 'stone fruits', 'nuts', and 'spice'. Do not hedge: instead of 'youthful', plump for either 'young' or 'developing'. Similarly, avoid broad, imprecise, subjective, or fanciful terms such as 'mineral', 'fairly high', 'feminine', and 'broad-shouldered'. In short, be as precise and concrete as you can. At the same time, do not fall into the opposite trap of being overly technical by, say, providing an estimate of the residual sugar level in grams per litre. Describe each wine in the absolute, without referencing the other wines in the flight. For instance, avoid writing that a wine is 'more aromatic than the previous wine'— unless specifically asked to compare the wines.

Try in as far as possible to be consistent and coherent within your tasting note. It is easy to inadvertently contradict yourself, sometimes even within the same sentence, for example, by describing the hue as '*deep* lemon' but the colour intensity as only 'medium'. More generally, if you think that a wine is obviously young, do not write down notes such as petrol or marzipan that suggest a fair bit of development.

Take care not to confuse a descriptor with a conclusion. 'Likely fermented in stainless steel' is a conclusion not a descriptor, and used as a descriptor is unlikely to attract a mark. Also unlikely to attract marks are negative descriptors such as 'no sediment', 'no tannins', and 'no evidence of new oak'.

In general, when concluding, it is not nearly enough to 'get it right'. To score full marks, you also need to back up your conclusions with evidence, explanations, and context, in proportion to the allocated number of marks. Should your conclusions prove incorrect, your reasoning could ensure that you score at least partial marks. You are unlikely to be given rare, unusual, or atypical wines, so do not stray too far off the beaten track with an Alto Adige Sylvaner, a Mornington Nebbiolo, or a Bío-Bío Gewurztraminer.

If you are also asked for a quality assessment, do not hold back from being critical. But be sure to back up your conclusions with evidence and explanations. For instance, do not merely state that a wine 'will not improve with age', but argue that it is 'lacking the concentration and structure for further ageing'. Similarly, do not merely state that a wine is 'balanced', but explain that 'the full body and high alcohol are offset by the high acidity'. Verify that your quality assessment is externally and internally coherent. If you noted further up that a probable Bordeaux has green tannins, do not conclude that it is at the level of a classed growth; or if you claim that a wine is of poor quality, do not argue that it will improve with age.

Ahead of the exam, it can be useful to draw up differential lists for recurring problem areas such as 'mineral whites' (Chablis, Muscadet, Savennières, Sancerre, Riesling...), 'aromatic whites' (Gewurztraminer, Pinot Gris, Viognier, Muscat, Torrontes...), 'light reds' (Pinot Noir, Gamay, Grenache, Tempranillo, Nebbiolo...), 'soft reds' (Gamay, Pinot Noir, Dolcetto, Barbera, Valpolicella...), and 'spicy reds' (Southern Rhône blends, Northern Rhône Syrah, Rioja, Chianti, Nebbiolo...). For each variety or style, write down the most important distinguishing features. Everyone is different, with different trouble areas, triggers, and tricks, so it is important that you draw up your own lists.

For example, here is a list for spicy reds.

Châteauneuf-du-Pape (Grenache dominated blend)

- *N Rhône Syrah: darker fruit, black pepper, higher acidity, lower alcohol, chewier tannins*
- *Rioja: brick red, less herbal, lower alcohol, more oaked and often with American oak*

- *Chianti: brighter with higher acidity, higher and firmer tannins, drier finish*
- *Nebbiolo: rust-red tinge, more floral, higher acidity, much higher tannins*

You can then rejig the list to put it in terms of another variety or style:

Chianti

- *Nebbiolo: rust-red tinge, more floral, higher acidity, much higher tannins*
- *Châteauneuf-du-Pape: garrigue, less cherry fruit, lower acidity, lower and softer tannins*
- *Rioja: brick red, less bright, lower acidity, softer tannins, more oaked and often with American oak*

Here are some more differential lists to get you started. Try, with the help of your peers, to formulate such lists in your tastings. Start with just a couple of varieties or styles, and then, over time, gradually extend and refine the list.

Chablis

- *Muscadet: paler, slight effervescence, lees character, lighter body, lower acidity and alcohol, less mineral*
- *Savennières: more aromatic, fuller body, higher alcohol, bitter afternote*
- *Sancerre: more aromatic, notes of gooseberry and grass*
- *Riesling: much more aromatic, petrol, possible residual sugar*

Gewurztraminer

- *Viognier: no pink tinge, more stone fruit, less exotic, often less oily, dry, lacks bitter finish*
- *Pinot Gris: pear or stone fruit, no lychee, often less oily, higher acidity, greater structure*

- *Muscat: grapey, orange blossom, lighter body, lower alcohol, often drier*
- *Torrontes: lacks lychee note, less oily, more mineral*

Pinot Noir

- *Gamay: blue tinge, estery notes, lower acidity, alcohol, and tannins, rarely oaked*
- *Grenache: spicier, higher alcohol, lower acidity*
- *Tempranillo: brick red, less finely etched fruit, lower acidity, often oaked with American oak*
- *Nebbiolo: rust-red tinge, fuller body, much higher tannins*

Gamay

- *Pinot Noir: no blue tinge or estery notes, higher acidity, alcohol, and tannins, often oaked*
- *Dolcetto: darker colour, more 'Italian' cherries and bitter almonds, lower acidity, higher alcohol and tannins, drier finish*
- *Barbera: more cherry than strawberry, higher acidity, more often oaked, drier finish*
- *Valpolicella: sour cherry note, higher acidity*

Cabernet Sauvignon (e.g. Left Bank Bordeaux)

- *Merlot: plums, no cassis or green pepper, more earth and less gravel, lower acidity, higher alcohol, softer tannins*
- *Syrah: black pepper, no cassis or green pepper, lower acidity, less structured*
- *Cabernet Franc: more aromatic, lighter fruit, lesser structure and tannins*
- *Cahors: inkier, earthy mineral notes, higher tannins*
- *Argentine Malbec: fuller body, higher alcohol, lower acidity, softer tannins*

Is blind tasting a sport?

Wittgenstein famously claimed that games cannot be defined. But, in 1978, Bernard Suits managed, more or less successfully, to define a game as 'a voluntary attempt to overcome unnecessary obstacles'.

In that much, sports resemble games. They also resemble games in that they take place outside of 'real life', and have no tangible product: when they do have a tangible product, such as fish in angling, then this is largely incidental, and the fish are returned to the water.

There are games like scrabble or monopoly that are clearly not sports. But if not all games are sports, are all sports games, as Suits claimed? While many sports like football and golf are also games, some sports like running, skiing, and rock climbing are less obviously so—other than in that they are voluntary and unnecessary. In ordinary language, we speak of 'playing football' or 'playing a round of golf', but not of 'playing running' or 'playing skiing'. And if we are running from a lion, our running is not even a sport, let alone a game.

Culture and politics aside, what is it that makes a sport a sport? If scrabble and monopoly are not sports, then this is surely because they do not involve any physical activity, or because physical activity is not their primary purpose and any physical activity incurred is merely secondary or incidental.

In 2015, the English Bridge Union (EBU) challenged a decision by Sport England not to recognize bridge as a sport—a decision that deprived bridge from government and lottery funding. The EBU lost their High Court battle on the grounds that bridge does not involve physical activity any more than, as Sport England argued, 'sitting at home, reading a book'.

But physical activity on its own is not enough. The primary purpose of working out on a cross-trainer is physical activity, but this is classed as exercise rather than sport. What is needed for sport is not mere physical activity, but skill in the exercise of physical activity, with some athletes going so far as to test the limits of human performance.

In 2005, Sport England recognized darts as a sport, presumably because darts involves skill as well as physical activity. By that account, video gaming, although targeted at a representational world, might also make the cut. Chess on the other hand is unlikely to constitute a sport because, although it involves some physical activity, this physical activity is not particularly skilled, and, in any case, is not the primary purpose of chess. It is perfectly possible to get someone to move our chess pieces for us and still be counted as playing chess: in that much, the physical activity associated with playing chess is not central or even secondary but merely incidental.

If I, as an amateur, decide to go skiing for a couple of days, is my skiing exercise or sport? The answer depends on my own attitude, whether I am skiing primarily to keep fit, or for the sheer thrill of pushing myself or simply being in the world: and I think that this potential for thrill, for exaltation, for a certain kind of joy—rather than just panting and sweating—is an important part of what makes a sport a sport.

Well, what if I meet a friend and we resolve to race each other down the mountainside? Does this competitive dimension make my skiing more of a game and therefore more of a sport? A person who develops a certain skill, whether in skiing or in baking or in any field of human endeavour, naturally wishes to measure that skill in competition with others who also lay claim to that skill. It is this competitive aspect that makes many sports so compelling to watch, although competition is by no means essential to popular spectator sports such as gymnastics and figure skating. What's more, a sport need not make compelling watching to be counted as a sport: angling, cricket, golf, canoeing, and weight lifting are not the most exciting to watch, but are nonetheless sports.

So where does that leave blind tasting? Fiercely fought competitions are popping up all around the world, and some of these competitions even have audiences. So can blind tasting be counted as a sport? Scrabble and monopoly are not sports because they do not involve any physical activity, but blind tasting clearly does involve some kind of physical activity, namely, tasting—and, as the name suggests, tasting is its primary purpose and not merely secondary or incidental. What's more, this physical activity is highly skilled, and, in some cases, can be said to test the limits of human physiology or performance.

It might be objected that the physical activity involved in blind tasting is not locomotor but gustatory, involving not the musculoskeletal system in tandem with the cardiovascular system but 'passive' senses such as olfaction, taste, and touch. It might further be objected, and this is an argument that I myself have made, that the real limitation in blind tasting is not in the tasting apparatus as such but in the cognitive appraisal of the wine, and thus that blind tasting is more like chess than snooker or darts (although snooker and darts also involve important cognitive elements). Finally, it might be added that the thrill or joy in blind tasting lies more with the cognitive aspect than the tasting aspect, although that does depend on the wine.

But unlike with chess, with blind tasting it is not possible to delegate the physical component: you cannot get someone to do the tasting for you and still be counted as blind tasting. In that much, blind tasting is more of a sport than chess, which the International Olympics Committee already recognizes as a sport.

As any athlete will attest, cognition is an important part of any sport: why create arbitrary distinctions between the primarily physical and the primarily mental, or between the musculoskeletal system and the specialized senses? Are the nose and the tongue and the brain not also part of the body? And are they not also trainable, fatiguable, fallible, mortal? Chess, bridge, and maths have their associations, players, teams, training, rules, competitions, professionals, spectators, drama, and tears—everything, in fact, but a skilled, primary physical activity. And blind tasting even has that.

Now pass me a napkin.

Wine ratings

A wine rating is a summary of the appraisal of a wine by one or more critics, most notoriously Robert Parker, who, until his retirement in

2019, assigned 'Parker points' on a scale of 0 to 100. Since the 1970s, the practice of rating wines on a 100-point scale has proliferated. Other scales, including 0-to-20 and 0-to-5 (sometimes featuring stars in lieu of numbers), are also frequently used. Certain websites enable consumers to emulate critics by contributing to 'community' notes and scores. In competitions, wines are generally tasted blind by a panel of critics, usually alongside other wines from the same appellation or region. In theory, a rating is merely intended to supplement a tasting note; in practice, the tasting note—if it even exists—is often ignored or omitted, with the wine reduced to nothing more than a headline number.

Wine ratings convey information simply and efficiently, guiding the purchasing decisions of novices in particular. Assuming strict single-blind conditions at the time of tasting, they reflect performance rather than price or reputation. Scores can be compared, which encourages producers to compete and improve their offerings, and rewards them for doing so. Wines with 90-plus points are much more likely to shift, and those with scores in the high 90s can develop cult followings. Château Tirecul la Gravière, in Monbazillac, became an overnight reference after Parker gave 100 points to its 1995 Cuvée Madame.

However, wine ratings can be criticized on the triple grounds of concept, procedure, and consequences. While a numerical score can come across as scientific, it merely reflects the personal preferences and prejudices of one or several critics, and it may be that grading wines is as misguided as ranking people in a beauty pageant. For what is beauty, and can it be reduced to a number? Like the contestants in the pageant, the wines are often very young, and scores cannot fully account for the delights and disappointments that they are yet to reveal. In any case, the most beautiful boy or girl is probably not on the stage, but sitting at home buried in *War and Peace*. Many of the most hallowed producers shun competitions, partly on ideological grounds, but mainly because they have little to gain and much to lose.

Scores are influenced not only by personal preferences and prejudices, but also by the context and conditions of the tasting, and, in a panel, by the group dynamics, with junior judges exquisitely sensitive to every 'um' and 'aah' of the distinguished panel chair. The number that comes out of this process might be of existential import to the producer, who has toiled for a year, indeed, several years, to make his or her wine, but in fact reflects no more than a few seconds of tasting with no or very little time for discussion and debate. In competitions, there is also a financial incentive to dish out medals, which encourage further paid entries and increase sales of medal stickers. As a result, there has been a devaluation of wine scores over the years, so that scores of less than 80 are now uncommon.

As for consequences, wines that garner the highest scores fall prey to speculators and are traded like financial commodities, effectively removing them from the marketplace. More gravely, ratings tend to favour the sort of wines that are able to stand out on a fatigued, tannin-coated palate, at the expense of more delicate wines, which are likely to be more elegant, more interesting, more faithful to terroir, and better suited to the table. This phenomenon contributed in no small measure to the homogenization, or 'Parkerization', of wine styles as producers vied to obtain the highest scores—although this is no longer quite the problem it used to be.

Wine ratings have played an important role in the rise of wine culture, but their grip seems to be loosening, if not quite fading, as consumers become more and more experienced and knowledgeable. To me, a score of 98 can also function as a signal for caution.

STYLISTIC PROFILES: WHITE WINES

As discussed, the deductive approach to blind tasting rests on three pillars: accurate analysis of the wine, knowledge and experience of the most important grape varieties and wine styles, and the linking of the two to arrive at a best guess.

The most important grape varieties and wine styles are the subject of the second and larger part of this book. What follows is merely a synopsis for easy reference in blind tasting practices. You can download it as a crib sheet from https://neelburton.com/blind-wine-tasting-resources/

Riesling

Germany, Mosel

Mosel Riesling is pale in colour, possibly with a touch of effervescence. On the nose, it is intensely fragrant, more floral than fruity with notes of stony rainwater and sherbet. On the palate, it is filigree and delicate, with a mineral or salty finish. Alcohol is very low and acidity very high, but balanced by sugar and extract. Sweeter examples may be botrytized. Rieslings from the Saar and Ruwer valleys are steelier than those from the Middle Mosel. Drier styles are becoming more common.

Germany, Rheingau

Compared to Riesling from the Middle Mosel, Riesling from the Rheingau is a lot sturdier: deeper in colour with a firmer structure and texture, riper fruit, and higher alcohol. It is commonly made in an austere, completely dry style.

France, Alsace

Alsatian Riesling tends to be drier, richer in extract, and higher in alcohol than Riesling from across the Rhine. It is often tight, steely, and inexpressive in its youth, with aromas of mineral, apple, citrus fruits, stone fruits, jasmine, and honey. With age, it opens out and develops a complex bouquet dominated by pure fruit flavours and appealing petrol or kerosene notes, typically with a long, dry finish that is carried on the tail of a backbone of high acidity.

Austria, Wachau or Kremstal or Kamptal

Like Alsatian Riesling, which it most resembles, Austrian Riesling is dry with high acidity, medium-to-high alcohol, and pronounced minerality. However, it is typically less austere and dominated by riper stone fruit. 'Hints of lime' is another common tasting note. Riesling from Kremstal and Kamptal is often fuller than that from Wachau.

Australia, South Australia, Clare Valley or Eden Valley

Clare Valley or Eden Valley Riesling is pale lemon and lime green in colour. Spritz in the glass speaks of fermentation in stainless steel, which is common in Australia. The wines are characterized by searing acidity and mineral austerity. Unlike, say, Rheingau Riesling, their fruit profile leans very strongly towards lime, whether this be, depending on ripeness, lime zest, fresh lime juice, or lime cordial. The best examples are complex enough to overlie this 'limeyness' with floral, appley, and waxy notes, and are further distinguished by a talcum or chalky texture (from lees ageing) and a long, dry, and acidic finish. Some examples exhibit a mineral pungency derided by critics as 'fly spray'. Clare Valley Riesling is generally considered to be drier and leaner than that from Eden Valley, although the two styles are difficult to distinguish.

New Zealand, e.g. South Island, Nelson

When it comes to Riesling, New Zealand looks more to Europe than to Australia, with generally lighter and more delicate styles. The wines are typically crisp and clean with a fresh lime character, as opposed to the pungent lime cordial note of many Australian Rieslings. There are, however, a range of styles, including delicate, Mosel-like styles and late harvest dessert styles. The climate preserves Riesling's searing acidity. With age, the best examples develop appealing petrol notes. Note that Riesling, from wherever it is, is never oaked.

Gewurztraminer

France, Alsace

Gewurztraminer (or Gewürztraminer in Alsace, with a trema) is gold in colour, sometimes with a pinkish tinge. The nose is intense and often reminiscent of Turkish delight, or an oriental bazaar or perfume shop, with notes of spice and rose petals, lychee, grapefruit, peach kernel, and smoky bacon. On the palate, it is opulent with high alcohol, but can, especially in hotter vintages, seem flabby and lacking in acidity. It ranges in sweetness from dry to very sweet, but, owing to its aromatic profile, can be sweeter than it is. It is never oaked. Gewurztraminer is readily confused with Viognier, but has a more exotic profile and a slightly bitter finish.

Pinot Gris/Pinot Grigio

France, Alsace

Alsatian Pinot Gris is deep lemon in colour, often with a pinkish tinge. The nose is fairly aromatic, with notes of spice and pear or stone fruit, hints of honey and smoke, and a certain earthy minerality. The palate combines the spiciness and alcohol of Gewurztraminer with some of the structure and acidity of Riesling. The wines often have a distinct oily texture. They range in sweetness from dry to sweet and are never oaked.

Italy, Friuli-Venezia-Giulia

Compared to Pinot Gris, Pinot Grigio is lighter in colour with less ripe fruit on the nose. On the palate, it is leaner with a tighter structure and higher acidity. It is invariably dry and unoaked, with faint notes of apple, pear, lemon, white peach, white flowers, and bitter almond, and, often, a clean and mineral finish.

New Zealand, South Island

New Zealand Pinot Gris is much closer to Alsatian Pinot Gris than to Italian Pinot Grigio. It is usually dry or off-dry, with notes of apple, pear, honeysuckle, white pepper, and spice. Examples from the North Island in particular may bear the oiliness of an Alsatian Pinot Gris. There are often suggestions of lees stirring or barrel ageing.

Chardonnay

France, Burgundy, Chablis

Chablis is pale lemon in colour, sometimes with a greenish tinge, with notes of citrus fruits, green apple, honeysuckle, cream, and, often, a characteristic stony or smoky minerality ('wet stone'). The palate is lean, dry, and austere with marked acidity, which is a key distinguishing feature. New oak is usually absent. Top examples are weightier and, especially with increasing age, can be difficult to distinguish from their counterparts in Beaune.

France, Burgundy, Beaune

Beaune is lemon in colour with primary notes of ripe apple and citrus fruits. French oak is common, contributing notes of vanilla, toast, and, along with *bâtonnage*, butter. The wine is full-bodied, with crisp acidity and medium-to-high alcohol. It is potentially intense, complex, and lengthy, developing notes such as minerals, spice, tropical fruits, lemon tart, and toffee. Puligny-Montrachet is tight and structured and mineral. Chassagne-Montrachet is perhaps slightly richer, fruitier, and nuttier. Meursault, in contrast, is broad and buttery and rather extravagant, although some producers favour leaner styles.

France, Burgundy, Mâcon

As with Chablis, much Mâcon is unoaked. However, Mâcon is much less acidic than Chablis. Compared to Beaune and especially to Chablis, it is deeper in colour, with riper aromas and a fuller and softer body. The Pouilly wines, which are often oaked, tend to be richer and riper on the one hand, and finer and more complex on the other.

USA, California, Napa Valley

Napa is hotter and sunnier than Burgundy, leading to wines with a darker colour, fuller body, higher alcohol, and lower acidity. Until recently, the fashion was for highly concentrated, heavily oaked wines. Napa Chardonnay typically exhibits notes of baked apple and tropical fruits with vanilla, toast, butter, or coconut from oak ageing. Cool climate Chardonnay reminiscent of Chablis is made in certain sites in Sonoma, Mendocino, and Monterey.

Australia e.g. New South Wales, Hunter Valley

Australian Chardonnay is often made in an ultra-clean style. Oak, when used, can seem almost clinical in its application. Wines from warmer regions tend to be dominated by fig, melon, and tropical fruits, while those from cooler regions tend more towards fresh apple, citrus fruits, and flowers, often with ripe stone fruit on the palate. Australian Chardonnay tends to lack the yoghurt or 'dairy' note often found in New Zealand expressions. Modest examples may betray added tartaric acid or the crude use of oak staves or chips. Overall, the best sites for Chardonnay are in the Hunter Valley, the regions around Port Phillip Bay, Tasmania, Adelaide Hills, and Margaret River.

New Zealand, e.g. South Island, Marlborough

New Zealand Chardonnay exhibits ripe (although not tropical) fruit and high acidity. Typical notes are ripe apple and stone fruit, sometimes with a distinct yoghurt note. The finest examples evince Burgundian winemaking techniques, especially oak ageing, with American oak less common than it used to be. Chardonnay from the North Island is often riper, but it is hard to generalize.

Chile, e.g. Coquimbo, Limarí

The cool climate expression of Chardonnay from Limarí, Casablanca, and San Antonio (especially Leyda) has become Chile's signature style of Chardonnay. The wines are lean, restrained, and elegant with notes of both citrus and tropical fruits. Top producers favour Burgundian techniques, with the current fashion being for more subtle oaking. The best examples can be difficult to distinguish from well-made Mâcon. Chardonnay from warmer sites in the Central Valley are lower in acidity and higher in alcohol, with more overt tropical fruits.

Viognier

France, Northern Rhône, Condrieu or Château-Grillet

Condrieu is gold to deep gold in colour. High alcohol and a full, almost oily body are balanced by an intense perfume of candied peach, apricot, orange blossom, anise, acacia, and violets. Although dry, the richness and high alcohol can produce an impression of sweetness. Acidity is not as high as in Chardonnay and can be distinctly low. Many examples remain unoaked. Château-Grillet is more Burgundian than Condrieu: drier, lighter, more delicate, less perfumed, and oaked.

Marsanne and Roussanne

France, Northern Rhône, e.g. Hermitage, Crozes-Hermitage, Saint-Joseph

Marsanne and Roussanne are found in a number of regions outside their native Rhône Valley, including Savoie, the Languedoc, California, Washington, Victoria, and Swartland. They are often blended with each other, as in Hermitage and the Northern Rhône, or with other varieties such as Grenache Blanc, Viognier, or Chardonnay. Marsanne is full-bodied or 'waxy', with high alcohol and low acidity and notes of glue and marzipan. Roussanne is much higher in acidity and more aromatic, with notes of herbal or floral tea, pear, apricot, and honeysuckle. White Hermitage, which is mostly Marsanne, is rich yet textural and mineral, and with age develops complex notes of honey, wax, and hazelnuts.

Melon de Bourgogne

France, Loire, Muscadet

Muscadet is pale, sometimes almost watery, in colour, with a slight effervescence that can prickle on the tongue. On the nose, it is distinctly unaromatic. On the palate, it is dry and light-bodied with high acidity and a touch of minerality or saltiness, especially on the finish. Lees ageing contributes yeasty or nutty aromas and a rounder texture, and top examples can also exhibit notes such as smoke, honey, and dried papaya. Under AOP regulations, alcohol content is capped at 12%. Muscadet is often confused with Chablis, which is however more mineral, with higher acidity and alcohol. I like to think of Muscadet as a wine with a lot of negative space, in a good way.

Chenin Blanc

France, Loire, Vouvray or Coteaux du Layon

Vouvray is made in a range of styles. In the sweeter styles, the high acidity may be masked by residual sugar. With increasing age, aromas of green apple, quince, and acacia blossom surrender to complex tertiary aromas such as honeysuckle, fig, and lanolin. Botrytis is less common than in Coteaux du Layon, which also tends to be fuller in body, sweeter, and lower in acidity. Compared to Sauternes, which is typically associated with peach and honey, the sweet wines of the Loire are more often associated with apple, quince, and apricot, together with a much higher natural acidity and rather less sugar and alcohol.

France, Loire, Savennières

Savennières is gold in colour with concentrated notes of apple, pear, chamomile, warm straw, cooked fruits, beeswax, grilled almonds, and, with age, old cognac (musty lanolin, 'wet dog') and petrol. On the palate, it is dry and unoaked with high acidity and alcohol and a long mineral finish with a slightly bitter afternote. Compared to dry Vouvray, it is more austere with a fuller body and higher alcohol.

South Africa, Western Cape, e.g. Stellenbosch

Much South African Chenin is rather generic, but some producers focus on quality expressions similar to those from the Loire, including rich, bone dry wines reminiscent of Savennières and sweet, botrytized wines reminiscent of Coteaux du Layon. Owing to the warmer and sunnier climate, the emphasis is more on tropical fruits than on apples. Classic notes of honey and nuts can come through in the best examples, but the musty character typical of the Loire is mostly absent. In general, acidity, although still high, is lower, and alcohol is higher. Some premium examples may be lightly oaked.

Sauvignon Blanc

France, Loire, Sancerre or Pouilly-Fumé

Sancerre is pale lemon in colour, possibly with a green tinge. Notes of gooseberry and grapefruit are accompanied by hints of blackcurrant leaf, nettles, cut grass, and smoke. The nose is sometimes shorthanded as 'cat's pee on a gooseberry bush'. On the palate, Sancerre is dry and light-bodied with high acidity, medium alcohol, and a mineral finish. Oak is usually absent. In practice, it is very difficult to distinguish Sancerre from Pouilly-Fumé across the river, although the latter does tend to be smokier. Compared to, say, Marlborough Sauvignon Blanc, Sancerre and Pouilly-Fumé are more smoky and mineral with less overt fruit and a cooler fruit profile.

France, Bordeaux, Graves

White Graves combines the opulence of Semillon with the verve of Sauvignon Blanc, and is substantial and refreshing both at the same time. The wine can be complex with intense aromas of citrus fruits, peach, acacia, beeswax, and hazelnut. On the palate, it is medium in body, acidity, and alcohol, often with discernible oak influence and lees character. Compared to Loire Sauvignon Blanc, Sauvignon Blanc from Bordeaux is more expressive of tropical fruits and less so of grass and minerals.

New Zealand, South Island, Marlborough

Compared to Sauvignon Blanc from the Loire, Sauvignon Blanc from New Zealand is typically riper, higher in alcohol, and less chalky or mineral. It has a clean, pungent aroma with notes of gooseberry, passion fruit, asparagus, fresh grass, and blackcurrant leaf. Acidity is high but somewhat disguised by a smooth texture and, often, a touch of residual sugar that contributes roundness rather than sweetness. Body is medium and alcohol medium-to-high. The finest examples can boast a more 'serious' austerity, and, as in Bordeaux, may be fermented and matured in oak. Sauvignon Blanc from the North Island is often lighter in style and driven more by tropical fruit.

South Africa, Western Cape, e.g. Walker Bay

If Marlborough Sauvignon Blanc is ripe and expressive and Loire Sauvignon Blanc is lean and mineral, then South African Sauvignon Blanc falls somewhere in between. While the gooseberry and nettle is unmissable, the wine is less overt than Marlborough yet fuller in body than Loire. Quality examples with complexity and minerality hail from cooler regions, in particular Walker Bay, Cape Agulhas, and the Cape Peninsula. Oaked Sauvignon Blanc, so-called Fumé Blanc or Blanc Fumé, is produced throughout South Africa.

Chile, Aconcagua

Most Chilean Sauvignon Blanc is vinified in stainless steel. It neither matches New Zealand Sauvignon Blanc for punchiness nor Sancerre for restraint, but is instead distinguished by grapefruit and a nettle or smoky herbal note. Wines from warmer sites are often dominated by tropical fruit aromas and can be rather flabby.

USA, California

Californian Sauvignon Blanc is high in alcohol with medium-to-low acidity. Tropical fruits such as guava, mango, and pineapple overlie the nettle and gooseberry character of the grape variety. The oaked 'Fumé Blanc' style is popular.

Semillon

France, Bordeaux, Graves

See above, under Sauvignon Blanc.

France, Bordeaux, Sauternes or Barsac

Sauternes is intense, complex, and long, with notes of apricot, peach, passion fruit, orange marmalade, honey, honeysuckle, acacia, hazelnut, and vanilla. In time, the colour transmutes from gold to amber and copper, and notes such as old books, caramel, and crème brulée are not uncommon. On the palate, crisp acidity balances the intense sweetness, rich creaminess, and high alcohol. Barsac is difficult to distinguish from Sauternes but is often lighter, fresher, and less sweet. Note that Sauternes and Barsac are varying blends of Semillon and Sauvignon Blanc, and, in some cases, Muscadelle.

Australia, New South Wales, Hunter Valley

The Hunter Valley produces a unique style of Semillon that is very pale in colour with notes of flowers, citrus fruits, fennel, and fresh grass, high acidity, and low alcohol. The wines are dry and often quite textural on the palate. The best examples are extraordinarily lengthy. Although austere and flinty in their youth, with age they develop a complex bouquet of toast, nuts, beeswax, and tarragon. Owing to this toast, aged Hunter Valley Semillon can seem to have been oaked, but this is almost never the case.

Australia, Western Australia, Margaret River

In Margaret River, Semillon is typically blended with Sauvignon Blanc and aged in new French oak. The wines are full-bodied with medium-to-high alcohol, crisp acidity, and intense flavours of peach and honey from the Semillon and herbs and gooseberry from the Sauvignon Blanc. Compared to Graves, they are made in a 'cleaner' style with more intense, finely etched flavours. They are likely also to be fuller in body and higher in alcohol. This 'cleaner' style of winemaking—some have used the word 'clinical'—is typical of Australia as a whole.

Australia, South Australia, Barossa

Barossa Semillon is entirely different from Hunter Valley Semillon. The hot climate favours the development of rich wines with low acidity, medium-to-high alcohol, and notes of peach jam, mangoes, and coconut or vanilla from new, often American, oak.

Petit Manseng

France, South-West France, Jurançon

Jurançon is golden in colour, often with a greenish tinge. The nose delivers a medley of tropical fruits such as mango, pineapple, and guava along with flowers and sweet spice, and perhaps even beeswax, banana, and coconut. Acidity is very high but sweetness varies considerably according to vintage conditions and time of harvest. Sweet Jurançon is more akin to Vouvray than to nearby Sauternes, both in terms of acid structure and aroma profile. Dry Jurançon is often mistaken for New World Sauvignon Blanc, but is less herbaceous.

Albariño

Spain, Galicia, Rías Baixas

Albariño is pale to medium in colour with hints of gold and green. On the nose, it is aromatic, with notes of lime, apple, white peach, almonds, honeysuckle, and jasmine. On the palate, it is medium in body with high citrusy acidity, medium alcohol, and a dry or pithy mineral finish. Oak is usually absent. In blind tasting, Albariño is often arrived at by exclusion. Compared to Riesling, it is fuller in body and lacks the tartness and petrol notes; compared to Pinot Gris, it is drier and higher in acidity; compared to Viognier, it is lighter in body and much higher in acidity; and compared to Grüner Veltliner, it is less acidic and austere and lacks the white pepper note.

Garganega

Italy, Veneto, Soave Classico

Soave is typically straw in colour, with notes of citrus fruits and almonds and hints of flowers and spice, a body ranging from light to fairly full, crisp acidity, medium alcohol, no or little residual sugar, and a mineral or creamy finish with a slightly bitter edge. Top examples are rich, long, and complex. Oak is usually absent. Soave is often confused with Pinot Grigio, but is higher in acidity.

Grüner Veltliner

Austria, Wachau or Kremstal or Kamptal

Grüner Veltliner from Wachau is pale gold with hints of green. It is usually dry with notes of celery, white pepper, spice, and minerals. Depending on ripeness, fruit can range from apple and grapefruit to distinctly tropical fruits. Body is medium-to-full, with high acidity and medium-high to high alcohol. Oak is typically absent. Top examples can develop honeyed and toasty aromas with age. Grüner Veltliner from Kremstal and Kamptal is often fuller than that from Wachau.

Furmint

Hungary, Tokaj

Compared to Sauternes, with which it is often confused, Tokaji Aszú is a darker, copper colour with higher acidity and notes of apricot, orange zest, barley sugar, spice, and tea.

Hungary, Tokaj

Dry furmint is lemony in colour, with notes of smoke, pear, and lime, and hints of mandarin, apricot, honey, and spice. On the palate, it is light and crisp, with high acidity, medium-high or high alcohol, and a mineral backbone. The finish can be quite long. It is not so difficult to identify so long as one remembers to remember it!

Torrontés

Argentina, e.g. Salta

Torrontés is often pale gold in colour. On the nose, it presents a floral Muscat-like bouquet with notes of rose, jasmine, peach, and citrus fruits. On the palate, it is typically full-bodied and dry to off-dry depending on the style. The best examples are fresher and higher in acidity. Torrontés is often confused with Muscat or Gewurztraminer, but is less grapey than Muscat and lacks the distinctive lychee note of Gewurztraminer. Also, compared to Gewurztraminer, the palate is less oily and more mineral.

STYLISTIC PROFILES: RED WINES

Pinot Noir

France, Burgundy, Côte de Nuits

Pinot Noir is aromatic with a light-to-medium body, high acidity, and silky tannins. Côte de Nuits is reputed for its savoury fleshiness and mushroom and farmyard aromas. The character varies from commune to commune although there is much overlap. For instance, Gevrey-Chambertin is noted for its deep colour, power, and structure: full, rich, but also silky and delicately perfumed. Chambolle-Musigny is lighter, brighter, more delicate, more elegant, and more seductive. Nuits-Saint-George is full, firm, and dominated by black rather than red fruits.

France, Burgundy, Côte de Beaune

Compared to Côte de Nuits, Côte de Beaune is lighter, suppler, more fruit-driven, and quicker to mature. That said, red Corton (which is the only red wine Grand Cru in the Côte de Beaune) and Pommard tend to be more muscular and tannic, and more akin to Côte de Nuits. While the soils of Pommard are rich in marl, those of nearby Volnay are rich in limestone. As a result, Volnay is especially soft and fragrant, similar to (but lighter than) Chambolle-Musigny in the Côte de Nuits.

New Zealand, Martinborough or Marlborough or Central Otago

Ultra-clean fruit and high acidity are the hallmarks of New Zealand Pinot Noir. More ambitious examples can develop notes of earth and game. Pinot Noir from Central Otago is deep violet in colour with notes of black fruits and cherry and maybe a hint of greenness. On the palate, it is full-bodied for Pinot Noir, often with high alcohol and firm, round tannins. Marlborough Pinot Noir is lighter in colour and weight, and dominated by red fruits such as cranberry and raspberry, with finely etched, peppery tannins. Martinborough Pinot Noir is often from older vines and most akin to Burgundy. It is weightier than Marlborough and more complete and complex than Central Otago, with notes of cherry, plum, game, spice, and chocolate.

Australia, e.g. Victoria, Yarra Valley

Australian Pinot Noir is very clean and fruit-driven with good acidity. Unfortunately, it is sometimes marred by high alcohol—or, at least, alcohol that is too high in relation to its light body. The best examples avoid jammy fruit and tend to more earthy notes, often accompanied by eucalyptus or herbal mint. Much Australian Pinot Noir hails from the cooler regions of the Port Phillip zone in Victoria.

USA, Oregon, e.g. Willamette Valley

Oregon Pinot Noir is characterized by purity of fruit, florality, and, often, an herbaceous pine needle note. Maturation in new French oak is more common than in Burgundy. As with Burgundy, acidity is very high but tannin structure is generally softer. After several years of cellaring, very fine examples can develop *sous-bois* and other appealing tertiary notes.

USA, California, Sonoma

Sonoma Pinot Noir is the benchmark style for California. In particular, Russian River Valley Pinot Noir is classically vibrant in colour with notes of cherry, berry fruits, earth, and mushroom. Compared to Burgundy, it is fuller in body, richer in fruit, and lower in acidity.

Gamay

France, Burgundy, Beaujolais

Beaujolais is typically pale in colour with a blue tinge. It is light in body, medium-to-high in acidity, medium-to-low in alcohol, and low in tannins. Most Beaujolais is made by semi-carbonic maceration, which contributes estery notes of banana and bubblegum to the red fruits of the Gamay grape. However, cru wines tend to be made by traditional vinification and can be oaked, making them more tannic and difficult to recognize as Beaujolais. Beaujolais is easily confused with regular Valpolicella and other red wines that can be made by semi-carbonic maceration. Compared to Beaujolais, regular Valpolicella is higher in acidity and dominated by a sour cherry note.

Cabernet Franc

France, Loire, Chinon or Bourgueil or Saumur

Loire Cabernet Franc is light purple to purple in colour with a nose of raspberries and pencil shavings. With age, it develops earthy, spicy, and animally notes. Unripe examples may be marred by a bitter greenness or herbaceousness. On the palate, the wine is light or medium in body with high acidity, medium alcohol, and fine and powdery tannins. Chinon and Bourgueil tend to be more structured than Saumur, but in practice the three appellations are almost impossible to tell apart. All three appellations are noted for their limestone soils, but, especially in Chinon and Bourgueil, include lower vineyards on clay, gravel, or sand. So rather than by appellation, the wines vary more by soil type, and, of course, by producer. Outside the Loire, Cabernet Franc is often blended with Cabernet Sauvignon or Merlot. Cabernet Franc is most readily confused with Cabernet Sauvignon, which is less aromatic, with darker fruit and greater structure and tannins.

Cabernet Sauvignon

France, Bordeaux, Left Bank, Pauillac

Pauillac is bluish purple in its youth and brickens with age. On the nose, it is complex, dominated by notes of cassis (blackcurrant), green pepper (bell pepper), cedar, chocolate, cigar-box, and vanilla from new French oak. On the palate, it is powerful but elegant, with a medium body, fairly high acidity, medium alcohol, fine and structured tannins, and a long, astringent finish. Other Left Bank villages overlap in style and are difficult to distinguish from Pauillac. Archetypal Margaux is floral, exuding a perfume of acacia and violets. Saint-Julien offers a compromise between the power of Pauillac and the magic of Margaux, with, classically, a silkier texture and drier finish. Saint-Estèphe, which is often richer in Merlot, is likely to be deeper in colour and fuller or coarser in texture, with more rustic tannins, a touch more acidity, and a touch less perfume. Moulis is soft and fleshy, with more power but less finesse than Margaux, and maturing more quickly. Listrac is firmer and more tannic, similar to Saint-Estèphe but less ripe and more rustic, and also maturing more quickly. Compared to those of the Médoc, the wines of the Graves tend to be lighter in colour, body, and tannins, with more fragrance, more Merlot character, and hints of smoke, minerals, and red brick or terracotta.

USA, California, Napa Valley

Napa is comparatively hot and sunny, leading to wines with a darker colour, fuller body, higher alcohol, and lower acidity than their French counterparts. The tendency is for highly concentrated, full-bodied wines with significant French or American oak. Inspired by Left Bank Bordeaux, Napa Cabernet Sauvignon aims at structure and elegance. It is typically deep in colour with a flavour profile of concentrated ripe or jammy dark berries overlain by a fresh greenness often manifest as menthol. Merlot can contribute plum and milk chocolate notes, Cabernet Franc flint and herbal notes, and Petit Verdot floral and spicy notes. Alcohol can be very high, but, in finer examples, remains in balance.

Australia, South Australia, Coonawarra

Coonawarra Cabernet Sauvignon tends to fairly high levels of alcohol although the variety's characteristic acidity is retained. The fruit profile is ripe, with notes of concentrated blackcurrant and plum, verging on prune in hot vintages, coupled with a classic cedar note and eucalyptus rather than green pepper. Tannins are structured and fine-grained but less austere or chalky than in Bordeaux. Shiraz is sometimes used to round out the mid-palate in the same way that Merlot is used in Bordeaux.

Australia, Western Australia, Margaret River

Compared to Coonawarra, Margaret River is more akin to Left Bank Bordeaux and more likely to have been blended with Merlot and Cabernet Franc. Alcohol levels can still be high but the fruit is less likely to be stewed. Fresh green pepper replaces eucalyptus, tannins are firmer, and the use of French oak is more common.

Chile, Central Valley or Aconcagua

Chilean Cabernet Sauvignon is deep purple with aromas of fresh cassis and, often, a signature smoky, herbaceous note. Top examples are aged in French oak, adding notes of cedar, vanilla, and toast. Cool nights lead to crisp acidity, and warm days to high alcohol and riper, softer tannins than Bordeaux.

South Africa, Western Cape, e.g. Stellenbosch

South African Cabernet Sauvignon can be made as a varietal wine or blended with other grape varieties. Compared to Bordeaux, it is deeper in colour, fuller in body, and lower in acidity, with riper or jammier fruit flavours. The nose and palate are characterized by an intense note of blackcurrant with some of the green pepper character of Bordeaux along with an earthy or smoky signature that is particular to South Africa. The use of French oak is common.

Merlot

France, Bordeaux, Right Bank, Pomerol

This classic Merlot blend is deep ruby in colour with notes of fresh plum and other black and red fruits, spice, truffles, and vanilla from new French oak. On the palate, it is rich, often opulent, with lower acidity and softer tannins than Left Bank Bordeaux. Alcohol can be high in hotter vintages. Compared to Pomerol, which is sometimes compared to fruitcake, Saint-Emilion is drier and more tannic and less obviously from the Right Bank. It also tends to contain less Merlot and more Cabernet Franc and Cabernet Sauvignon. The Saint-Emilion satellites such as Montagne Saint-Emilion and Lussac Saint-Emilion are similar to Saint-Emilion, if more rustic.

Chile, Central Valley

Compared to Merlot-dominated Right Bank Bordeaux, Chilean Merlot is deeper in colour with notes of ripe plum, cherry, currants, chocolate, and mint. The minty note is analogous to the herbaceous quality typical of Chilean Cabernet Sauvignon and Carménère, and may be passed on from nearby garrigue and eucalyptus. On the palate, the wine is full-bodied with high alcohol, balanced acidity (though often adjusted), and soft and silky tannins that are not, however, without grip. Some of the finer examples of Chilean Merlot come from Maipo and Colchagua.

Malbec

France, South-West France, Cahors

Cahors is easily mistaken for Bordeaux, but is darker in colour with more plum, chocolate, and mineral notes, and heavier tannins that can make it austere in its youth. With age, it develops aromas of earth and *sousbois* with meaty, animally undertones. Other commonly cited descriptors include violet, gentian, ink, and liquorice. On the palate, acidity is high but body and alcohol are only medium. Top examples are aged in varying proportions of new oak.

Argentina, Mendoza

Argentine Malbec is deep in colour, perhaps even inky black. All Malbec is characterized by a plummy fruit profile, but whereas Cahors tends to earthy mineral notes of ink and iron, Argentine Malbec is riper, almost jammy, with spicy notes of cinnamon and nutmeg. On the palate, it is full-bodied with soft and velvety tannins, high alcohol, and, in many cases, medium-low acidity. The use of new French oak is common.

Carmenère

Chile, Rapel Valley, Colchagua

The best examples of Chilean Carmenère are deep ruby in colour with notes of cherry, blueberry, spice, black pepper, green pepper, and tobacco. Acidity is low, alcohol is high, and tannins are soft and silky. Cabernet Sauvignon is often co-opted for extra acidity and tannin structure, and field blends with Merlot are common.

Syrah/Shiraz

France, Northern Rhône, Hermitage

Hermitage is dark, full-bodied, and tannic, with intense aromas of soft black fruits accompanied by red fruits, smoke, black pepper and other spices, leather, cocoa, and coffee. With age, it develops a sweetness of fruit and gamey complexity. Heavy oak is unusual. Crozes-Hermitage is typically softer and fruitier than Hermitage. Saint-Joseph from the area of Mauves can be very similar to Hermitage, but most Saint-Joseph is lighter and dominated by black fruits and pepper. Traditional Cornas is fuller and richer than Crozes-Hermitage or Saint-Joseph, but more rustic and robust than Hermitage. Côte-Rôtie marries power and finesse, with a complex nose of raspberry, blueberry, blackberry, plum, bacon, green olives, violets, and leather. Northern Rhône reds are often confused with Bordeaux, which tends to be higher in acidity with drier and grippier tannins and green or leafy Cabernet notes.

Australia, South Australia, Barossa Valley or McLaren Vale

Barossa Shiraz is very dark in colour. On the nose, it typically exudes jammy or stewed black fruits, milk chocolate, sweet spice, black pepper, and eucalyptus or menthol. On the palate, it is rich and opulent, with high alcohol, soft acidity, and chunky, velvety tannins. The use of new American oak is traditional, but there is a trend towards new French oak and old oak. Compared to Barossa Shiraz, McLaren Vale Shiraz is less enormous, with a flavour profile of chocolate, mocha, earth, and spice that is more savoury than sweet.

South Africa, Western Cape

South African Shiraz is typically rich and ripe, with a sweetness of fruit reminiscent of Barossa Shiraz. Compared to its Australian counterparts, South African Shiraz is often smokier, with savoury notes of game, leather, and tar: not unlike Northern Rhône, but 'supercharged'. Both French oak and American oak are commonly used. Rhône blends with Grenache and Mourvèdre are increasingly common, as are cool climate expressions from areas such as Walker Bay.

Grenache

France, Southern Rhône, Châteauneuf-du-Pape or Gigondas

Red Châteauneuf-du-Pape is typically Grenache blended with other grape varieties, most commonly Syrah, Mourvèdre, and Cinsault. It is medium-to-deep ruby in colour, with notes of red and black fruits, game, tar, leather, and garrigue. On the palate, it is rich and spicy, with dusty or powdery tannins and a higher alcohol and lower acidity than Bordeaux or Hermitage. Significant new oak ageing is the exception rather than the rule. The wine is tight in its youth but softens and opens up after about seven years, and can improve for several more years, sometimes decades. Gigondas is a rich and powerful Grenache blend that is more rustic and animally than Châteauneuf-du-Pape. Some people, unfairly, think of Gigondas as junior Châteauneuf-du-Pape, and of neighbouring Vacqueyras as junior Gigondas. Vacqueyras often contains less Grenache than Gigondas.

Spain, Catalonia, Priorat

Priorat is very dark in colour with an intense aroma of ripe but savoury black and red fruits, minerals, earth, spice, liquorice, chocolate, and, in some cases, vanilla from new French oak. On the palate, it is full-bodied with high alcohol; crisp acidity; big and chewy tannins; and a long, dry, and structured finish.

Australia, South Australia, Barossa or McLaren Vale

Grenache thrives in the heat of South Australia, yielding varietal wines with notes of strawberry jam and ginger or white pepper, very high alcohol, and powdery, mouth-coating tannins. However, in most cases it is blended with Shiraz and Mourvèdre to produce full-bodied wines not unlike their inspirations in the Southern Rhône, with notes of ripe strawberry and plum fruit, game, pepper, cloves, liquorice, and herbs.

Mourvèdre

France, Provence, Bandol

Red Bandol consists of at least 50% Mourvèdre, usually completed by Grenache and Cinsault. The wine is dark in colour with savoury notes of black fruits, vanilla, spice, liquorice, garrigue, leather, red meat, and earth. On the palate, it is full-bodied, intense, and structured, with a high alcohol in the order of 14–15%. It is aged in old oak for at least 18 months prior to release.

Dolcetto

Dolcetto is deep ruby to purple in colour. It is soft and fruity, with notes of black cherry, soft spice, and liquorice; low acidity; high alcohol; and a characteristic dry, bitter almond finish. It is often thought of as Italy's best answer to Beaujolais, but is generally darker, drier, and more tannic than Beaujolais, with a more 'Italian' aroma profile of cherries and bitter almonds.

Barbera

Barbera ranges from light and delicate to heavy and powerful. It is more often deep ruby in colour with an intense and mouth-filling fruitiness. Notes of black and red cherries are complemented by cocoa, earth, leather, and soft spice. On the palate, it is very high in acidity with medium alcohol, low or medium tannins, and a dry finish. Some modern examples are aged in oak.

Nebbiolo

Italy, Piedmont, Barolo or Barbaresco

Although full-bodied, Barolo is light in colour, typically with a brick- or rust-red tinge that can make it seem older, sometimes much older, than it truly is. The nose is potentially very complex and often shorthanded as 'tar and roses'. Other notes include damson, mulberry, dried fruit, violets, herbs, dark chocolate, liquorice, and, with increasing age, leather, camphor, tobacco, *sousbois*, mushroom, and truffle. The palate is defined by medium-to-high alcohol, high acidity, and, above all, very high tannins, which, in the best of cases, translate into a silky or velvety texture. Barbaresco is similar to Barolo, if generally more aromatic and refined, with softer fruit and suppler, riper tannins. Although tight and tannic in its youth, it requires less cellaring time than Barolo.

Corvina

Italy, Veneto, Amarone della Valpolicella

Amarone is deep ruby in colour. The wine is rich, full-bodied, and concentrated with high alcohol, crisp acidity, velvety tannins, and a long and bitter finish. Its complex flavour profile is often compared to that of port, with notes of stewed cherries, raisins, dark chocolate, and liquorice—although, of course, Amarone is not fortified. A more modern, or 'international', style of Amarone is also made, which is softer and purer in fruit, with noticeable new oak influence. Other styles of Valpolicella include Classico, Ripasso, and Recioto.

Sangiovese

Italy, Tuscany, Chianti or Brunello di Montalcino

Chianti is typically medium ruby with notes of cherry and other red fruits, plum, clove, and herbs—and, with increasing age, tealeaves, tobacco, and leather. Top examples may display additional accents derived from maturation in new French oak. On the palate, body is medium, acidity high, alcohol medium-to-high, and tannins firm. The finish is agreeably dry with a note of bitter almonds. Compared to Chianti, Brunello is darker and richer, more full-bodied, tannic, and alcoholic, and, in many cases, more complex. Chianti is often confused with Châteauneuf-du-Pape, but has higher acidity and higher and firmer tannins.

Tempranillo

Spain, Rioja

Rioja is often pale in colour, brick-red or garnet with a bronzing rim. On the nose, it is dusty with notes of cooked strawberries and raspberries, tobacco leaf, game, nuts, leather, soft spice, and vanilla and coconut from American oak (although some producers are now using French oak). On the palate, it is medium in body with medium-to-low acidity, medium alcohol, ripe and silky tannins, and a spicy or savoury finish. Compared to traditional Rioja, international style Rioja generally spends less time in oak and is denser in colour and fruit, with more plum and blackberry.

Spain, Ribera del Duero or Toro

The Tempranillo of Ribera del Duero has thicker, darker skins than that of Rioja, and is also higher in acidity. Compared to most Rioja, the wines are dark and brooding: more full-bodied, concentrated, alcoholic, and tannic, and dominated by dark berries and plums rather than red fruits. Toro is similar in style to Ribera del Duero, but more exuberant and (often) more rustic, with a signature spicy note.

Spain, Navarra

Navarra is often similar to Rioja, if perhaps more international in style, with a deeper colour, darker blackberry fruit from the blending of grape varieties such as Cabernet Sauvignon and Merlot, and, in many cases, French rather than American oak.

Pinotage

South Africa, Western Cape, e.g. Paarl

Pinotage is deep ruby or purple in colour, sometimes with a bluish tinge, with notes such as plum, prune, fruitcake, bacon, rooibos tea, and smoke. On the palate, it is medium-to-full-bodied with medium acidity and high alcohol and tannins. The use of French or American oak is common. The best examples bring out the grape variety's character and complexity, with remarkable notes of banana, coffee bean, clove, and boiled sweets emerging with increasing bottle age. Pinotage has a tendency to retain volatile esters during vinification, which can result in unpleasant paint-like aromas. Critics often deride it as pungent and alcoholic with coarse tannins, but this need not be the case.

Zinfandel

USA, California, Sonoma

Zinfandel is deep ruby or purple in colour with notes of strawberry or brambly fruit, fresh cream, black tea, thyme or other herbs, and, often, coconut from American oak. On the palate, it is full-bodied with high alcohol, moderate acidity, and high tannins. Top examples are lengthy with a mineral core and savoury finish. Early-harvested or cool-climate examples are paler and tend to herbal green notes and angular tannins. Zinfandel is a clonal variation of Primitivo from Puglia, Italy. Compared to Zinfandel, Primitivo exhibits a more savoury, dried-fruit profile with, on the palate, a drier entry and more substantial tannins.

Blaufränkisch

Austria, e.g. Burgenland, Mittelburgenland

Blaufränkisch is usually dark purple in colour with notes of redcurrants or cherries, blackberry, pepper and spice, and liquorice. On the palate, body is medium, acidity high, alcohol medium, and tannins firm and gripping. Some examples are aged in new French oak.

Zweigelt

Austria, e.g. Burgenland, Neusiedlersee

Zweigelt is fresh and fruit-driven. It is often deep ruby, with notes of red cherries and soft spice such as cinnamon and nutmeg. On the palate, it is light-to-medium bodied with a supple acidity reminiscent of Barbera (but less high), medium alcohol, and soft and subtle tannins. Oak is usually absent.

PART II: FRANCE AND SPARKLING WINES

6

ALSACE

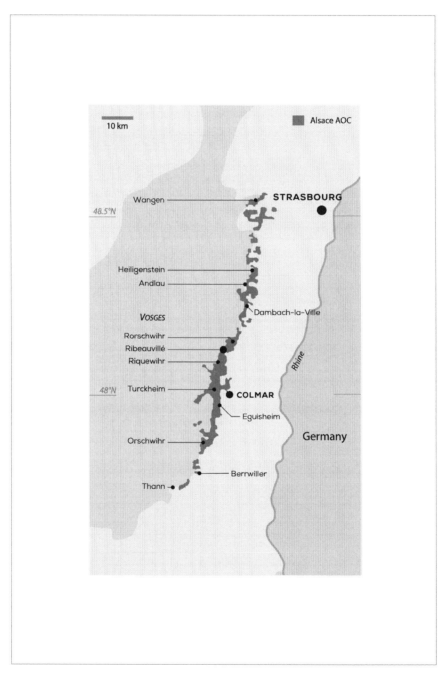

Alsace

*I*n the 1st century the Romans established the region of Alsace, then part of the province of Germania Superior, as a centre of viticulture. In more recent history, Alsace has at times been German and at other times French, but at all times, and above all, proudly Alsatian. Despite the centralizing tendency of the French Republic, the region still retains a strong and separate identity, with its own language, culture, cuisine, and wine tradition, which revolves around not French but Germanic grape varieties. Alsatian wines are, for the most part, single varietal white wines, with the most prized made from Riesling, Gewurztraminer, or Pinot Gris. As in Germany, it is common for the grape variety to be prominently displayed on the front label. If the variety does not feature on the front label, this usually means that the wine is a blend of several varieties, sometimes labelled as *Gentil* or more modest *Edelzwicker*.

The lie of the land

The vineyards of Alsace are framed by the Vosges Mountains to the west and the River Rhine to the east, and centred on the picturesque towns of Colmar and Ribeauvillé, which lies ~16km [~10mi] north of Colmar and ~70km south of the regional capital of Strasbourg. The best vineyards are at the foot of the Vosges, forming a narrow strip that stretches from north to south over a distance of more than 100km. The slopes generally face east, but hills and lateral valleys give rise to a number of south-facing and north-facing inclines. Indeed, many of the best vineyards have a south-east to south-west orientation. The slopes are usually worked by hand, with mechanical harvesting confined to the plains of the Rhine.

Climate

Alsace sits in the rain shadow of the Vosges, which shelter the region from the prevailing Atlantic winds. Colmar receives less than 500mm [20in] annual rainfall, which makes it the second driest place in France after Perpignan in the far south. While summers are hot, winters are long and harsh, as may be expected in such a northerly and continental location (although Alsace is actually south of Champagne). Dry autumns favour the finesse associated with extended ripening. The principal threats to the harvest are spring frosts and summer hailstorms.

Soils

The vineyards of Alsace run along a collapsed fault line, and so the soils are very varied, sometimes even within a single vineyard. The soils on the plain are for the most part alluvial, but those higher up can be almost anything. Rockier **flint, granite, and schist soils** are associated with a mineral, petrol, and gunflint character, and are best suited to Riesling. Heavier **clay and marl soils** are associated with weight and broad fruit flavours, and are best suited to Gewurztraminer. **Limestone soils** are associated with finesse, and are best suited to Muscat. Producers often choose grape varieties according to their terroir, but also seek to diversify plantings to minimize the impact of a poor harvest for any one variety.

Grape varieties

The seven major grape varieties are Riesling, Gewurztraminer, Pinot Gris (formerly 'Tokay'), Pinot Blanc, Pinot Noir, Sylvaner, and Muscat. Over the years, there has been a trend to replace plantings of Sylvaner, once the commonest variety, with Pinot Gris, Pinot Noir, and Riesling. All the wines are white except for those made from Pinot Noir, which are light red or rosé.

A good quality sparkling wine, **Crémant d'Alsace**, is also made by the traditional method (Chapter 12), and has come to account for about a quarter of the region's production. Grapes for Crémant d'Alsace are picked at the beginning of the harvest season, and permitted varieties include Pinot Blanc, Pinot Gris, Pinot Noir, Riesling, and Chardonnay.

Finally, there are **late harvest wines**, which may be classified as either *Vendange Tardive* (VT, 'Late Harvest', similar to *Auslese* in Germany) or

Sélection de Grains Nobles (SGN, 'Selection of Noble Berries', similar to *Beerenauslese* in Germany and made from botrytized grapes). Only the four so-called 'noble' varieties, namely, Riesling, Gewurztraminer, Pinot Gris, and Muscat, are permitted for late harvest wines, whether VT or SGN. Late harvest wines account for a very small fraction of total production, even in vintages that are favourable to late ripening and noble rot. Straw wine (*vin de paille*, a wine made from dried grapes) and ice wine are also made, but in even smaller quantities.

Appellations

The French and European classification systems are introduced in Appendix A. Almost the entire production of Alsace is *Appellation d'Origine Protégée* (AOP) as there is no *Indication Géographique Protégée* (IGP) designation for the region. To make life simple, there are only three AOPs: **Alsace AOP** and **Crémant d'Alsace AOP**, which cover the entire region, and the more restrictive **Alsace Grand Cru AOP** (~4% of production), which covers 51 named vineyards, from Rangen in the south to Steinklotz almost 100km further north, and from Kanzlerberg at just 3ha to Schlossberg at over 80ha. 37 Grand Crus lie in the southern administrative *département* of Haut-Rhin, and 14 in the northern *département* of Bas-Rhin, north of Ribeauvillé. With a couple of minor exceptions, only the four noble grape varieties are permitted for Grand Cru wines.

Some producers relinquish the Grand Cru designation in favour of historical names such as Clos Sainte Hune, which is part of Grand Cru Rosacker and perhaps the most vaunted name in Alsace wine. Other historical and highly regarded clos, such as Clos des Capucins and Clos Hauserer, fall outside of Grand Cru demarcations. The village of Rorschwihr counts 12 historical crus, and proudly rejected the Grand Cru designation when it was offered two large Grand Crus instead of 12 smaller ones. The creation of Cru and Premier Cru tiers is currently being discussed, and could be a boon to producers in villages such as Rorschwihr. Terms such as *Réserve Personnelle* and *Cuvée Spéciale* have no legal status, but producers can include them to indicate a wine of higher quality. They can also include the name of a particular *lieu-dit*, or locality.

While crémant is entered into champagne bottles, still wine is entered into tall and slender bottles called *flutes d'Alsace*. Unlike in Germany, this is actually an appellation rule. The one exception is for Pinot Noir, which can also be entered into Burgundy bottles.

Wine styles

Compared to their German counterparts, the white wines of Alsace tend to be fuller in body and higher in alcohol, and also dryer—although perhaps not quite as dry as they used to be. They are mostly unblended, unoaked, and unsoftened by a malolactic conversion, and tend therefore to be highly expressive of varietal character and terroir. It used to be difficult to gauge the sweetness of a particular wine, but since 2021 sweetness levels must be displayed, with labels stating 'sec', 'demi-sec', 'moelleux' (12-45g/l sugar), or 'doux'. Producers tend to have a house style: for example, Trimbach and Léon Beyer are known for their bone-dry wines and Rolly Gassmann for a rich and velvety sweetness. Other leading houses include Blanck, Agathe Bursin, Albert Mann, Hugel, Josmeyer, Marcel Deiss, Ostertag, Schlumberger, Valentin Zusslin, Vincent Stoeffler, Weinbach, and Zind-Humbrecht. It is said, or used to be said, that Protestant houses make dry, mineral wines, whereas Catholic ones favour rounder, richer styles, and thus that you can tell a winemaker's religion from his or her style and vice versa. Independent wine growers account for a mere 20% of the region's production, with the remainder accounted for by co-operatives and négociants.

Riesling is the most blue-blooded of the four noble grape varieties, and also the most highly reflective of terroir. Alsatian Riesling tends to be drier, richer, and higher in alcohol than Riesling from across the Rhine. It is often steely and inexpressive in its youth, with aromas of mineral, apple, citrus fruits, stone fruits, jasmine, and honey. With age, it develops a complex bouquet dominated by pure fruit flavours and appealing petrol or kerosene notes, typically with a long, dry finish that rides home on a backbone of high acidity.

Gewurztraminer, spelt Gewürztraminer in Alsace, is easy to recognize, as it is opulent with high alcohol and smells like an oriental bazaar or perfume shop. For just these reasons, it can seem sweeter than it is. In hot vintages, it can be flabby and lacking in acidity, and this too can contribute to an impression of sweetness. Blind tasters often look out for a pink tinge to the golden hue, but this is not invariably present or visible. Typical notes include spice, rose petals, lychee, grapefruit, peach kernel, and smoky bacon. Despite its relative lack of acidity, Gewurztraminer can be ageworthy. It is commonly used in VT and SGN, but most of the production is dry or off-dry.

Pinot Gris is noted for aromas of spice and pear or stone fruit with hints of honey and smoke and a certain earthy minerality. Alsatian Pinot Gris is much fuller and richer than Italian Pinot Gris ('Pinot Grigio'), which is often crisp and lean. Among Alsatian wines, it sits in the middle, combining the spiciness and alcohol of Gewurztraminer with some of the structure and acidity of Riesling. Like Riesling and Gewurztraminer, it can improve with age. Pinot Gris can achieve high levels of sugar, and, like Gewurztraminer, is commonly used in VT and SGN.

Pinot Blanc is often blended with a similar variety called Auxerrois, with the blend labelled as Pinot Blanc. Auxerrois can be thought of as an understudy of Chardonnay. At best, it is round and medium-bodied with hints of ripe apples, pears, and spice, and a clean and refreshing finish. Although distinctly Alsatian, Pinot Blanc has less body than Gewurztraminer or Pinot Gris, less acidity and precision than Riesling, and less aromatic intensity than either of the three. It is not intended for ageing.

Once upon a time, **Pinot Noir** from Alsace was pale, thin, and unripe. Today, the trend, driven by rising temperatures and Burgundian prices, is for darker and richer offerings, and from more premium sites. Marcel Deiss, Albert Mann, and Valentin Zusslin make some of the most inspiring examples. In May 2022, after a ten-year-long process, the

Grand Crus of Hengst and Kirchberg were authorized for Pinot Noir—Alsace's first red grand crus!

Sylvaner is a humble variety, although there are some fine examples. Indeed, since 2005, it has been permitted in Grand Cru Zotzenberg, prompting some to label it as the 'comeback kid' of Alsace. Typical examples are lean and fresh with hints of citrus and white flowers, sometimes marred by a slight bitterness or earthiness. Wines made from Sylvaner are not intended for ageing.

Alsatian **Muscat** is usually a blend of Muscat Ottonel and Muscat Blanc à Petits Grains [Muscat de Frontignan, Moscato d'Asti...], which together make up just 3% of the region's vineyards. Muscat Blanc à Petits Grains was held in high regard by the Greeks, Romans, and Phoenicians, and is perhaps the oldest grape variety still in cultivation. Alsatian Muscat is delicate and floral, with a light body and low alcohol. Although it is dry, the signature grapy aroma produces an impression of sweetness. Other notes include apple, orange, mandarin, rose (from geraniol and other terpenes), white pepper, and mint. The intensity of the nose rarely follows through on the palate, particularly since acidity is often lacking. Alsatian Muscat is not intended for ageing. A handful of houses can make a VT or SGN in certain years.

Although it is difficult to generalize across grape varieties and styles, stronger vintages in Alsace include 1989, 1990, 1997, 1998, 2000, 2005, 2007, 2009, 2012, 2015, 2016, 2017, 2018, 2019, and 2020. Weaker vintages include 1991, 1999, and 2003. It has been said that the 2015 vintage is better even than 2005, 1959, 1947, and 1834, and (from old records) as good as 1540!

7

BURGUNDY

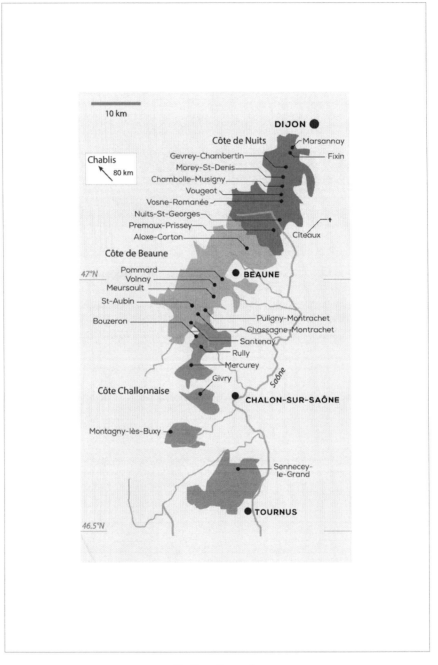

Northern Burgundy

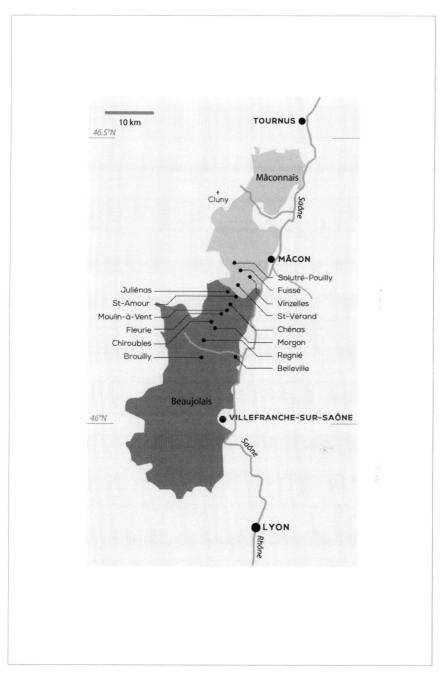

Southern Burgundy

*T*he Celts were already making wine in Burgundy when the
Romans conquered Gaul in 51 BCE. To supply their soldiers
and colonists, the Romans propagated the vine all along the east-facing
slopes of the Saône river valley. After the fall of the Western Roman
Empire, the monasteries moved in, and, by the gradual accretion of
land, became the dominant force in winemaking. In his *History of the
Franks* (591 CE), Gregory, Bishop of Tours, compared Burgundy to the
Roman Grand Cru Falernian: 'Dijon has all around it abundant springs,
and on the west are hills, very fertile and full of vineyards, which
produce for the inhabitants such a noble Falernian that they disdain
wine of Ascalon.'

The Benedictines, who founded the Abbey of Cluny in 910, and the
reformist Cistercians, who founded the Abbey of Cîteaux in 1098,
became especially implicated in winemaking. Mindful of the subtle
influences of terroir, these brothers in God began to document vineyard
and vintage variations with fastidious care. In 1336, the Cistercians
created the first enclosed vineyard in Burgundy, the Clos de Vougeot.
The monks invested so much time, effort, and skill into their wine that
the Avignon popes began to take notice, purchasing vast volumes to
ease the pangs of their Babylonian captivity. To uphold the quality of
his country's wines, Philip II the Bold, Duke of Burgundy (d. 1404),
banned the cultivation of the 'vile and disloyal' Gamay grape and the
use of manure as fertilizer (which, by increasing yields, decreased
concentrations). Thenceforth, red Burgundy could only be made from
Pinot Noir. Meanwhile, white Burgundy was being made from not
Chardonnay but Fromenteau, an ancestor of Pinot Gris.

In the eighteenth century, roads improved, easing the export of wine
out of landlocked Burgundy. Burgundy began to vie with Champagne,
which was then predominantly still and red, for the lucrative Paris
market. It became so fashionable that, in 1760, the Prince de Conti
acquired the Domaine de la Romanée and appended his name to the
already famous estate.

After the absorption of Burgundy into the French crown in the late fifteenth century, the Church began, both figuratively and literally, to lose ground. In the late eighteenth century, revolutionaries auctioned off the Church's remaining lands. Owing to the *Code Napoléon*, which stipulates that any inheritance be equally divided between all children, these new, laical holdings became ever smaller. Today, there are no fewer than eighty growers in the Clos de Vougeot, with some owning just a few rows of vines. This extreme parcellation has not occurred in Bordeaux, where many properties are owned by, or structured as, companies, and where the vineyards are not individually delineated and registered. The small size of many Burgundian holdings makes négociants and co-operatives an important part of the landscape. Great négociant houses such as Bouchard Père et Fils, William Fèvre, Louis Jadot, Louis Latour, Joseph Drouhin, Faiveley, and Chanson Père et Fils do own some vineyards (which are often among the best), but the law limits the extent of their holdings and they remain reliant on smaller growers and producers. William Fèvre sometimes has two bottlings of the same cru, one labelled 'Domaine William Fèvre' made from their own grapes and the other labelled simply 'William Fèvre'.

In 1847, Louis-Philippe of France gave the village of Gevrey the right to append to its name that of its most celebrated Grand Cru, Chambertin. Not to be outdone, other villages soon followed suit, whence all the double-barrelled names in the area: Chambolle-Musigny, Morey-Saint-Denis, Puligny-Montrachet, and so on. In 1855, the year of the Bordeaux Classification, one Dr Jules Lavalle published an influential book with the snappy title, *Histoire et statistique de la vigne et des grands vins de la Côte-d'Or*. It included an unofficial classification of the vineyards of Burgundy, which, in 1861, informed the classification adopted by the Beaune Committee of Agriculture. Upon the introduction of the French AOP/AOC system in 1936, most of the vineyards in the top tier of this classification acceded to the lofty Grand Cru status.

Like other wine regions, Burgundy then started to suffer, first from phylloxera, which arrived in Meursault in 1878, then from the Great Depression, and finally from the Second World War. German troops had been instructed to steer clear of 'first growths', leading to the hasty creation of the Premier Cru designation. Because the demarcation line with the Free Zone ran through the Côte Châlonnaise, there were, until 2020, no Premier Crus in the more southerly Mâconnais. Upon returning to their land, growers enriched their vineyards with chemical fertilizers. This worked well at first, but then potassium accumulated in the soil, leading to a fall in acidity in the grapes and wines.

The lie of the land

Burgundy has 96 AOPs, ~25% of the total number of AOPs in France and almost twice as many as Bordeaux. But if one excludes Beaujolais (12 AOPs), the actual area under vine is only a small fraction of that in Bordeaux, ~28,000ha versus ~120,000ha [1ha = 2.47ac]. To the north, just south of the regional capital of Dijon, lies the most illustrious section of the *vignoble bourgignon*, the Côte d'Or, which is the name of both the *département* and the wine growing area. The Côte d'Or consists of the northerly Côtes de Nuits, which is most reputed for its red wines and encompasses the great majority of the red Grand Cru vineyards, and the southerly Côtes de Beaune, which is most reputed for its white wines. Still further south is the Côte Chalonnaise, with some of the best bargains in Burgundy, then the Mâconnais, and, finally, the Beaujolais, which stretches almost as far south as Lyon. The picture is completed by Chablis, a satellite of Burgundy that is closer to Champagne than to the Côte d'Or.

Climate

The climate in Burgundy is northerly and continental, with cold winters, hesitant springs, and potentially hot summers. East-facing slopes, long summer days, and, in good years, a dry and sun-drenched September, help to compensate for the short growing season. Aside from spring frosts, other hazards include heavy rain in May and June and hailstorms in late summer. Unsurprisingly, there can be a lot of variation between vintages and even between vineyards. While the marginal climate presents a number of difficulties, the overall cool temperatures preserve acidity and promote the development of complex aromatic compounds. Without its marginal climate, Burgundy would not be Burgundy.

Grape varieties

The principal grape varieties of Burgundy are Pinot Noir for the reds and Chardonnay for the whites. Otherwise, Gamay goes into making Beaujolais, and there is also some Aligoté. The locals say that Pinot Noir is a white variety in disguise, and Chardonnay a red variety in disguise, and, almost uniquely, taste the reds before the whites.

Pinot Noir

The name Pinot Noir is thought to allude to the grapes themselves, which are tightly clustered into bunches resembling pinecones. As the variety is ancient and prone to mutations, there are a great number of clones for growers to choose from. Even a single clone can give rise to multiple expressions, and Pinot Noir is more reflective of terroir than perhaps any other grape variety. But it is not easy to work with: as the Californian winemaker André Tchelistcheff put it, 'God made Cabernet Sauvignon whereas the devil made Pinot Noir.' The vine is intolerant of heat and drought and does best in cooler climates, especially when planted on well-drained limestone soils as in the Côte d'Or, its spiritual home and its highest expression. As it flowers early, it is vulnerable to spring frosts and *coulure* (failure of grape development) and *millerandage* (uneven grape development); and as the grapes are tightly bunched and thin-skinned, they are prone to rot and disease and hail damage. Pinot Noir is relatively lacking in pigment and tannin, which accounts for the characteristic pale colour and a reliance on high acidity rather than tannins for definition on the palate; if the grapes are overripe, the result is a soft and jammy offering that is flabby and lacking in interest. Planting densities, especially in Burgundy, are very high: up to 12,000 vines/ha, with the vines, which are single or double Guyot trained, less than 1m (3.3ft) apart. The wines are light to medium in body, silky, and aromatic, and distinguished by their savoury fleshiness and farmyard notes.

Chardonnay

Unlike Pinot Noir, Chardonnay is relatively easy to work with, and, worldwide, it is more widespread than any other grape variety including Cabernet Sauvignon. It tends to do best on chalk, clay, and limestone, which are all plentiful in its Burgundian homeland. Chardonnay has a 'neutral' or 'malleable' profile, and is sometimes compared to a mirror that reflects its terroir as well as the skill and ambition of the winemaker—especially with regard to fermentation temperature, malolactic fermentation, lees contact and stirring, oak treatment, and bottle ageing. Yields in excess of 50hl/ha are easily achieved, and ought to be restricted to concentrate the grapes. The choice of rootstock is important for restricting vigour and, on limestone, for reducing the risk of chlorosis. Like Pinot Noir, Chardonnay buds and flowers early, which makes it vulnerable to spring frosts and to *coulure* and *millerandage*. The use of frost protection systems is common, especially in Chablis. As Chardonnay is thin-skinned, it is prone to rot and hail damage; but as it ripens early (just after Pinot Noir), it can often be harvested before the autumn rains settle in. Another reason not to delay harvest is to preserve acidity, which declines rapidly once full ripeness has been reached. Even within Burgundy itself, Chardonnay is made into a number of styles, from lean, racy, mineral Chablis to round, rich, buttery Meursault. The best Chardonnays from Mercurey, Montagny-lès-Buxy, or Rully in the Côte Chalonnaise can rival those of the Côte de Beaune, as can those from the Pouilly area in the Mâconnais.

Aligoté and other white varieties

Aligoté plays second fiddle to Chardonnay, and has been relegated to poorer vineyard sites at the top and bottom of the slopes. Aligoté wines can be labelled as Bourgogne Aligoté AOP or, in Bouzeron in the Côte Chalonnaise, as Bouzeron AOP. Yields for Bouzeron are capped at 45hl/ha, compared to 60hl/ha for Bourgogne Aligoté. The wines are light with faint notes of apples and lemons, and high, often angular, acidity—although some of Burgundy's most hallowed names, such as Aubert de Villaine and Lalou Bize-Leroy, are proving that Aligoté can do much better than that. Kir, or *vin blanc cassis,* is traditionally made by adding crème de cassis to Aligoté.

Other, less common, white varieties in Burgundy are Pinot Blanc, Pinot Gris, Melon de Bourgogne, and Sauvignon Blanc, which, for the delight of blind tasters, has a variety-specific appellation in Saint-Bris. The Nuits-Saint-Georges La Perrière Premier Cru from Domaine Henri Gouges is made from a white mutation of Pinot Noir, called Pinot Gouges. The mutation was discovered by Henri Gouges, mayor of Nuits-Saint-Georges, an early advocate of domaine bottling and one of the people charged with delineating the crus of Burgundy. So as not to seem biased or corrupt, he determined that no vineyards in the village should accede to Grand Cru.

Appellations

~61% of the wine produced in Burgundy is white, ~31% is red (together with a very little rosé), and the rest is sparkling.

The wines of Burgundy can be divided into four levels: regional or generic, village or commune, Premier Cru, and Grand Cru. There are 7 regional AOPs, 44 commune AOPs (which encompass the Premier Crus), and 33 Grand Cru AOPs. The first account for 52% of the vineyard area, the second for 46.6%, and the third for just 1.4%. Within this, Premier Cru vineyards, or *climats*, of which there are 662, account for ~11% of the vineyard area.

The 7 regional AOPs are Bourgogne, Bourgogne Aligoté, Bourgogne Passe-tout-grains (rosé and red wines made from Pinot Noir and up to 2/3 Gamay), Côteaux Bourguignons (aka Bourgogne Grand Ordinaire or Ordinaire, and less restrictive than Bourgogne), Bourgogne Mousseux, Crémant de Bourgogne, and Mâcon, which includes Mâcon Villages for wines produced in 11 communes. In addition, there are 13 *Dénominations Géographiques Complémentaires* within Bourgogne AOP (e.g. Bourgogne Chitry, Bourgogne Côte Chalonnaise, Bourgogne Côte d'Or...) and 27 within the Mâcon AOP (e.g. Mâcon-Vergisson, Mâcon-Verzé, Mâcon-Vinzelles...) There is no such thing as a regional *Vin de Pays* and there is no *Vin de Pays* for the *département* of the Côte d'Or; but there is a *Vin de Pays* for the Sâone-et-Loire and for the Yonne.

The broad **Côte de Nuits-Villages** and **Côte de Beaune-Villages** are considered as village or commune appellations rather than regional appellations. Côte de Nuits-Villages is a red wine appellation that can be used by five communes, two in the extreme north of the Côte de Nuits (Fixin, Brochon) and three in the extreme south (Prissey, Corgoloin, Comblanchien). Except for Fixin, they cannot use their own name. Côte de Beaune-Villages is also a red wine appellation, available to a number of communes in the Côte de Beaune (all the communes except Aloxe-Corton, Beaune, Volnay, and Pommard). Unlike with Côte de Nuits-Villages, these communes can choose between Côte de Beaune-Villages and their own name.

Next up are the **village or commune AOPs** that apply to a specific commune. Examples include Pommard AOP, Chambolle-Musigny AOP, and Pouilly-Fuissé AOP. For a commune AOP, the vineyard or *climat* can be included on the label, but must be in smaller lettering, except if it is a Premier Cru. A wine from a Premier Cru vineyard such as les Perrières in Meursault may be labeled as MEURSAULT LES PERRIERES or MEURSAULT PREMIER CRU. The latter designation, MEURSAULT PREMIER CRU, can also be used for a blend from several Premier Cru vineyards in Meursault.

At the peak of the pyramid are the 33 **Grand Crus**, which, unlike the Premier Crus, are independent of the commune appellation. In the Côte d'Or (so excluding Chablis Grand Cru AOP), all but one of the red Grand Crus are in the Côte de Nuits, and all the white Grand Crus (of which there are fewer) are in the Côte de Beaune. A couple of the red Grand Crus, namely, Le Musigny and Corton, also produce some white wine. The red Grand Crus occupy 356ha, and the white Grand Crus 194ha. Some of the largest Grand Crus are Corton (~98ha), Corton-Charlemagne (~52ha), and Clos de Vougeot (~51ha); the smallest is La Romanée at a mere 0.85ha. Although every producer in, say, Clos de Vougeot is entitled to label his or her wine as GRAND CRU CLOS DE VOUGEOT, their wines sell at very different prices.

Wine styles

Chablis

Chablis is in the Yonne, around 100km to the north-west of Dijon. The vineyards spread out across some twenty communes centred on the small town of Chablis in the valley of the River Serein. The climate is cooler than in the Côte d'Or, and the use of sprinklers and smudge pots to defend against frost is widespread. The soil consists of a limestone bed overlain by either Kimmeridge or the younger Portland clay. **Kimmeridge clay** is more sought-after, and consists of clay, limestone, and fossilized shells. Only Chardonnay is planted in Chablis, which, for a time in America, became synonymous with the grape variety.

There are, mercifully, just four appellations: Petit Chablis AOP, Chablis AOP, Chablis Premier Cru AOP, and Chablis Grand Cru AOP. In recent decades, the area classified as Chablis AOP, which accounts for the bulk of production, has controversially been expanded to include land on Portland clay. There are forty Premier Cru vineyards, although the smaller ones may be labelled under the name of a nearby larger one. There are 17 such 'umbrella' Premier Crus, including Montée de Tonnerre, Fourchaume, Vaillons, and Montmains. The seven Grand Cru vineyards—Blanchot, Bougros, Les Clos, Grenouilles, Preuses, Valmur, and Vaudésir—form part of a single Grand Cru AOP and occupy just over 100ha on the south-western aspect of the slope along the right-bank of the Serein. The Grand Cru wines most reliably capture the gunflint quality [*gout de pierre à fusil*] for which Chablis is rightly reputed.

Chablis winemakers privilege terroir over winemaking, and tend to avoid exposing their wines to significant oak treatment. Some Grand Cru and Premier Cru wines do come into contact with new oak, but much less so than their counterparts in Beaune, and the charring of the barrels is lighter. About a third of total output is overseen by the co-operative La Chablisienne, which makes quality wines at all levels. In the glass, Chablis is classically pale lemon in colour with or without a greenish tinge. On the nose, there are citrus fruits, green apple, honeysuckle, cream, and a characteristic stony or smoky minerality. The palate is lean, dry, and austere with pronounced acidity, which is a key distinguishing feature. The best examples are very long-lived, although may in their adolescence go through a closed, wet-wool phase.

Other than La Chablisienne, notable producers of Chablis include Brocard, William Fèvre, Joesph Drouhin, Billaud-Simon, Raveneau, Vincent Dauvissat, Dampt, Droin, Christian Moreau, Louis Michel, Maison Verget, Pattes Loup, and Alice et Olivier de Moor.

Côte d'Or: Côte de Nuits

The vineyards of the Côte d'Or, with the romantic walled town of Beaune more or less at their centre, run the length of an east-facing limestone escarpment, whence 'Côte d'Or' ('Golden Slope', and also 'Oriental Slope'). The limestone escarpment divides the mountains of the Morvan to the west from the plain of the River Saône to the east. The soils at the top of the escarpment are too sparse, and those on the plain too fertile, for greatness. Thus, the best vineyards are mid-slope, at altitudes of 250–300m, where the vines also benefit from better sun exposure and water drainage. The monotony of east-facing vineyards is broken by a number of streams and dry valleys, or *combes*, which cut across the escarpment and alter the aspect of certain vineyards.

The Côte de Nuits is the northern part of the Côte d'Or, from Dijon to just south of Nuit-Saint-Georges. Of its 14 communes, six produce Grand Cru wines, with the commune of **Gevrey-Chambertin** boasting no less than nine Grand Crus, all carrying 'Chambertin' in their name. The largest is Charmes-Chambertin, followed by Chambertin and Chambertin-Clos de Bèze (which can be labelled as Chambertin). Gevrey also has 26 Premier Crus, and a Premier Cru from a more reputed producer might fetch a higher price than a Grand Cru from a less reputed one. All in all, the wines of Gevrey are noted for their deep colour, power, and structure: full, rich, but also silky and delicately perfumed.

Morey-Saint-Denis, immediately south of Gevrey, boasts four Grand Crus: Clos de la Roche, the largest and most reputed; Clos Saint Denis;

and Clos de Tart and Clos des Lambrays, which, unusually, are both monopoles (in single ownership). Clos de Tart and Clos des Lambrays are easy to recognize by their planting, in that the rows run north-to-south i.e. perpendicular to the slope, which is unusual in Burgundy. Another Grand Cru, Bonnes Mares, mostly sits in Chambolle-Musigny. Morey-Saint-Denis also counts 20 Premier Crus, the most reputed of which is Clos des Ormes, just below Clos de la Roche. In 2014, LVMH bought Clos des Lambrays for a rumoured €11.5m per hectare; and in 2017, the Groupe Artémis bought the adjacent Clos de Tart for a rumoured €26–30m per hectare—making it the fourth owner of Clos de Tart in 876 years. These movements have set alarm bells ringing in Burgundy, with long established winemaking families threatened by large corporations and associated price inflation.

Compared to those of Gevrey, the wines of **Chambolle-Musigny** can be described as feminine, that is, lighter, brighter, more delicate, more elegant, and more seductive, and not unlike those of Volnay in the Côte de Beaune (which are however somewhat lighter). As in Volnay, the soils are relatively rich in limestone, and Le Musigny is the only Grand Cru in the Côte de Nuits for both red and white wine. Bonnes-Mares, the other Grand Cru in Chambolle, is larger but less reputed than Le Musigny, which has been monikered 'queen of all Burgundy', and described as 'an iron fist in a velvet glove', or, again, 'a peacock's tail' that unfurls on the palate. Some of the 25 Premier Crus in Chambolle, especially Les Amoureuses (which borders on Le Musigny) and Les Charmes, are so highly regarded as to fetch Grand Cru prices.

The smallest village in the Côte de Nuits, **Vougeot**, contains its largest Grand Cru, the Clos de Vougeot, which, at 50.6ha, accounts for the bulk of the commune's production. Named for the River Vouge separating Vougeot from Chambolle, the Clos de Vougeot comprises a château which, since 1945, has played host to the *Confrérie des Chevaliers du Tastevin*, an outfit devoted to upholding standards in Burgundy. Most highly regarded is the top, north-western corner of the vineyard, which surrounds the château and borders on Le Musigny and Grands Echezeaux; less regarded is the bottom section, to the east and bordering on the D974 (formerly the N74). This, together with the large number of producers with a stake in the Clos de Vougeot, means that wines labelled 'Clos de Vougeot' can vary enormously in style, quality, and price.

The communes of **Vosne-Romanée** and Flagey-Echezeaux together count eight Grand Crus, among which the iconic Romanée-Conti. There is no separate appellation for Flagey-Echezeaux, and the village and Premier Cru vineyards in this commune fall under the Vosne-Romanée AOP. Vosne itself has six Grand Crus: Romanée-Conti and La Tâche, which are both monopoles of Domaine de la Romanée-Conti; La Romanée, which is a monopole of Comte Liger-Belair; Romanée-Saint-Vivant; Richebourg; and La Grande Rue, a monopole of Domaine Lamarche and upgraded to Grand Cru only in 1992. Flagey has a further two Grand Crus, Grands Echezeaux and Echezeaux. The smallest of these eight is La Romanée at 0.85ha, corresponding to about 300 cases a year, and the largest by far is Echezeaux at ~35ha. As with the Clos de Vougeot, large size and fragmentation mean that Echezeaux wines vary considerably in style, quality, and price. Vosne-Romanée Premier Crus are highly regarded, and those further up the hill, such as Aux Raignots and Cros Parentoux, tend to be fresher in style. I was lucky in 2018 to taste, with Aubert de Villaine, Romanée-Conti from the barrel. The wine seemed like a game of chess: an intricate reticulum of moving flavours, with negative space between the pieces.

Nuits-Saint-Georges lies at the southern end of the Côte de Nuits, stretching for 5 kilometres to Prémaux-Prissey. The Nuits-Saint-Georges appellation covers both communes, and can apply to red or white wine (although white wine is only 3% of production). For historical reasons (see mayor Henri Gouges, above), there are no Grand Crus but as many as 41 Premier Crus, including the highly regarded Les Saint Georges, Les Vaucrains, and Les Cailles, which lie just south of Nuits-Saint-Georges. These wines are richer and more structured than those from the north of the appellation, which are more similar to neighbouring Vosne-Romanée in style. In general, the wines of Nuits-Saint-George are full and firm, and dominated by black rather than red fruits. The Côte de Nuits borrows its name from Nuits-Saint-Georges, as does the lunar St. George crater.

In the north of the Côte de Nuits, in the shadow of Gevrey, lie the communes of Fixin ('Fissin') and Marsannay. The **Fixin** AOP covers Fixin and Brochon for both red and white wines, although white wine production is tiny. Five vineyards are Premier Cru and the rest are at village level. In style, Fixin is similar to Gevrey, if somewhat less intense and refined. Created in 1987, the **Marsannay** AOP covers vineyards in Marsannay-la-Côte, Couchey, and Chenôve. The AOP can apply to red, rosé, and white wine, although red wine accounts for two-thirds of production and rosé for most of the rest. All the vineyards are at village level, making Marsannay the only village level appellation for rosé. Compared to other red wines in the Côte de Nuits, Marsannay is often softer and fruitier.

Notable producers in the Côte de Nuits include Arlaud, Ghislaine Barthod, Albert Bichot, Bruno Clair, Château de la Tour, Clos de Tart, Comte Georges de Vogüé, Jean-Jacques Confuron, Domaine du Comte Liger-Belair, Dugat-Py, Claude Dugat, Dujac, Fourrier, Henri Gouges, Anne Gros, François Lamarche, Domaine des Lambrays, Leroy, Méo-Camuzet, Denis Mortet, Frédéric Mugnier, Geantet-Pansiot, Perrot-Minot, Ponsot, Domaine de la Romanée-Conti, Rossignol-Trapet, Emmanuel Rouget, Georges Roumier, Sylvain Pataille, and Armand Rousseau.

Côte d'Or: Côte de Beaune

The soils in the Côte d'Or are essentially a mixture of limestone and marl. In the Côte de Beaune, limestone tends to pre-dominate, making it more suitable to the cultivation of Chardonnay than the Côte de Nuits. The Côte de Beaune contains all but one of the white Grand Crus. Even so, red wine production predominates. Red wines from the Côte de Beaune are lighter, suppler, more fruit-driven, and quicker to mature than those from the warmer Côte de Nuits. That said, red wines from Corton (which is the only red Grand Cru in the Côte de Beaune) and from the commune of Pommard tend to be more muscular and tannic and akin to those from the Côte de Nuits.

To the north of Beaune itself, the **hill of Corton** sits between the communes of Aloxe-Corton, Pernand-Vergelesses, and Ladoix. It is home to three partially overlapping Grand Crus: Corton for red and white wine, Corton-Charlemagne for white wine, and the little used Charlemagne for white wine. Corton-Charlemagne mostly occupies the higher parts of the hill, which are better suited to Chardonnay. Excluding Chablis Grand Cru, Corton-Charlemagne is the largest white wine Grand Cru in Burgundy.

Pommard is a red wine-only commune that lies just south of Beaune. Quality is variable, but better examples can offer good value for money. Most highly rated are the Premier Crus Rugiens and Epenots, which are being considered for Grand Cru status. The muscular red wines of Pommard are often contrasted to the delicate and perfumed wines of nearby **Volnay**, which is the most southerly red wine-only appellation of the Côte d'Or. While the soils of Pommard are rich in marl, those in Volnay are rich in limestone, leading to soft and fragrant wines similar to (but lighter than) those of Chambolle-Musigny in the Côte de Nuits. Among the most highly regarded Volnay Premier Crus are Clos des Chênes, Caillerets, Bousse d'Or, Champans, Santenots, and the Clos des Ducs monopole.

Further south, the communes of Puligny-Montrachet, Chassagne-Montrachet, and Meursault yield some of the finest whites in the world. **Puligny-Montrachet** boasts four Grand Crus of which two, Montrachet and Bâtard-Montrachet, extend south into **Chassagne-Montrachet**, which also has a Grand Cru of its own, Criots-Bâtard-Montrachet. Some look upon Le Montrachet ['Bare Mountain'] as the best Chardonnay in the world: Alexandre Dumas Père deemed that it should be drunk 'on your knees and head uncovered', and it is customary for workers to scrape their clogs or boots before leaving the vineyard. Puligny-Montrachet is tight, structured, and mineral, and hard to distinguish from Chassagne-Montrachet, which is perhaps slightly richer, fruitier, and nuttier. **Meursault** is broad and buttery and rather extravagant, although some producers do favour leaner styles. While there are no Grand Crus in Meursault, there are some highly performing Premier Crus, especially Perrières, Genevrières, and Les Charmes. The three appellations admit of red wines, although production is negligible in Meursault and anecdotal in

Puligny-Montrachet. At the southern end of Chassagne-Montrachet, red wine production once again takes over, and also predominates further south in **Santenay**. In a side-valley to the west is **Saint-Aubin**, which focuses more on white wine production. The vineyards are higher than in other parts, such that the village performs especially well in warmer years. Some of the wines, especially from the eastern side of the valley, are redolent of Chassagne-Montrachet. Both Santenay and Saint-Aubin have a high proportion of Premier Cru sites.

In blind tastings, it is very difficult to tell communes apart, perhaps even more so than for the Haut-Médoc. The punter who can habitually distinguish Côte de Beaune from Mâconnais for whites and Côte de Nuits from Côte de Beaune for reds is already doing a good job.

Notable producers in the Côte de Beaune include Bonneau du Martray, Coche-Dury, Comte Armand, Comte Lafon, Domaine d'Auvenay, Domaine de Courcel, Domaine des Croix, Domaine de la Pousse d'Or, Joseph Drouhin, Hubert Lamy, Leflaive, Lucien Le Moine, François Mikulski, and Ramonet.

Burgundy vintages are seldom all good or all bad. In any given year, white wines may do much better than red, or vice versa, and Chablis or Beaujolais may tell another story from the Côte de Nuits and Côte de Beaune. For the Côte de Nuits and Côte de Beaune, stronger vintages for red wines include 1989, 1990, 1993, 1999, 2002, 2005, 2009, 2010, 2012, 2015, 2016, 2017, 2018, and 2019. Stronger vintages for white wines include 1992, 1995, 1999, 2000, 2002, 2005, 2009, 2010, 2014, 2015, 2016, 2017, 2018, and 2019.

Mâconnais

The climate of the Mâconnais is considerably warmer than that of Chablis or even the Côte d'Or. The relief is not as marked as in the Côte d'Or, and vineyards are mixed in with other forms of farming. The most reputed wines are from the south of Mâcon, in an area that rises into three limestone peaks: the Mont de Pouilly, the Roche de Solutré, and the Roche de Vergisson. The Roche de Solutré, which is a prehistoric and pilgrimage site, is picturesque, and well worth the gentle hike to its 493m summit.

Chardonnay predominates, but Gamay and Pinot Noir are also found, especially in areas that are richer in sand and clay. The vines are pruned as simple Guyot, with the cane trained *en arcure* [in an arc], which helps to delay budding (especially of terminal buds) and protect against frost. Aside from the regional AOP (Mâcon and Mâcon-Villages) and the 27 *Dénominations Géographiques Complémentaires* (see above), there are **five commune-specific appellations** (white wines only): Pouilly-Fuissé, Pouilly-Vinzelles, Pouilly-Loché, and Saint-Véran to the west of Mâcon, and Viré-Clessé to the north. In 2020, 22 Premier Crus were announced for Pouilly-Fuissé, covering about a quarter of the vineyard area—the first Premier Crus in the Mâconnais, and the first new ones in Burgundy since 1943.

Compared to Beaune, Mâcon is more variable in quality. It tends to be deeper in colour with riper aromas and a fuller body, and less if any oak. The Pouilly wines tend to be richer and riper on the one hand, and finer and more complex on the other. Owing to their sought-after smoky, flinty, or 'wet stone' character, they are, I think, easier to confuse with Chablis than with Beaune. **Pouilly-Vinzelles** (~40ha) and **Pouilly-Loché** (~30ha) are exclaves of the much larger **Pouilly-Fuissé** (~760ha), and the wines from these three appellations are very similar in style. Vinzelles with its two castles was known to the Romans, who called it *Vincella*, or 'Small Vine'. The soils in Vinzelles tend to be more ferrous, which can translate into spicier, broader wines. Neighbouring Loché can be labelled as Vinzelles, making it harder to find. Saint-Véran envelopes Pouilly-Fuissé like a scarf (or a bun) with wines that tend to a leaner, fresher style. Owing to an administrative cock-up in 1971, the village name is 'Saint-Vérand' but the appellation 'Saint-Véran', without the 'd'. Viré-Clessé to the north of Mâcon varies in style, but the best examples, especially from Viré, are easily mistaken for Pouilly-Fuissé—as are the best examples from Saint-Véran.

Notable producers in the Mâconnais include Domaine de la Soufrandière and the related négoce Bret Brothers (very classic regional style), Guffens-Heynen and the related négoce Verget, Chagnoleau, Denogent, Ferret, Rijckaert, and Valette.

It's all too easy to underestimate the Mâconnais but the best wines can be as good as anything in Burgundy, at a fraction of the price. In 1866, Dr Jules Guyot wrote a report for the French ministry of agriculture in which he compared the potential of Meursault to that of Pouilly-Fuissé, and it says something that he put it that way round.

Côte Chalonnaise

The Côte Chalonnaise is named for the town of Chalon-sur-Sâone, an important Celtic and, later, Roman trading centre. The vineyards, which are interspersed with other forms of agriculture, are planted along a 25km stretch of undulating land that divides the Côte de Beaune to the north from the Mâconnais to the south.

The geology and climate, and even the aspect of the vineyards, facing the rising sun, are similar to those of the Côte d'Or, and four of the five village-level AOPs (from north to south, Rully, Mercurey, Givry, and Montagny) are rich in Premier Crus. Many of the more reputed sites were only replanted in recent decades, making the Côte Chalonnaise a growing source of high quality, value Burgundy for those in the know.

Mercurey produces more wine than any other village-level AOP: so important is Mercurey that the Côte Chalonnaise used to be called the 'Région de Mercurey'. As in **Givry** to the south, production is mostly of red wine, which is noted for its deeper colour, fuller body, and spicy cherry notes. Further south, the area of **Montagny** is devoted to white wine production, and boasts as many as 49 Premier Crus. To the north of Mercurey, **Rully** produces more white than red wine, and is also an important source of Crémant de Bourgogne. **Bouzeron** in the north of the region is a bit of a curio in that it is the only village-level AOP for Aligoté, although has no Premier Crus.

Notable producers in the Côte Chalonnaise include Pierre & Marie Jacqueson, Dureuil-Janthial, François Lumpp, Jean-Baptiste Ponsot, Domaine Faiveley, Domaine Ragot, Domaine Feuillat-Juillot, Domaine du Cellier aux Moines, and Domaine de Villaine.

Beaujolais

Beaujolais, named for Beaujeu, the historical capital of the province, is important by volume, and, more and more, by reputation. 98% of the production is red, and almost all of that is made from the thin-skinned Gamay grape, which, in the Middle Ages, was driven south onto the granite soils of Beaujolais by the edicts of Philip the Bold and, later, Philip the Good. Although it is thought of as Burgundy, most of the region lies in Auvergne-Rhône-Alpes. The climate is more similar to that of the Rhône, and the vines, traditionally, are trained in bush. The northern part, to the north of Villefranche, features rolling hills of granite and schist. The southern part, or Bas-Beaujolais, is flatter and more fertile, with soils rich in sandstone and clay interspersed with patches of limestone. Owing to a combination of gradient and soil type, the grapes ripen earlier and more completely in the northern part, which contains all the region's village level vineyards as well as its ten Crus.

Beaujolais is typically pale in colour with a blue tinge. It is light in body, medium-to-high in acidity, medium-to-low in alcohol, and low in tannins. Most Beaujolais is made by semi-carbonic maceration, which contributes estery notes of banana and bubblegum to the red fruits of the Gamay grape. In contrast, Cru wines tend to be made by traditional vinification and can also be oaked, making them more tannic and tricky to recognize as Beaujolais.

Whereas most Beaujolais ought to be drunk within the year, the **Crus** benefit from some cellaring, with the best approaching Burgundy in style and substance. Believe it or not, the French have a whole verb for a red wine that takes on Burgundian characteristics, 'pinoter', as in, *Un Beaujolais qui pinote*. Moulin-à-Vent, Morgon, Juliénas, and Chénas are the most long-lived Crus, and can improve over ten or fifteen years. Moulin-à-Vent enjoys the best reputation, followed by Morgon. Moulin-à-Vent counts 18 climats, and Morgon six—the most notable of which is Cote du Py. The other six Crus are St Amour, Chiroubles, Fleurie, Regnié, Côte de Brouilly, and Brouilly, which contains the notorious *Pisse Vieille* vineyard. According to local lore, a devout Catholic woman once misheard the priest's exhortation '*Allez! Et ne péchez plus*' ('Go! And sin no more') as '*Allez! Et ne pissez plus*' ('Go! And piss no more'). Upon learning of this, her husband is supposed to have exclaimed, '*Pisse Vielle!*' ('Piss, old woman!'). Côte de Brouilly is an enclave of Brouilly on the slopes of the dormant Mount Brouilly volcano, and, compared to Brouilly, produces richer, more expressive wines. The Beaujolais Crus do not correspond to individual vineyards as in the rest of Burgundy, but to entire areas of viticulture. The largest cru, Brouilly, extends over 1,257ha; the smallest, Chénas, over 249ha. The other two Beaujolais appellations are Beaujolais AOP and Beaujolais-Villages AOP in a defined area in the north.

Beaujolais Nouveau is not an appellation but a style: simple, fruity, and destined for early release and immediate drinking. After a short fermentation, it is bottled and put on sale, by decree, from midnight on the third Thursday of November. Beaujolais Primeur is another, less commercially important *vin de primeur* that can only be sold after 31 January. In theory, Beaujolais Nouveau and Beaujolais Primeur can be produced from any area of Beaujolais except the ten Crus; in practice, much of it comes from the Bas-Beaujolais. Beaujolais fell victim of the one-time success of Beaujolais Nouveau, which, in the end, caused lasting damage to the region's reputation.

Notable producers of Beaujolais include Labruyère, Château des Jacques, and Château du Châtelard in Moulin-à-Vent; Lapierre, Jean Foillard, Louis-Claude Desvignes, Mee Godard, Jean-Marc Burgaud, and Dominique Piron in Morgon; Michel Chignard, Domaine du Vissoux, and Domaine de la Grand'Cour in Fleurie; and Château Thivin in Côte de Brouilly. Also Liger-Belair and the Graillot sons at Domaine de Fa.

8

THE RHÔNE

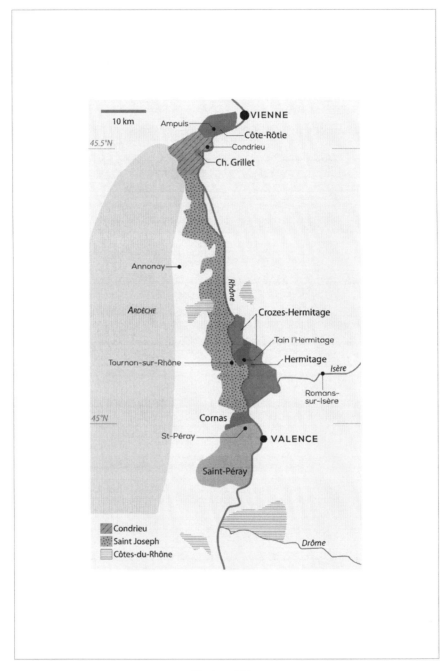

Northern Rhône

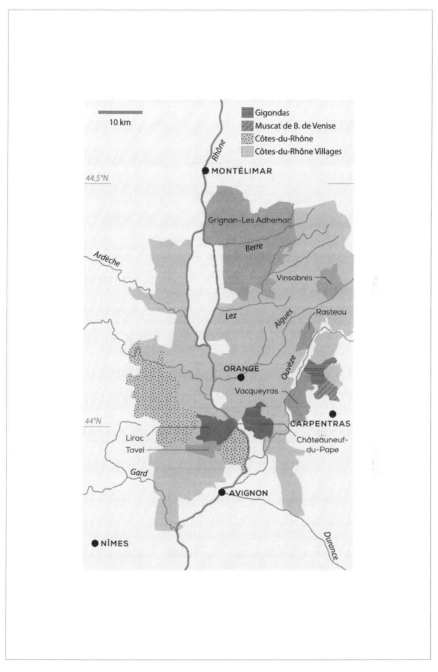

Gigondas
Muscat de B. de Venise
Côtes-du-Rhône
Côtes-du-Rhône Villages

10 km

44.5°N

Rhône

MONTÉLIMAR

Grignan-Les Adhemar

Berre

Ardèche

Vinsobres

Lez

Aigues

Rasteau

Ouvèze

ORANGE

Vacqueyras

44°N

CARPENTRAS

Lirac

Châteauneuf-
du-Pape

Tavel

Gard

AVIGNON

NÎMES

Durance

Southern Rhône

*T*he first century naturalist Pliny the Elder noted that, in the region of Vienne, the tribe of the Allobroges produced and exported a highly prized wine. After the fall of the Western Roman Empire, Rhodanian viticulture fell into long-term decline, to be revived from 1308 when Clement V migrated the papal court to Avignon. His successor John XXII did much to improve viticultural practices, and wines from the area came to be known as 'Vin du Pape' and, after John erected his famous castle, 'Châteauneuf-du-Pape'. But the Avignon popes also loved their Burgundy: when Petrarch wrote to Urban V pleading for his return to Rome, the pontiff replied that the best Burgundy did not percolate south of the Alps.

In the fifteenth and sixteenth centuries, Lyon and its hinterland began to prosper. However, from 1446, Burgundy banned Rhône wines on the grounds that they were *très petits et pauvres*, effectively restricting access to northern markets. In the seventeenth and eighteenth centuries, Rhône wines began to develop a following in Paris and London, so much so that leading Bordeaux producers such as Château Lafite took to enriching their wines with Hermitage. Some of these blends came to fetch even higher prices than their thinner counterparts. Today, Château Palmer and Château La Lagune in Bordeaux have created revival cuvées of this historical *Hermitagé* style.

In the wake of phylloxera, quality plummeted, and the practice of passing off inferior wine as Châteauneuf-du-Pape became depressingly common. By 1880, only 200 hectares of vines remained in the entire appellation. In 1924, Baron Le Roy of Château Fortia founded the *syndicat des vignerons de Châteauneuf- du-Pape* and, in 1929, the *syndicat des Côtes-du-Rhône*. In 1933, he succeeded in defining and delimiting the appellation of Châteauneuf-du-Pape, thereby restoring the quality and reputation of the wines. In that same year, he co-founded the *Académie du vin de France*, and, in 1935, together with former agriculture minister Joseph Capus, the *Institut national des appellations d'origine* (INAO), which did for France what Le Roy had done for Châteauneuf.

The Northern Rhône too had suffered a severe decline, only to be revived in the late twentieth century (much later than the Southern Rhône) by such figures as Marcel Guigal and Robert Parker. Auguste Clape, who passed away in 2018, was the first in Cornas to bottle his own wines. Back in 1982, Condrieu counted a mere 14ha of vines, versus ~135ha today, and those 14ha contained most of the world's Viognier! Still today, compared to Burgundy and especially Bordeaux, the Rhône retains a rustic and agrarian feel.

The Northern Rhône

The entire Rhône region is defined and united by the River Rhône, which arises in the Alps, drives into and out of Lake Geneva, and veers south to carve out the *couloir rhodanien*, a valley that separates the Alps from the Massif Central. The Northern Rhône, or *secteur septentrional*, stretches ~80km from Vienne in the north to Valence in the south. This area differs significantly in climate, topography, and geology from the Southern Rhône, or *secteur méridional*, which stretches ~70km from Montélimar in the north to Avignon in the south. The Northern and Southern Rhône are not contiguous, and there is a gap of ~30km between them.

The Northern Rhône, where the river valley is steep and narrow, is much more dramatic than the Southern Rhône, with terraced vineyards that can only be worked by hand. The subsoil consists of granite and gneiss and the topsoil is sparse and prone to erosion by heavy rains. Most of the appellations of the Northern Rhône lie on the western (east-facing) slope: all, in fact, but Hermitage and Crozes-Hermitage, which lie on the eastern slope, just north of Valence and the confluence with the River Isère. In some areas, plantings reach into lateral valleys which offer shelter from the full force of the Mistral, a cold, dry gale that picks up as it funnels down the Rhodanian corridor. Winters are cold and summers warm, but tempered by the Mistral and less hot than in the Southern Rhône.

The Northern Rhône accounts for only a small fraction of the total production of the Rhône, which, after Bordeaux, is the second largest quality region of France. Despite this, it is home to some of the region's most celebrated wines. Except in the small white wine appellations of Condrieu, Château-Grillet, and Saint-Péray, red wines predominate, and are made of Syrah or a majority blend of Syrah with one or two of three white wine grapes: Viognier, Roussanne, and Marsanne. Of the red wines, Côte-Rôtie can be blended with up to 20% Viognier (although 0-5% is more typical), Crozes-Hermitage and Hermitage with up to 15% Marsanne and Roussanne, and Saint-Joseph with up to 10% Marsanne and Roussanne. Cornas, in contrast, cannot be blended, and is invariably pure Syrah. Of the white wines, Condrieu and Château-Grillet are made from Viognier; and Saint-Péray and the white wines of Hermitage, Crozes-Hermitage, and Saint-Joseph are made from Marsanne and Roussanne. There are, at least officially, no rosés in the Northern Rhône.

Hermitage

Hermitage is the grandest appellation of the Northern Rhône and the spiritual home of Syrah. The name 'Syrah' has led to speculation about distant and exotic origins, but DNA typing has revealed it to be an offspring of Dureza and Mondeuse Blanche. According to lore, the Chevalier de Stérimberg returned wounded from the Cathar Crusade, and was granted permission by Blanche of Castile, Queen consort of France, to build a small refuge and chapel in which to eke out his days as a hermit. This hermitage lent its name to the appellation, which rises from Tain l'Hermitage and runs along the southern aspect of a steep granite hill that captures the best part of the sun. The appellation, which stands at a mere 137ha (cf. Château Lafite, 107ha), is divided into a number of *climats*; and traditional Hermitage, such as that of JL Chave, is a blend from several of these climats. Hermitage is dark, full-bodied, and tannic, with intense aromas of soft black fruits accompanied by red fruits, smoke, black pepper and spice, leather, cocoa, and coffee. After about ten years, it develops a certain sweetness of fruit and gamey complexity. Significant new oak ageing is more the exception than the rule. The best examples from top vintages, such as the famous La Chapelle 1961, keep for decades, and very old Hermitage can be very difficult to distinguish from top claret of a similar age. White

Hermitage, which is mostly Marsanne, is rich yet textural and mineral, and with age develops complex notes of honey, wax, and hazelnuts. A few producers make a straw wine in some years, which, owing to scarcity, fetches high prices. Other than Chave, top producers of Hermitage include Chapoutier, Delas Frères, Bernard Faurie, Ferraton, Remizières, and Marc Sorrel.

Crozes-Hermitage

Compared to Hermitage, Crozes-Hermitage and Saint-Joseph are large appellations which together account for most of the production of the Northern Rhône. Crozes-Hermitage stretches across eleven villages centred on Tain-l'Hermitage. Over 90% of production consists of unblended red wines, which are generally softer and fruitier than Hermitage. The best examples are complex and full-bodied and similar to Hermitage, and can offer good value for money. However, wines from vineyards on flatter land, or made by semi-carbonic maceration, are usually less impressive. Among the best Crozes-Hermitage are Domaine Aléofane, Laurent Combier, Domaine des Entrefaux, Domaine de Thalabert, Les Chassis, and the offerings of the late Alain Graillot. The co-operative Cave de Tain is very important in Crozes-Hermitage, as is Jaboulet.

Saint-Joseph

The heart of Saint-Joseph lies around the communes of Tournon, on the right bank opposite Tain l'Hermitage, and Mauves, a bit further south—indeed, Saint-Joseph used be called *vin de Mauves*. Today, the appellation is named for the vineyard of Saint-Joseph, itself named for the patron saint of manual labour and scorned husbands. After the creation of the appellation in 1956, the area under vine expanded six-fold, so that Saint-Joseph is just as variable as Crozes-Hermitage. The grapes ripen less fully than in Hermitage across the river, resulting in lighter wines with notes of black fruits and pepper. Saint-Joseph is mostly intended for early drinking. Notable producers of Saint-Joseph include Pierre Gonon, Jean-Louis Chave, Pierre et Jérôme Coursodon, Bernard Gripa, Domaine Monier-Perréol, and Domaine du Tunnel.

Côte-Rôtie

The sturdy wines of Hermitage are often contrasted with the more sybaritic ones of Côte-Rôtie, which lies in the area of Ampuis, right up in the north of the Northern Rhône. Owing to a bend in the river, the vineyards face south-east on a slope that is even steeper than in Hermitage. Aspect and incline combine to maximize sun exposure, whence the name Côte-Rôtie ['Roasted Slope']. The site is also protected from the Mistral, more properly called *la bise* in the Northern Rhône and 'Mistral' in the Southern Rhône. Although they can be destructive, these northerlies reduce rot, pests, and disease. Côte-Rôtie is subdivided into two main areas, the Côte Brune on dark, iron-rich schist, and the Côte Blonde on pale granite and schist. According to lore, the areas were named for the brown- and blonde-haired daughters of a local lord. Just like those girls, the wines have their own characters, with Côte Brune more tannic and full-bodied and Côte Blonde softer and more elegant. Traditionally, Côte-Rôtie was often a blend of Côte Brune and Côte Blonde, but in recent years there has been a trend towards single vineyard wines. It is above all the single vineyard wines of Guigal, namely, La Mouline, La Landonne, and La Turque (aged in new oak for an eye-popping 42 months), which, in the early 1980s, led to the revival of the appellation and region. Côte-Rôtie is 100% Syrah or a blend of Syrah and a small amount (typically ~5%) of Viognier, which some say imparts a floral fragrance to the wine. The wines marry power and finesse, with a complex nose of raspberry, blueberry, plum, bacon, green olives, violets, and leather. Other than Guigal, top producers include Pierre Benetière, Domaine Clusel-Roch, Yves Cuilleron, Yves Gangloff, Jean-Michel Gérin, Domaine Jamet, Domaine Jasmin, Domaine Pichat, Nicolas Perrin, Michel and Stéphane Ogier, René Rostaing, and Jean-Michel Stephan.

Cornas

At the other end of the Northern Rhône, south of Saint-Joseph, lies the highly regarded appellation of Cornas, which is smaller even than Hermitage. 'Cornas' is Celtic for 'burnt earth', cf. Côte-Rôtie. The land forms a natural amphitheatre which captures sunlight and protects against the *bise*. Cornas is invariably pure Syrah, as the appellation does not encompass white wines and blending is not permitted. The wines are fuller and richer than Crozes-Hermitage or Saint-Joseph, and more rustic and robust than Hermitage and Côte-Rôtie. The fresher and more fruit-forward style of Cornas pioneered by Jean-Luc Colombo can be drunk earlier than traditional Cornas of the sort championed by Auguste Clape, the icon of the appellation. Other top producers include Thierry Allemand, Alain Voge, Noel Verset, and Vincent Paris.

Condrieu, Château-Grillet, and Saint-Péray

The white wines of the Northern Rhône (including white Hermitage, Crozes-Hermitage, and Saint-Joseph), though relatively scarce, often make an appearance in blind tasting exams and competitions.

Condrieu is a small appellation entirely given to Viognier. It extends south from Côte-Rôtie on steepish slopes with a south and south-eastern aspect. The best areas are those that include a fine layer of *arzelle*, which consists of decomposed chalk, flint, and mica. Condrieu is characterized by a pronounced perfume of candied peach, apricot, orange blossom, anise, acacia, and violets; a full, almost oily body; and high alcohol. Modern Condrieu is usually dry, although the richness and high alcohol can lead to an impression of sweetness. Acidity is not as high as for Chardonnay and can be on the lower side. Oak is often absent, as perhaps it should be in such an aromatic wine. Condrieu ought to be drunk within the first three years of release, before it loses its freshness and perfume. Leading producers include Georges Vernay, Yves Cuilleron, Yves Gangloff, Stéphane Montez, André Perret, and François Villard.

At the southern end of Condrieu lies the enclave of **Château-Grillet**, a mere 4ha of a soil that is lighter and more fragmented than in Condrieu. This too is a land of Viognier, planted in a natural granite amphitheatre which, as in Cornas, captures the sun and protects against the *bise*. Château-Grillet is a monopole and there is just the one wine, matured in oak for up to 24 months before being entered into signature brown bottles. The wine is more Burgundian than Condrieu: drier, lighter, more delicate, less perfumed, and more evidently oaked. It can improve over a decade or more.

The last appellation in the Northern Rhône is **Saint-Péray**, which is, again, a very small appellation. It lies at the southern end of the region, across the river from Valence. Quite unlike Condrieu, Saint-Péray is typically light and acidic, although the best examples can be gently floral. Sparkling traditional method Marsanne and Roussanne blends still account for almost half of the appellation's output.

Stronger vintages in the Northern Rhône include 1990, 1991, 1995, 1998, 1999, 2000, 2001, 2003, 2005, 2007, 2009, 2010, 2013, 2015, 2016, 2017, 2019, and 2020.

The Southern Rhône

In the Southern Rhône, the Rhodanian corridor opens up into a rugged landscape with sheltered valleys and diverse mesoclimates. The macroclimate is Mediterranean with mild winters and hot and dry summers. Drought is a perennial problem. Rather than orchards as in the Northern Rhône, vineyards are interspersed with olive groves, lavender fields, and *garrigue* [Mediterranean scrub]. Some of the best vineyards are on alluvial deposits overlain by polished stones called *galets*, which reflect sunlight, store solar heat, and improve drainage and water retention.

Unlike the Northern Rhône, which is dominated by its eight crus, the Southern Rhône puts out a great deal of modest Côtes-du-Rhône and IGP-Vin de Pays. There are also a number of satellite appellations such as Côtes du Ventoux and Côtes du Luberon, which are not dissimilar to Côtes-du-Rhône. The only appellation of the Southern Rhône that can compete with the likes of Hermitage and Côte-Rôtie is Châteauneuf-du-Pape, which is a blend of up to 13 grape varieties. In contrast, the entire Northern Rhône counts just four grape varieties (Syrah, Viognier, Marsanne, Roussanne). Other notable cru appellations of the Southern Rhône include Gigondas, Vacqueyras, and Tavel.

Châteauneuf-du-Pape

Châteauneuf-du-Pape alone puts out more wine than the entire Northern Rhône. Its ~3,200ha stretch across an undulating plateau on the left bank of the Rhône, from Orange in the north to Sorgues in the south. The other three communes of the appellation are Courthézon, Bédarrides, and, largest of all, Châteauneuf-du-Pape. Of the 134 *lieu-dits*, the most famous is La Crau, which is principally held by Domaine du Vieux Télégraphe. The soils are diverse. La Crau, for instance, is rich in *galets* deposited by Alpine glaciers and polished by the Rhône over the millennia. Some 95% of production is red and the remaining 5% is white. Château de Beaucastel takes great pride in growing and blending each and every one of the 13 permitted varieties (8 black and 5 white), but many producers use just three or four, typically Grenache, Syrah, Mourvèdre, and Cinsault. Some, most notably Château Rayas, use only Grenache. Unlike in the Northern Rhône, the vines are trained in bush, or *gobelet*, for greater resistance to wind and drought. Some of the vines are centenarian. Grenache accounts for over 70% of plantings, Syrah for 10%, and Mourvèdre for 7%. Syrah typically brings colour and spice to a blend, while Mourvèdre contributes structure and elegance. Grenache, which is prone to oxidation, is vinified in large cement tanks. The other varieties are most commonly vinified in wood. The wines may be matured in tanks, barriques, demi-muids, or foudres.

Red Châteauneuf is medium to deep ruby in colour, with notes of red and black fruits, game, tar, leather, and garrigue. On the palate, it is rich and spicy, with dusty or powdery tannins and a higher alcohol and lower acidity than Bordeaux or Hermitage. Significant new oak ageing is more the exception than the rule. The wine can be tight in its youth but softens and opens up after about seven years, and can improve for several more years, sometimes decades. Vinification by carbonic maceration or semi-carbonic maceration results in a lighter, earlier drinking style. White Châteauneuf—which can be made from Clairette, Grenache Blanc, Bourboulenc, Roussanne, Picpoul, and Picardin—ranges in style from lean and mineral to rich and oily, and is difficult to generalize about.

Top producers of Châteauneuf-du-Pape other than those already
mentioned include André Brunel, Clos des Papes, Clos du Mont-Olivet,
Château La Nerthe, Domaine de la Janasse, Domaine du Pegaü,
Domaine de Marcoux, Domaine Pierre André, and Domaine Saint
Préfert.

Stronger vintages in Châteauneuf-du-Pape include 1990, 1995, 1998,
2000, 2001, 2005, 2006, 2007, 2009, 2010, 2012, 2015, 2016, 2017, 2018, and
2019. 2016 is especially good.

Gigondas

Gigondas ranks second in prestige in the southern Rhône and can be
similar to Châteauneuf-du-Pape. The town of Gigondas, founded by the
Romans for the recreation of the soldiers of the Second Legion [Lat.
jocunditas, pleasure, enjoyment], lies at the foot of the picturesque
Dentelles de Montmirail. This small chain of mountains divides the
appellation's 1,200ha into two distinct areas, one being cooler than the
other. Most of the production is red wine, and the rest rosé. Red
Gigondas is typically heavy in Grenache (up to 80% of the blend), but
also contains a minimum of 15% Syrah and/or Mourvèdre and a
maximum of 10% of other Rhône varieties. The wines are rich and
powerful and more rustic and animally than Châteauneuf-du-Pape.
The best examples, such as those from Château de Saint Cosme,
Domaine de la Bouïssière, or Domaine la Roubine, can improve for
around a decade.

Vacqueyras

If Gigondas can be thought of as junior Châteauneuf-du-Pape, then
nearby **Vacqueyras** can be thought of as junior Gigondas. The best
vineyards of the 1,400ha appellation are on the Plateau de Garrigues. As
in Gigondas, most of the production is red wine, although small
amounts of rosé and white wine are also made. Vacqueyras typically
consists of at least 50% Grenache (so often less Grenache than
Gigondas), completed by smaller proportions of Syrah, Mouvèdre, and
Carignan.

Tavel

Across the river from Châteauneuf-du-Pape lies the commune and appellation of Tavel, which, uniquely in the Rhône, produces only rosé. In the course of history, Tavel has found favour with, among others, the Avignon popes, Louis XIV, Balzac, and Hemingway. The principal elements in the blend are Grenache and Cinsault, although eight further varieties are also permitted. The rosé is made by the *saignée* method, which involves 'bleeding off' some of the must of a red wine in the making after it has had some limited skin contact—a process that can also serve to 'concentrate' the red wine. Tavel ought to be drunk chilled. Better examples are structured and full-bodied, but, at the same time, bone-dry and refreshing. Alcohol is high, at around 13.5%. Tavel is often drunk young but, unusually for a rosé, can improve for several years.

Côtes-du-Rhône

The discussion so far has focused on cru wines, which, in the Southern Rhône, also include Lirac, red Beaumes de Venise (promoted 2005), Vinsobres (promoted 2005), red Rasteau (promoted 2010), and Cairanne (promoted 2015). However, much of the wine produced in the Rhône falls under the more modest generic appellation of Côtes-du-Rhône, which remains of tremendous commercial importance. In principle, the AOP can apply to red, rosé, and white wine from anywhere from Vienne to south of Avignon, so long as the alcohol is 11% or more and the yield does not exceed 52hl/ha (vs. 35hl/ha for Châteauneuf-du-Pape). In the main production area south of Montélimar, appellation rules stipulate a minimum of 40% Grenache and a combined minimum of 70% Grenache, Syrah, and Mouvèdre. There is also a more restricted appellation of Côtes-du-Rhone Villages with stricter regulations for alcohol levels, yields, and varieties. Within this higher appellation, a certain number of villages can also display their name on the label, for example, SABLET, APPELLATION COTES-DU-RHONE VILLAGES PROTEGEE. A significant amount of Côtes-du-Rhone is made by carbonic maceration, and some of that is released *en primeur* to compete with Beaujolais Nouveau. Côtes-du-Rhone wines are very diverse, and the best, which are getting better, can offer astounding value for money. Some of the region's leading producers also make superlative Côtes-du-Rhône, sometimes from vines bordering a cru, or young vines in a cru. Examples include Château de Fonsalette (Château Rayas), Coudoulet de Beaucastel (Chàteau de Beaucastel), and Equivoque (Domaine Jamet).

9

BORDEAUX

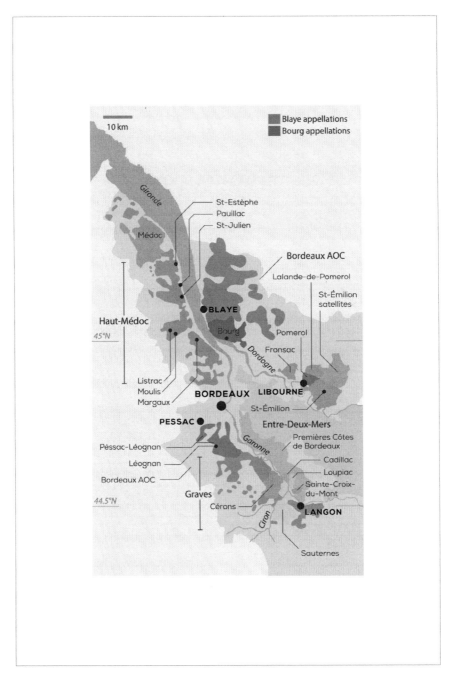

Bordeaux

*T*he region of Bordeaux in Aquitaine lies around the confluence of the Rivers Garonne and Dordogne. This confluence gives rise to the Gironde estuary, the largest estuary in Europe, which flows north-west for some 65km before merging into the Bay of Biscay.

It is the Romans who first brought the vine to Bordeaux, as attested by the first century naturalist Pliny the Elder and the fourth century rhetorician Ausonius, who is still remembered by Château Ausone in Saint-Emilion. In 1152, Henry II of England married the formidable Eleanor of Aquitaine, bringing Aquitaine under English rule and 'claret' (red Bordeaux) into fashion. By the end of the Hundred Years' War in 1453, France had regained the Bordelais, but the English thirst for claret never slaked.

In the seventeenth century, Dutch traders drained the marshland around the Médoc, which soon overtook the Graves as the pre-eminent viticultural area. Pierre de Rauzan, a *grand bourgeois* and manager of Château Latour until his death in 1692, accumulated the land that later became Châteaux Pichon Longueville Comtesse de Lalande, Pichon Longueville Baron, Rauzan-Ségla, and Rauzan-Gassies. Later, Nicolas Alexandre, marquis de Ségur, acquired the epithet *Prince des vignes* after coming into possession of the Médoc properties of Châteaux Lafite, Latour, Mouton, and Calon-Ségur. He turned some pebbles from Pauillac into coat buttons, which Louis XV once mistook for diamonds. #TrueStory

In 1855, Napoleon III ordered a classification of the top châteaux of Bordeaux for the *Exposition Universelle de Paris*. Bordeaux brokers ranked 61 châteaux into five *crus* or 'growths' based on a *savant mélange* of price and reputation. All 61 châteaux are in the Haut-Médoc bar one, Haut Brion in the Graves.

In the late nineteenth century, the Bordelais suffered from oidium, or powdery mildew, followed by phylloxera. Phylloxera required vines to be replanted onto American rootstocks, and the grape varieties that tolerated this best, such as Cabernet Sauvignon, Cabernet Franc, and

Merlot, became dominant. But then came downy mildew and black rot, followed by war, economic depression, more war, the Great Frost of 1956, and an oil crisis. By the late twentieth century, many châteaux found themselves in disrepair and in dire need of the restoration and regeneration that is still under way.

The lie of the land

The Bordeaux region, which boasts ~110,000ha of vineyards and 65 appellations, can be divided into three main sub-regions. The Right Bank describes the area north of the Dordogne and Gironde, with Libourne at its centre. The Left Bank describes the area south of the Garonne and Gironde, with Bordeaux itself at its centre. Finally, the Entre-Deux-Mers is the larger and relatively undistinguished area between the Dordogne and the Garonne. The Left Bank is subdivided into the Médoc downstream of Bordeaux; the Graves upstream; and, also upstream, Sauternes, Barsac, and Cérons. By far the most notable areas on the Right Bank are Saint-Emilion and Pomerol, which are both very close to Libourne.

Climate

Like the Rhône valley, Piedmont, Veneto, and Oregon, Bordeaux is on the 45th parallel, about halfway between the Equator and the North Pole. The climate is maritime, with high humidity from the Bay of Biscay and local river systems predisposing to both noble and ignoble rot: powdery mildew, downy mildew, grey rot, black rot, and eutypa dieback. Winters are short and mild, and summers increasingly warm. For all that, severe frost in the winter of 1956 decimated the vines. During the growing season, the main threats to the size and quality of the harvest are spring frosts, unsettled weather around flowering time in June, midsummer heat spikes and storms, and September rains. April 2017 saw the worst frost damage since 1991, with many growers, especially in the Right Bank and Entre-Deux-Mers, losing most if not all of their crop. Devastating April frosts returned all over France in 2021 and 2022, in what seems to be becoming a pattern.

Soils

The subsoil of the Bordelais is mostly limestone. On the Left Bank, the topsoil is likely to consist of quartz-rich gravel over clay and marl. The last ice age deposited five major gravel banks, four in the Haut-Médoc (in Saint-Estèphe, Pauillac, Saint-Julien, and Margaux) and one in Pessac-Léognan in the north of the Graves. Aside from being rich in minerals and microorganisms, these gravels reflect light, retain heat, and improve drainage. Further south on the Left Bank, the topsoil is mostly a mixture of clays and sands. On the Right Bank, the topsoil is more likely to consist of clay and limestone, but here too there are some gravelly areas. Compared to gravel, clay is damper, reflects less light, and retains less heat. As a result, the fruit ripens later, and is more susceptible to frost and rain. Gravel soils are best suited to Cabernet Sauvignon and Sauvignon Blanc, clay soils to Merlot and Semillon.

Grape varieties

Cabernet Sauvignon, Merlot, and other black varieties

People often think of Bordeaux as a Cabernet Sauvignon dominated blend from the Médoc, but the most planted black variety in Bordeaux is in fact, and by far, Merlot (~66% vs. ~22%). Merlot flowers and ripens earlier than Cabernet Sauvignon. As it is thinner in skin, it is more prone to rot. It is high yielding, and requires hard pruning if it is to produce wines of distinction. Cabernet Sauvignon is a smaller grape with a much higher skin-to-pulp ratio, whence the deeper colour and higher tannins. If Cabernet Sauvignon is Apollonian, Merlot is Dionysian. The sugar and alcohol in Merlot are higher, which together with the lesser tannins make for a certain ripeness, softness, and early approachability. Merlot suffers more in hotter vintages, which lead to excessive alcohol; but Cabernet Sauvignon suffers more in cooler vintages, which lead to overpowering pyrazine (or green pepper) notes. The other four permitted black grape varieties are Cabernet Franc (~9%), which is especially prominent in Saint-Emilion and Pomerol, Malbec (~980ha), Petit Verdot (~490ha), and Carmenère (~6ha).

Sauvignon Blanc, Semillon, and other white varieties

White wine production in the Bordelais has fallen to 11% of the total production of ~6m hectolitres. The main white varieties are Semillon (~46%), Sauvignon Blanc (~46%), and Muscadelle (~5%). Compared to Semillon, Sauvignon Blanc is higher yielding, thicker in skin, lighter in body, and higher in acidity and aromatic intensity. But Semillon is more prone to noble rot and better suited to oak, and predominates for sweet white wines. Other permitted white varieties are Colombard, Ugni Blanc, Merlot Blanc, Mauzac, and Ondenc.

Viticulture

The number of growers in Bordeaux has declined to ~5,600, with a significant proportion making their wines with at least some help from a co-operative. At the same time, the average holding size has increased to ~20ha. Some estates can be much larger, with many, including Lafite, spreading over more than 100ha. The other three first growths of the Médoc are also quite large, with Mouton-Rothschild at 78ha, Margaux at 78ha, and Latour at 65ha. The fifth and final first growth, Haut Brion in the Graves, is a 'mere' 46ha. In the Sauternes, Yquem is 103ha, Suduiraut 90ha, Rieussec 75ha, and Climens 29ha. Châteaux in Saint-Emilion and Pomerol tend to be smaller, with, for example, Cheval Blanc at 36ha, Angelus at 23ha, Pétrus at 11ha, and the bijou Le Pin at a mere 2ha. In addition, the Right Bank is associated with a number of very small producers, called garagistes, whose wines can (also) fetch exorbitant prices.

Vine densities are often very high, with up to 10,000 vines per hectare in the Médoc. Single Guyot training predominates on the Right Bank, and double Guyot on the Left Bank. Common viticultural practices include spraying, de-leafing, and green harvesting. Hand harvesting is the norm at top châteaux. The harvest kicks off in September in all but the hottest years, and may extend into October, with, in general, Merlot first, Cabernet Franc next, and Cabernet Sauvignon last. Sauvignon Blanc and Semillon for dry wines are harvested earliest of all, and for sweet wines latest of all, with the selective harvesting of botrytized grapes sometimes stretching into November.

Vinification and maturation

Vinification is led by the *maître de chai*, or cellar master, sometimes assisted by a wine consultant. Almost all Bordeaux wines are blended, with the individual components of a blend vinified separately.

After harvesting, bunches are sorted in the vineyard or winery to remove any diseased or unripe fruit and extraneous material. The bunches are then de-stemmed and the grapes crushed.

Fermentation is carried out on the skins by ambient rather than cultured yeasts, most often in a stainless steel vat. The vat is held at a temperature of ~30°C, and fermentation completes over ~14 days. *Remontage* [pumping over] and sometimes also *pigeage* [punching down] serve to increase extraction. Once fermentation is complete, the wine is left to macerate on the skins for several more days. The malolactic conversion takes place either in the fermentation tank or in barrique. Micro-oxygenation is sometimes used at the fermentation stage to defuse green and harsh tannins, although the best châteaux try to ensure that there are no green and harsh tannins in the first place. Micro-oxygenation can also be used at the later stage of élevage, in this case to avoid racking and control oxygen exposure.

With fermentation and maceration complete, the free-run juice is racked off, either by pumping or gravity, with any remaining matter entered into a basket [vertical] or pneumatic press. Compared to free-run juice, press wine is coarser and more likely to go into a lesser wine. The wine is left to mature for up to 18–20 months in medium-toast barriques, with racking off the lees every three months or so. A certain proportion of the barriques are new; at properties such as Lafite and Latour, that proportion is a full 100%.

Blending occurs either before the wine is entered into barriques or in January or February, in time for the *en primeur* tastings. The blending reflects not so much the harvest as the precise requirements of the vintage, with unused wine going into a lesser, second or third wine. For instance, Merlot can be used to flesh out the mid-palate of a Cabernet-Sauvignon dominated blend. Petit Verdot, which is used as a 'seasoning' variety, can enhance structure and tannins and contribute spiciness. Before bottling, the wine may be fined with egg whites or powdered albumen. It might also be filtered.

Bordeaux châteaux generally sell a large proportion of their wine as futures [*en primeur*] to négociants, who then sell it on to importers in several, increasingly pricey, batches, or *tranches*. This only marks the end of the beginning: the wine still needs several more years to mature in bottle, and will not be released from bond for another ~18 months.

For dry white wines, the imperative is often to preserve and enhance fruitiness, freshness, and varietal character. Depending on final style, possible differences include extended pre-fermentation skin contact (*macération pelliculaire*, pioneered by Denis Dubourdieu for Sauvignon Blanc), a cooler fermentation temperature, suppressed malolactic fermentation, and *bâtonnage* [lees stirring]. Sweet white wines are fermented very slowly to convert as much sugar as possible into alcohol before the fermentation arrives at a standstill or is cut short by cooling or sulphur dioxide. Depending on the vintage, some producers, including Château d'Yquem, might make use of cryoextraction, or freeze concentration.

Appellations and classifications

There are in essence three levels within the AOP structure, **regional** (Bordeaux AOP or Bordeaux Supérieur AOP), **district** (for example, Haut-Médoc AOP, Saint-Emilion AOP, Sauternes AOP), and **commune** (for example, Pauillac AOP and Margaux AOP, which are both within the Haut-Médoc AOP). Compared to Bordeaux AOP, Bordeaux Supérieur AOP requires older vines, a longer élevage of 12 months, and a slightly higher minimum alcohol of 10.5%. Taken together, the regional appellations account for almost half the vineyard area and production of the Bordelais.

The Médoc appellations only apply to red wines, even though the Médoc also makes some excellent white wines such as Château Margaux's Pavillon Blanc. Médoc AOP applies to the clayey northern Médoc; Haut-Médoc AOP to the larger, more gravelly southern Médoc. The Haut-Médoc AOP also encompasses the six commune appellations of Saint-Estèphe, Pauillac, Saint-Julien, Margaux, Moulis, and Listrac. Of the six, Saint-Julien and Pauillac have the highest proportion (more than 60%) of Cabernet Sauvignon plantings, and Listrac the highest proportion (around 60%) of Merlot plantings.

Various classifications are superimposed upon the AOP structure, most notoriously the **1855 Classification**, which has barely changed over the years. In 1973, Château Mouton-Rothschild acceded to first growth level, whence its revised motto, from *Premier ne puis, second ne daigne, Mouton suis* ['First I cannot, second I deign not, Mouton I am'] to *Premier je suis, second je fus, Mouton ne change* ['First I am, second I was, Mouton never changes']. Classed growths that regularly perform on par with the five first growths are referred to as 'super-seconds'. A list of super-seconds might include the Pichons, Léoville-Las-Cases, Ducru-Beaucaillou, Cos d'Estournel, Montrose, and Palmer. The 1855 Classification includes a separate chapter for the sweet wines of Sauternes and Barsac, which divides 26 estates into first and second growths with Château d'Yquem standing above and alone as a *Premier Cru Supérieur*. Médoc châteaux outside the 1855 Classification can apply for the five-year *Cru Bourgeois* classification, of which there are three tiers: *Cru Bourgeois Exceptionnel* (14 châteaux), *Cru Bourgeois Supérieur* (56 châteaux), and *Cru Bourgeois* (179 châteaux).

The classification of the Graves and that of Saint-Emilion are relatively recent, dating back, respectively, to 1953 and 1955. In the **Graves**, there are six châteaux that are classed for both their red and white wine (Bouscaut, Carbonnieux, Chevalier, Malartic-Lagravière, Latour-Martillac, and Olivier), seven for their red wine only (including Haut-Brion, the only Bordeaux château to feature in two classifications), and three for their white wine only—amounting in total to 16 châteaux and 22 wines. In **Saint-Emilion**, the classification is revised every ten years or so. It divides into *Premier Grand Cru Classé* (which further divides into

A and B categories, with only Ausone, Cheval Blanc, Angélus, and Pavie in the A category) and *Grand Cru Classé*. The latter should not be confused with Saint-Emilion Grand Cru AOP, which is only slightly superior to Saint-Emilion AOP. As for Pomerol, it continues to resist and defy classification—and yet Pomerol properties fetch the highest prices of all.

Vineyards in Bordeaux are not individually mapped and registered, as, say, in Burgundy. This means that, so long as the appended land is within the same AOP, a proprietor can expand his or her property's holdings and still retain the same status in the classification.

Wine styles

Pauillac

The 1,200ha of Pauillac are split into north and south by the Chenal du Gaer drainage channel. This Promised Land contains 18 classed growths, including the first growths Lafite, Latour, and Mouton; the Pichons; Duhart-Milon; and 12 disparate fifth growths. Most notable among these are Pontet-Canet, Grand-Puy-Lacoste, d'Armailhac, Lynch-Bages, and Clerc-Milon. At its best, Pauillac is the epitome of a Cabernet Sauvignon dominated blend. On the nose, it is complex, dominated by notes of cassis, green pepper, cedar, chocolate, cigar box, and vanilla from new French oak. On the palate, it is powerful yet elegant, with a medium body, fairly high acidity, medium alcohol, fine and structured tannins, and a long, astringent finish.

Saint-Julien

The Ruisseau de Juillac separates Pauillac from the 900ha of Saint-Julien to the south. The gravel is not quite as deep as in Pauillac, which might account for the absence of first growths. There are however 11 classed growths of which five second growths, including Léoville-Las Cases which borders on Latour and is regarded as first among the super-seconds. Other highly performing properties include Léoville-Barton, Léoville-Poyferré, Ducru-Beaucaillou, and Gruaud-Larose. *En bouche*, Saint-Julien is a seductive compromise between the power of

Pauillac and the magic of Margaux, and more consistent than either, with, classically, a silkier texture and drier finish.

Saint-Estèphe

Saint-Estèphe is the northernmost commune appellation of the Médoc, and its 1,200ha are separated from neighbouring Pauillac by the La Jalle du Breuil drainage channel. The gravel here is not quite as abundant as in Pauillac, Saint-Julien, or Margaux, with more clay, more moisture retention, and more Merlot. Saint-Estèphe is nonetheless home to five classed growths including second growths Cos d'Estournel and Montrose and third growth Calon-Ségur. Compared to Pauillac, Saint-Julien, or Margaux, Saint-Estèphe tends to be deeper in colour and fuller in texture, with more rustic tannins, a touch more acidity, and a touch less perfume. Owing to the moisture-retentive soils, it performs relatively better in hotter, drier years. Sociando-Mallet to the north of Saint-Estèphe sits on a gravelly *croupe* overlooking the Gironde, like all the best château of the Médoc; although a mere Haut-Médoc AOP, it has occasionally outclassed first growths in blind tastings.

Margaux

The 1,500ha of Margaux are not contiguous with Saint-Julien, lying a fair distance further south. Margaux counts more classed growths than any other commune, including Château Margaux, five second growths, ten third growths, three fourth growths, and two fifth growths. Soils and topography are more diverse than further north and quality is less consistent. Properties with a strong reputation, aside from Château Margaux, include Brane-Cantenac, Palmer, Rauzan-Ségla, and d'Issan. Archetypal Margaux is floral and seductive, exuding a refined perfume of acacia and violets.

Moulis and Listrac

Adjoining Margaux are the diminutive appellations of Moulis (550ha) and Listrac (650ha). Moulis and Listrac do not contain any classed growths, but the best properties are worth the detour and often offer excellent value for money. In Moulis, Chasse-Spleen (cf. Baudelaire, *Spleen et Idéal*) and Poujeaux are performing at classed growth level. In

Listrac, the best names include Clarke, Fourcas-Dupré, and Fourcas-Hosten. Moulis is soft and fleshy, with more power but less finesse than Margaux, and maturing more quickly. Listrac is firmer and more tannic, similar to Saint-Estèphe but more rustic with less ripe fruit, and also maturing more quickly. Although dominated by Cabernet Sauvignon, the wines of Moulis and Listrac often contain more Merlot than those of the other four communes.

Graves

On the Left Bank, south of Bordeaux, is the Graves, so named for its gravel soils. The northern enclave of **Pessac-Léognan**, an appellation created in 1987 under the aegis of André Lurton (d. 2019), encompasses all the leading Graves properties. Haut-Brion stands out as the only château outside the Médoc in the 1855 Classification. Its principal wine contains considerably more Merlot and Cabernet Franc than the other four first growths. Other high-performing properties include La Mission-Haut-Brion, Haut-Bailly, Smith-Haut-Lafite, Domaine de Chevalier, and Pape-Clément. Pape-Clément is the oldest wine estate in Bordeaux, and, in 2006, harvested its 700th vintage. It is named for Clement V, who was Archbishop of Bordeaux prior to becoming the first Avignon pope (and reviving viticulture in the Rhône). Compared to those of the Médoc, the wines of the Graves tend to be lighter in colour, body, and tannins, with more fragrance, more Merlot character, and hints of smoke, minerals, and red brick or terra cotta. With age, they develop autumnal notes of mushrooms, flowers, and potpourri.

Like their red counterparts, the **white wines of the Graves** can be among the finest in the world, combining the opulence of Semillon with the verve of Sauvignon Blanc, with intense aromas of citrus fruit, peach, acacia, beeswax, and hazelnut. On the palate, the wines are medium in body, acidity, and alcohol, with discernible oak influence and lees character. The relatively small amount of sweet wine produced in the Graves is labelled as Graves Supérieures AOP, a sweet wine appellation that is co-extensive with Graves AOP.

Stronger vintages for Left Bank Bordeaux include 1982, 1989, 1990, 1996, 2000, 2005, 2009, 2010, 2015, 2016, 2018, 2019, and 2020.

Sauternes and Barsac

Within the southern Graves lie the appellations of Sauternes and Barsac, which, since the eighteenth century, have been internationally reputed for their sweet white wines. Barsac is within Sauternes, and Barsac wines are entitled to either appellation. The other communes within Sauternes are Bommes, Fargues, and Preignac. The principal grape variety is Semillon, with Sauvignon Blanc for freshness and aroma, and, sometimes, a touch of Muscadelle for exotic perfume. The River Ciron, which emerges from a cool spring, courses along the Sauternes-Barsac boundary beneath a shady canopy before merging into the warmer Garonne. In the autumn, the temperature differential between these two waters gives rise to evening mists that linger until mid-morning and promote the development of noble rot. Some years see less mist, and so less rot, than others. This unpredictability, together with diminutive yields (typically just 12–20hl/ha), selective harvesting of individual berries with multiple pickings or *tries*, and soft demand for sweet wines can make it hard to turn a profit out of Sauternes, so that there has been a shift towards making dry white wine.

But the sweet wine is worth the heartache. Sauternes is intense, complex, and long, with notes of apricot, peach, passion fruit, orange marmalade, honey, honeysuckle, acacia, hazelnut, and vanilla. In time, the colour transmutes from gold to amber and copper, and notes such as old books, caramel, and crème brulée are not uncommon. On the palate, crisp acidity balances the intense sweetness, rich creaminess, and high alcohol. Barsac is difficult to distinguish from Sauternes but is often lighter, fresher, and less sweet.

The top name is of course Yquem, but other star performers include Fargues, Suduiraut, Rieussec, Lafon, and, in Barsac, Climens and Coutet. Stronger vintages for Sauternes include 1989, 1990, 2001, 2003, 2005, 2007, 2009, 2011, 2015, and 2016.

Similar if less distinguished wines are produced in the neighbouring regions of Cérons on the Left Bank, and Sainte-Croix-du-Mont, Loupiac, and Cadillac across the Garonne.

Entre-Deux-Mers

The bulk of the extensive area between the Garonne and Dordogne
falls under Entre-Deux-Mers AOP. In recent decades, Entre-deux-Mers
has seen a shift from dry white wine production to majority red wine
production. However, the AOP only applies to dry white wines, leaving
the red wines to be labelled as Bordeaux AOP. Entre-Deux-Mers AOP is
often Sauvignon Blanc, which compared to Loire Sauvignon Blanc is
more expressive of tropical fruits and less so of grass and minerals.

Pomerol

The Right Bank produces some of the world's greatest Merlot wines.
Pomerol is a tiny appellation of ~800ha. Demand far outstrips supply,
with some labels selling for considerably more than Left Bank first
growths. At the heart of Pomerol is a plateau of gravel and clay. To the
west, sandier soils yield somewhat lighter wines. The subsoil contains
seams of iron-rich clay known as *crasse de fer*, a major feature at
Château Pétrus. Merlot accounts for ~80% of plantings (~95% at Pétrus),
with most of the remainder made up by Cabernet Franc and, to a lesser
extent, Cabernet Sauvignon. Pomerol is deep ruby in colour with notes
of fresh plum and other black and red fruits, spice, truffles, and vanilla
from new French oak. On the palate, it is rich, often opulent, with lower
acidity and softer tannins than Left Bank Bordeaux. Alcohol can be
high in hotter vintages. Other than Pétrus, top producers include
Trotanoy, Le Pin, Vieux Château Certan, Lafleur, Gazin, l'Evangile, and
La Conseillante. More affordable is La Croix de Gay, Nénin, and Clos
René.

Across the Barbanne stream to the north of Pomerol is the somewhat
larger Lalande de Pomerol AOP, which can sometimes match or at least
evoke Pomerol or Saint-Emilion.

Saint-Emilion

Adjoining Pomerol to the south-east is the larger ~5,500ha appellation
of Saint-Emilion, with the heavenly town of Saint-Emilion at its centre.
~3,800ha are classified as Saint-Emilion Grand Cru AOP, with yields
capped at 40hl/ha (vs. 45hl ha) and a minimum alcohol of 11% (vs.

10.5%). Like Bordeaux Supérieur AOP, Saint-Emilion Grand Cru AOP is, in fact, close to meaningless. The highly heterogeneous soils can be divided into four sections: the limestone-rich **plateau** of Saint-Emilion; the surrounding **slopes** of limestone and clay; the **border** with Pomerol with its five gravel mounds (two at Cheval Blanc and three at Figeac); and the **plains** to the west and south with lighter, and much inferior, soils of sand and alluvium. The average holding in Saint-Emilion is larger than in Pomerol, but still small by Bordeaux standards. Merlot is less dominant than in Pomerol: Cabernet Franc accounts for ~30% of plantings, and Cabernet Sauvignon for ~10%. Cheval Blanc is, famously, Cabernet-Franc dominated, and Ausone (named for Ausonius), which is on the plateau, also contains a high proportion of Cabernet Franc. A third exception-that-proves-the-rule is Figeac, with less Merlot than Cabernet Franc or Cabernet Sauvignon. Compared to Pomerol, Saint-Emilion is drier and more tannic and less obviously from the Right Bank.

Saint-Emilion has four satellites to the north and north-east, the largest being Montagne Saint-Emilion and Lussac Saint-Emilion. The wines here are similar to Saint-Emilion, if more rustic, and can represent excellent value for money.

To the west of Pomerol and Libourne are the appellations of Fronsac and Canon-Fronsac. Fronsac is about the same size as Pomerol, and Canon-Fronsac much smaller. Both appellations, and Canon-Fronsac in particular, are reputed for powerful but refined Merlot-dominated wines.

Stronger vintages for Right Bank Bordeaux include 1989, 1990, 1995, 1998, 2000, 2001, 2004, 2005, 2006, 2008, 2009, 2010, 2012, 2014, 2015, 2016, 2018, 2019, and 2020.

10

THE LOIRE

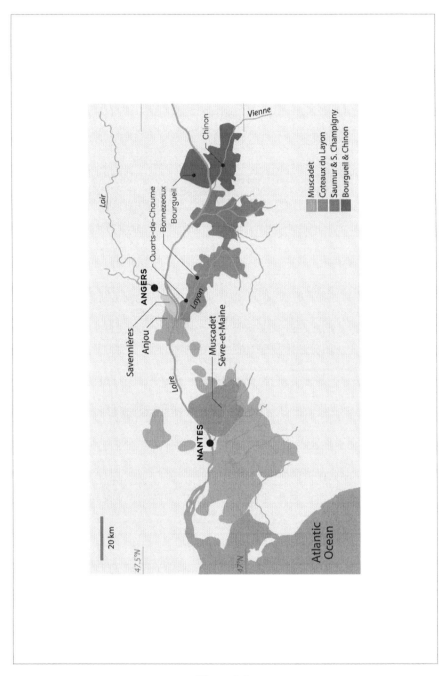

Western Loire

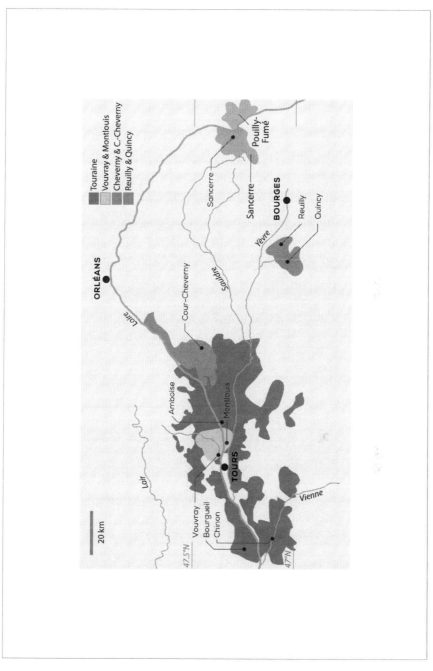

Eastern Loire

*T*he diversity of wines made in the Loire reflects variations in soils, climate, and grape varieties along the course of the River Loire. The bulk of production consists of white wines made from Chenin Blanc, Sauvignon Blanc, and Melon de Bourgogne (Muscadet), but there are also red wines made from Cabernet Franc, and rosé, sparkling, and dessert wines. In the first century, the Romans brought the vine to the Loire from the nearby regions of Bordeaux and Burgundy. The fourth century bishop St Martin of Tours is credited with spreading viticulture across the region. According to lore, his donkey stripped some nearby vines of their leaves, thereby establishing the practice of pruning! Proximity to Paris and the Atlantic facilitated trade. In the High Middle Ages, the English held the wines of the Loire in higher esteem than those of Bordeaux. Today, this most French of French regions, *le jardin de la France*, is unfairly neglected, and, for this reason, can offer excellent value for money.

The lie of the land

The Loire comprises 70,000ha of vines spread across ~500km and 14 administrative *départements*, from Muscadet near Nantes on the Atlantic coast to Sancerre and Pouilly Fumé to the south-east of Orléans in north central France. Sancerre is in fact closer to Burgundy than to Muscadet, not only in terms of distance but also of climate and culture. The Loire can be divided into four sections, from west to east along the river: The Nantais, Anjou-Saumur, Touraine, and Centre. The Nantais is mostly given to Melon de Bourgogne, Anjou-Saumur and Touraine to Chenin Blanc and Cabernet Franc, and Centre to Sauvignon Blanc.

Climate

The climate at this northerly latitude is distinctly marginal. Viticulture owes to the moderating influence of the Loire and its tributaries, along which the vineyards are huddled. The most prized sites are south-facing riverine slopes that receive the strongest sunlight. The mild, humid Atlantic climate of the Nantais contrasts with the continental climate of the Centre, with its cold winters and hot but short summers. Anjou is protected from the prevailing winds by the forests of the Vendée, and receives less rainfall than might otherwise be expected. Spring frosts and sustained autumn rains are all too common in the Loire, and vintage variation can be marked, with underripeness a perennial problem. According to a few winemakers I met, the town of Amboise, just to the east of Tours and once home to Leonardo da Vinci, is the climatic turning point of the Loire, with, to the west, Chenin Blanc and Cabernet Franc, and, to the east, Sauvignon Blanc and Pinot Noir.

Soils

Soils are very varied, as might be expected in a region that stretches over 500km. The soils of the Nantais are mostly sand with areas of clay, granite, schist, and gneiss; those of Anjou are mostly stony clay over schist; and those of Touraine are mostly flinty clay over limestone. The soils of Centre resemble those of Chablis, with areas of limestone, chalk, and Kimmeridge clay. In Saumur and Vouvray, the soils consist of *tuffeau*, a soft, free-draining, water-retaining calcareous rock. *Tuffeau jaune*, found in Chinon and Bourgueil, is sandier and softer than *tuffeau blanc* and especially suited to Cabernet Franc. The quarrying of *tuffeau* (mainly *tuffeau blanc*) to build the famous châteaux of the Loire created systems of caves that provide ideal conditions for wine storage and maturation.

Wine styles

The Loire can be thought of as a ribbon with crisp white wines at either end (Muscadet and Sancerre) and fuller-bodied white and red wines in the middle. The white wines tend to be made from Muscadet in the west, Sauvignon Blanc in the east, and Chenin Blanc in the middle. For red wines, Cabernet Franc is dominant, but Pinot Noir and Gamay become increasingly important further up-river. There are however a number of trend-breakers, such as Cour-Cheverny in Touraine which is entirely planted with the obscure Romorantin grape. Chardonnay,

Cabernet Sauvignon, and Grolleau, though seldom talked about, are not uncommon.

Sweet wines made from late harvest Chenin Blanc, which may be botrytized, are capable of great complexity and longevity. The most notable appellations for sweet wines are Vouvray and Coteaux du Layon with its sub-appellations of Bonnezeaux, Chaume, and Quarts-de-Chaume. Compared to Sauternes, which is typically associated with peach and honey, the sweet wines of the Loire are more often associated with apple, quince, and apricot, together with a much higher natural acidity and rather less sugar and alcohol.

The Loire is also an important producer of **sparkling wines**, third only to Champagne and Alsace. The most significant among these is Crémant de Loire, which is made by the traditional method (Chapter 12). Most Crémant de Loire is vinified in and around Saumur from blends of Chenin Blanc, Cabernet Franc, and Chardonnay, although a number of other traditional varieties are also permitted. Appellation rules call for manual harvesting and a minimum ageing period of one year (compared to nine months for, say, Saumur Mousseux). At its best, Crémant de Loire is long and complex with a floral, honeyed nose and nutty finish.

The Nantais: Muscadet

Muscadet is made from Melon de Bourgogne, a frost-resistant and early-ripening variety that came to dominate the area after the Great Frost of 1709. Of the three sub-regional appellations, Muscadet de Sèvre et Maine AOP is by far the most important. Melon de Bourgogne is fairly neutral, and lees ageing is often used to bring out greater flavour and texture, as is lees stirring and extended maceration. To drive up quality and reinvigorate the appellation, ten *crus communaux* have been established, including Clisson, Gorges, and Le Pallet.

Muscadet is pale, sometimes almost watery, in colour, with a slight effervescence that can prickle on the tongue. On the nose, it is distinctly unaromatic. On the palate, it is dry and light-bodied with high acidity and a touch of minerality or saltiness. Lees ageing contributes yeasty or nutty aromas and a rounder texture. Under AOP regulations, alcohol content is capped at 12%, the only instance of a maximum alcohol in France. Although the *sur lie* process helps to preserve freshness, most Muscadet is not intended for ageing. However, the finest examples can improve over many years and exhibit great depth and complexity, with notes such as smoke, honey, and dried papaya.

Top producers include Domaine de la Pépière, Luneau-Papin, Domaines Landron, Chéreau-Carré, Vincent Caillé, André-Michel Brégeon, Bruno Cormerais, Philippe Guerrin, Jerôme Bretaudeau, and Domaine de L'Ecu, where maverick Fred Niger is doing much more than making Muscadet. I like pairing Muscadet with seafood, especially oysters and mussels.

Anjou: Savennières, Coteaux du Layon

Anjou is associated with a broad spectrum of wines. But especially noteworthy are the dry Chenin Blanc of Savennières and the sweet, typically botrytized Chenin Blanc of Coteaux du Layon and more particularly Bonnezeaux and Chaume and Quarts-de-Chaume.

Historically, **Savennières** was sweet, but today the bulk of production is dry. Indeed, it is arguably the highest expression of dry Chenin Blanc, celebrated for its concentration, mineral intensity, and age worthiness. The crus of Savennières-Roche-aux-Moines AOP and Savennières Coulée-de-Serrant AOP are enclaves of Savennières AOP. Coulée-de-Serrant, first planted in 1130 by Cistercian monks and prized by Dumas's d'Artagnan, is a monopole that belongs to biodynamic beacon Nicolas Joly of Château de la Roche aux Moines, who describes himself on his business card as a 'Nature assistant and not wine maker'. Savennières is gold in colour with concentrated notes of apple, pear, chamomile, warm straw, cooked fruits, beeswax, grilled almonds, and, with age, old cognac (musty lanolin, 'wet dog') and petrol. On the palate, it is dry and unoaked with high acidity and alcohol and a long mineral finish that leaves a bitter afternote. Some producers favour malolactic conversion or maturation in new oak, leading to a diversity of styles. *Caveat emptor*: Savennières can be tight and austere in its youth, and may need several years to come out of its shell—although this, for many producers, is now less the case than it used to be. Other than Joly, top producers include Domaine du Closel, Damien Laureau, Thibaud Boudignon, Domaine des Baumard, Domaine de la Bergerie, and Domaine Eric Morgat.

The River Layon carved out a valley that encourages the development of noble rot, although some grapes are simply very ripe or encouraged to dry on the vine (*passerillage*). Successive pickings at harvest time ensure that all the grapes are bursting with sugar, acidity, and flavour. Within **Coteaux du Layon AOP**, six villages can append their name to that of the appellation or, alternatively, use the name 'Coteaux du Layon-Villages'. A further two villages—**Bonnezeaux and Chaume**— have their own separate appellations. There is also a third such sub-appellation, **Quarts-de-Chaume AOP**, for a sun-kissed enclave of Chaume in the form of an amphitheatre. The mesoclimate here is such that it is possible to ripen olives! Most of the land of Quarts-de-Chaume used to belong to the abbey of Ronceray d'Angers, which required tenant farmers to pay a tithe of one-quarter of annual production, whence 'Quarts-de-Chaume'. Compared to Vouvray, Coteaux du Layon tends to be fuller in body, sweeter, and lower in acidity. **Coteaux de l'Aubance**, along the River Aubance to the north, benefits from a similar schistous terroir. As in Coteaux du Layon, there is considerable variation in botrytis, sweetness, and quality. The wines are starting to give Coteaux du Layon a run for its money. Top producers in Coteaux du Layon include Pierre-Bise, Patrick Baudouin, Philippe Delesvaux, Domaine des Baumard, Château Soucherie, and Château de Fesles.

Rosé wines account for over half of Angevine production. First among them is Cabernet d'Anjou AOP, made from Cabernet Franc and Cabernet Sauvignon. Compared to Rosé d'Anjou, which is made predominantly from Grolleau, Cabernet d'Anjou tends to be drier with higher alcohol and greater complexity and ageing potential.

With the exception of Anjou-Gamay AOP, **red wines** are all made from Cabernet Franc and Cabernet Sauvignon. **Saumur-Champigny AOP** is very similar to neighbouring Chinon AOP and Bourgueil AOP, both in Touraine, and will be discussed alongside them.

Touraine: Vouvray, Chinon

The most notable appellations in Touraine are Vouvray and Montlouis for white wines, and, for red wines, Chinon, Bourgueil, and St-Nicolas-de-Bourgueil.

Vouvray AOP, on the right bank of the Loire just to the east of Tours, produces dry and sweet Chenin Blanc. A number of streams cut through the plateau of Vouvray, giving rise to sheltered south-facing slopes and promoting the development of noble rot. In more favourable vintages, production shifts to sweet and botrytized wines; in cooler, unfavourable vintages, it shifts to dry and sparkling or semi-sparkling wines (which however may also be sweet). Sparkling Vouvray is made by the traditional method, and can be either *pétillant* [semi-sparkling] or *mousseux* [fully sparkling]. The harvest often stretches into November, with successive pickings required for the sweet wines. Compared to Coteaux du Layon, botrytis is less common and there is greater reliance on ripeness. Sweet wines may be *moelleux* [soft], *doux* [sweet], or *liquoreux* [syrupy]. Dry wines may be *sec* [dry], *sec-tendre* [gently dry], or *demi-sec* [off-dry]. Vouvray is high in acidity, even though the acidity may be masked by sugar. Youthful Vouvray can be steely and unforgiving, although this is now less true than it used to be. With increasing age, aromas of green apple, quince, and acacia blossom surrender to complex tertiary aromas such as honeysuckle, fig, and lanolin. Vouvray, especially the sweeter examples, can have tremendous ageing potential, and on older vintages I have experienced notes such as bitter orange, truffle oil, and peat whisky. **Montlouis AOP**, on the opposite bank of the river, used to be part of Vouvray until it became a separate (and much smaller) appellation in 1938. Montlouis is similar to Vouvray in range and style, but tends to be less concentrated and lower in acidity. A lot of Vouvray is rather unimpressive; the best sites, such as Le Mont and Clos du Bourg (both owned by Huet), surmount the cliffs overlooking the river. Top producers in Vouvray and Montlouis include Huet, François Pinon, François Chidaine, Vincent Carême, Bernard Fouquet, Clos Naudin, Domaine de la Fontainerie, Domaine des Aubuisières, Domaine de la Taille au Loups, Clos de Meslerie, and Champalou.

Chinon is extolled in some verses by François Rabelais (d. 1553), its most famous son: *Chinon, trois fois Chinon: Petite ville, grand renom, Assise sur pierre ancienne, Au haut le bois, au pied la Vienne* ['Chinon, three times Chinon: Small town, great renown, perched on ancient rock, between the woods above and, below, the Vienne']. Chinon has forever been associated with red wine, but also produces a bit of rosé and a dash of white wine. The reds and rosés are Cabernet Franc with up to 10% Cabernet Sauvignon. The soils are diverse and complex. In essence, gravelly, alluvial soils on the river flats yield a lighter, more fruit-driven style, while higher areas rich in limestone and *tuffeau jaune* yield a richer, more structured style. Chinon offers a nose of raspberries and pencil shavings, although unripe examples, which are now less common, may be marred by a bitter greenness or herbaceousness. In time, it develops earthy, spicy, and animally notes. On the palate, it is light or medium in body with high acidity, medium alcohol, and fine and powdery tannins. New oak is possible but unusual. Top producers include Olga Raffault, Charles Joguet, Bernard Baudry, Philippe Alliet, Couly-Dutheil, Wilfrid Rousse, Château de Coulaine, and Domaine de Noiré. Their best wines can age for a decade or more.

Bourgueil AOP and the smaller **Saint-Nicolas-de-Bourgueil AOP** lie across the river from Chinon. The slopes are south-facing and sheltered from cold northerlies by forests. Like Chinon, this is mostly red wine territory although some rosé is also made. Bourgueil is Cabernet Franc with up to 10% Cabernet Sauvignon. As in Chinon, gravelly, alluvial soils on the river flats yield a lighter, more fruit-driven style, while higher areas rich in limestone and *tuffeau jaune* yield a richer, more structured style. Compared to Bourgueil, Saint-Nicolas-de-Bourgueil is likely to be lighter, more delicate, and more fruit-driven. Top producers in these appellations include Yannick Amirault, Max Cognard, and Delauney Druet.

Saumur-Champigny sits on a low plateau of free-draining *tuffeau*, and the soils are more uniform than in Chinon or Bourgueil. Saumur-Champigny is Cabernet Franc and up to 10% Cabernet Sauvignon or Pineau d'Aunis ('Chenin Noir'). Top producers in Saumur-Champigny and neighbouring Saumur (which also produces white wines from

Chenin Blanc) include Clos Rougeard, Domaine Guiberteau, Domaine du Collier, Domaine des Roches Neuves, and Antoine Sanzay.

Tasted blind, the four neighbouring appellations of Chinon, Bourgueil, Saint-Nicolas-de-Bourgueil, and Saumur-Champigny are very difficult to distinguish, and vary more by soil type (limestone vs river deposits) and producer than by appellation.

Centre: Sancerre, Pouilly-Fumé

The main grape variety in the Centre is Sauvignon Blanc, with smaller plantings of Pinot Noir and Chasselas. The most notable appellations are Sancerre AOP and Pouilly-Fumé AOP, which almost face each other across the Loire. **Sancerre** used to be famed for light-bodied red wines, but, since the mid-twentieth century, has built such a reputation for Sauvignon Blanc as to have become its spiritual home. Today, most Sancerre is Sauvignon Blanc, although red and rosé Pinot Noir is also made. **Pouilly-Fumé**, in contrast, is invariably Sauvignon Blanc. The soils of Pouilly-Fumé are richer in silex, translating into a smoky, gunflint aroma [*pierre-à-fusil*]. Moreover, the calcium-rich limestone imparts a certain chalky quality. Both silex and limestone reflect sunlight and retain heat, helping the grapes to ripen. Sancerre is pale lemon in colour, possibly with a green tinge. Notes of gooseberry and grapefruit are accompanied by hints of blackcurrant leaf, nettles, cut grass, and smoke. On the palate, the wine is dry and light-bodied with high acidity, medium alcohol, and a tapered, mineral finish. Malolactic conversion and oak ageing are unusual, and most Sancerre is intended for early drinking. In practice, it is very difficult to distinguish Sancerre from Pouilly-Fumé, although the latter does tend to be smokier from the richer silex. A lot of Sancerre is not much different from generic Sauvignon de Touraine AOP from the Middle Loire. At the other end of the spectrum, the villages of Bué, Chavignol, and Ménétréol-sous-Sancerre have achieved quasi cru status. Top producers include Didier Dagueneau, Henri Bourgeois, François Cotat, Lucien Crochet, Alphonse Mellot, Vincent Pinard, Gérard Boulay, and Vacheron. Wines labelled with just 'Pouilly' or 'Pouilly-sur-Loire' can be quite elegant, but are usually made from Chasselas rather than Sauvignon Blanc.

Sancerre Rouge, which occasionally crops up in blind tastings, is a very pale, light, and delicate Pinot Noir with herbal notes and a just-ripe raspberry fruit profile. In the shadow of Sancerre, Quincy was the first French white wine with an AOP: with soils of sand and gravel, the Sauvignon Blanc tends to be rounder and riper. Other nearby AOPs that produce Sancerre lookalikes are Reuilly and Coteaux du Giennois.

Owing to the geographical expanse and diversity of grape varieties and styles, it is very hard to generalize about Loire vintages. However, stronger overall years include 1989, 1990, 1996, 2005, 2009, 2014, 2015, 2016, 2017, 2018, 2019, and 2020.

11

OTHER NOTABLE FRENCH REGIONS AND APPELLATIONS

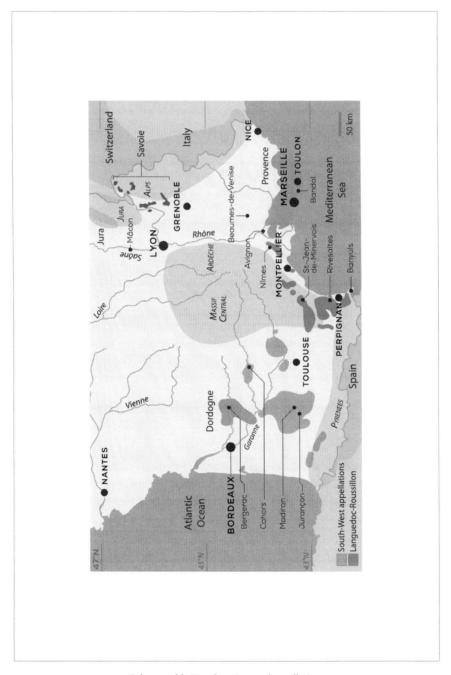

Other notable French regions and appellations

*J*ura is a small (~2,000ha) but diverse wine region in the foothills of the Jura Mountains, ~80km east of Burgundy. The climate is cooler than in Burgundy, although summers are fairly hot and sunny. The soils, which are rich in fossils, are clay and limestone with outcrops of marl. Five grape varieties are cultivated: **Chardonnay** and **Savagnin** for whites, and **Poulsard**, **Trousseau**, and **Pinot Noir** for reds. The reds, although vinified as reds, tend to be in colour more salmon than red.

The relative isolation of the Jura has led to the preservation of a number of distinctive wine styles. Most notable is *vin jaune* (~5% of production) made from very ripe Savagnin left to mature under a flor-like strain of yeast for six or more years before being bottled into 62cl clavelins. This process leads to oxidative nutty aromas similar to those of sherry— although, unlike sherry, vin jaune is not fortified. Other aromas include walnuts, honey, and 'curry'. Vin jaune can be made under the Arbois, Etoile, and Côtes du Jura appellations, but the richest examples are made under the exclusive **Château-Chalon** appellation, which is home to top producers Jean Macle and Domaine Berthet-Bondet. Vin jaune can last for decades, even centuries.

Also notable is a straw wine, or *vin de paille* (~1% of production), which, like vin jaune, can be made under the Arbois, Etoile, and Côtes du Jura appellations. This blend of Chardonnay, Poulsard, and Savagnin is pressed, normally in January, from dried grapes, and aged in oak for at least three years. It is rich and complex with high alcohol and dominant notes of honey and dried or confected fruits.

Macvin du Jura (~6% of production), which can be white (Chardonnay and Savagnin) or red (Poulsard, Trousseau, and Pinot Noir), is a *vin de liqueur* or mistelle made from the must of late harvest grapes. The must is aged in oak for 12 months without prior fermentation. Marc du Jura, which has to be made in the same winery, is then added in a ratio of 1:2, thereby arresting fermentation and preserving the natural sugars. Further oak ageing finishes the process by harmonizing the flavours.

To round up on the six Jura appellations: any style of wine can be made under the Arbois and Côtes du Jura appellations, which are the most quantitatively important. In contrast, only white wines (including *vin jaune* and *vin de paille*) can be made under the Etoile appellation, and only *vin jaune* under the Château-Chalon appellation. Macvin ['marc-vin'] du Jura is a regional appellation, as is **Crémant du Jura** (~28% of Jura production). This sparkling wine is made by the traditional method, most commonly from 100% Chardonnay. Poulsard and Trousseau are specialties of Arbois. Trousseau has travelled all the way down to Portugal and Madeira, where it is called Bastardo for being so difficult to grow. Recently, I blind tasted a Patagonian Bastardo (Trousseau) which I placed in Tenerife!

The bulk of Jura production (~60%) is accounted for by still 'regular' wines, with the whites enjoying a greater reputation than the reds. These whites, which can be very terroir driven, are made from Chardonnay and/or Savagnin, either by the classic method (*ouillé*, with the barrel headspace, or ullage, topped-up as in other wine regions) or under a veil of yeasts (*sous-voile,* with significant ullage). This oxidative, *sous-voile* style has long been the signature of this beautiful but isolated and often neglected wine region. Other than Jean Macle and Domaine Berthet-Bondet, leading producers include Jean-François Ganevat, Domaine Tissot, and Domaine du Pélican.

Savoie

Twenty years ago, the wines of Savoie were often thin and acidic, and good mostly for cutting through cheesy dishes such as the local fondue and raclette. On a trip to Chamonix, I was intrigued by some complex and unusual wines, and took a couple of days out of the skiing to visit some producers and find out more.

Before the Roman conquest, the vine was being cultivated in Savoie by the Gallic Allobroges. The region's 2,100ha (vs ~110,000ha for Bordeaux) are dispersed across four French départements: mostly Savoie and Haute-Savoie, and also Ain and Isère. Ain also contains the even smaller Bugey wine region, which is fairly similar to Savoie in terms of terroir, varieties, and styles. Although Savoie's wine producing areas are fairly disparate, they are united by their common Alpine landscape, with the vine cultivated on sheltered south-facing slopes and along moderating water bodies such as Lakes Geneva and Bourget. Stony soils provide good heat retention and water drainage, and I spotted the odd almond or apricot tree amid the vines.

White wine accounts for 70% of production, followed by red wine (20%), rosé (6%), and sparkling wine (4%). Only 5% of total production is exported, so the wines, though generally good value for money, are fairly hard to source. By far the most important appellation is **Savoie AOP**. The other two still wine appellations are **Roussette de Savoie AOP** (for the crus of Frangy, Monthoux, Marestel, and Monterminod) and **Seyssel AOP** (for the cru of Seyssel), although it is not clear even to the producers themselves why these two appellations are not subsumed under Savoie AOP. In 2009 growers in Crépy chose to have their AOP demoted so as to better market their wines as Savoie AOP. Crémant is becoming increasingly important, leading in 2014 to the creation of a fourth Savoie appellation, **Crémant de Savoie AOP**. Broadly, Crémant de Savoie is at least 40% Jacquère, with any remainder made up by Altesse and Chardonnay—although Chardonnay cannot make up more than 40% of the blend.

The Savoie wine region counts some **twenty crus**, from Ripaille and Marin on Lake Geneva in the north to Apremont, Les Abymes, Chignin, Montmélian, and Arbin in the south. The heart of the region is to the south, between the Bauges and the Chartreuse mountains in the valley of the Isère, in the so-called Cluse de Chambéry and Combe de Savoie. The soils here are predominantly limestone scree from crumbling mountains, including the picturesque Savoyarde in the Bauges and Mont Granier in the Chartreuse.

Over **twenty grape varieties** are cultivated, the most important being Jacquère, Altesse (Roussette), Bergeron (Roussanne), and Chasselas for the whites, and Mondeuse and Gamay for the reds. The high-yielding Jacquère accounts for half of plantings, while Chasselas is found in the north towards the Swiss border (Chapter 14). The Gringet grape is found only in Ayze, where it is made into a sparkling wine. Some of Savoie's indigenous varieties are endangered: there are, for example, just nine hectares of Persan left.

Jacquère wines are dry, crisp, and mineral, with notes of citrus fruits, white flowers, and wet stone. Some of the most 'Alpine' Jacquère expressions come from the aptly named crus of Apremont ['Bitter Mountain'] and Les Abymes ['The Abysses'], which lie on limestone scree from a thirteenth century landslide of Mont Granier that killed thousands.

Altesse underlies the Roussette de Savoie AOP. It is richer than Jacquère, with notes of honey, apricots, tropical fruits, and aniseed. According to lore, the variety was brought back from Cyprus as a royal dowry, whence the name 'Altesse' ['Highness']. Whatever the case, Altesse is capable of serious complexity, and, unlike Jacquère, improves with age, developing notes of toast and nuts. The Seyssel AOP is reputed for its floral sparkling wines made from Altesse, Chasselas, and Molette.

The cru of Chignin-Bergeron (not to be confused with the overlapping Jacquère cru of Chignin) is the only cru with a grape variety in its name: **Bergeron**, or Roussanne as it is known in the Rhône. Chignin-Bergeron is rich and honeyed, although more fresh and mineral, and less alcoholic, than Rhône Roussanne. It is capable of serious finesse and complexity, as, for example, in Louis Magnien's Grand Orgue cuvée.

The first century Columella wrote of Allobrogica, which probably corresponds to **Mondeuse**, as 'the grape that ripens amid the snow'. In 2000, there were just 200ha of Mondeuse left in France, although the variety has recovered somewhat. Mondeuse is often compared with the Piedmontese Refosco dal Peduncolo Rosso, though it is in fact more closely related to Syrah. It is deep in colour with notes of cherry, plum, violets, and spice, crisp acidity, and substantial tannins. Like Altesse and Bergeron, Mondeuse is ageworthy: at Louis Magnin, I tasted a 20-year-old Mondeuse that was still fresh. The finest Mondeuse is arguably from Arbin.

Notable producers in Savoie include Louis Magnin, André et Michel Quenard, Fabien Trosset, Céline Jacquet, Domaine Giachino, and Les Ardoisières (IGP Vin des Allobroges, just outside the Savoie AOP).

Provence

Most people associate Provence with its crisp and refreshing and ever so fashionable rosés, but it is the smaller, more peripheral appellations such as Bellet, Les Baux-de-Provence, Cassis, and, above all, Bandol that produce the region's most noteworthy wines.

The climate is Mediterranean with mild winters and hot, dry summers, and over 3,000 annual sunshine hours. The soils are very varied, with white varieties dominating outcrops of limestone as, for example, in Cassis. A diversity of varieties are cultivated, including Rhône varieties such as Mourvèdre, Syrah, Grenache, Cinsault, and Roussanne; Atlantic varieties such as Cabernet Sauvignon and Merlot; and more local varieties such as Tibouren for rosés and Rolle [Vermentino] for white wines. The largest appellations are Côtes de Provence to the east and Côteaux d'Aix-en-Provence to the west. Leading producers include Domaine de Trévallon to the south of Avignon, Domaine Richeaume to the east of Aix-en-Provence, and Château Simone which dominates the small, limestone-rich appellation of Palette near Aix-en-Provence.

To the south, between Marseille and Toulon, lies the sleepy fishing village of **Bandol**, which produces red wine, rosé, and a dash of white wine. The ~1600ha of vineyards on diverse soils of marl and limestone are sheltered by the Montagne Sainte-Victoire and the Massif de la Sainte-Baume to the north and the Chaine de Saint-Cyr to the west. Moist sea breezes make up for any shortfall in rain. The showcase variety is Mourvèdre, which ripens fully in this hot and dry climate. In contrast, Grenache runs the risk of over-ripening, and is usually planted on cooler, north-facing slopes. Yields are among the lowest in France, equivalent to no more than one bottle per vine.

Red Bandol consists of at least 50% Mourvèdre, usually completed by Grenache and Cinsault. Syrah and Carignan may also be included but are restricted to 15% of the blend and 10% individually. The wine is aged in old oak for at least 18 months prior to bottling. Red Bandol is dark in colour with notes of black fruits, vanilla, spice, liquorice, leather, red meat, and earth. On the palate, it is full-bodied, intense, and structured, with a high alcohol in the order of 14–15%. It greatly improves with age and can be cellared for a decade or more. The rosé, which is made from a similar blend (and has come to account for over 70% of the AOP's output), is spicy and earthy in character, and not dissimilar to Tavel from the Southern Rhône. Leading producers include Domaine Tempier, Domaine de la Bégude, Pibarnon, and Vannières.

Languedoc-Roussillon

When it comes to wine, the regions of Languedoc and Roussillon are often lumped together. Their vineyards hug the Gulf of Lyon from Banyuls on the Spanish border to near Nîmes in the East, straddling the Rivers Tech, Têt, Agly, Aude, Orb, and Hérault, and enveloping the cities of Perpignan, Narbonne, and Montpellier. Overall, the climate is Mediterranean, that is, hot and dry, with the dryness accentuated by the inland tramontane, which picks up as it funnels between the Pyrenees and the Massif Central.

Languedoc ['Language of Yes'] corresponds roughly to the old County of Toulouse, extending from the Garonne to the Rhône and northwards to the Cévennes and Massif Central. In viticultural terms, it can be divided into three topographical zones: the fertile coastal plains, the cooler hillsides and mountains, and the Atlantic corridor. The region is a right ragbag of terroirs, varieties, and appellations that puts out more wine than all Australia. Before the EU started paying growers to uproot vines, it was a major contributor to the European wine lake. However, its weakness has also been its strength, with ambitious and innovative winemakers moving on cheap land and shaking up the still dominant co-operatives. Some of the most iconic wines are made *hors appellation*, with both Mas de Daumas Gassac and Grange des Pères labelled as humble IGP Pays de l'Hérault. The enveloping IGP Pays d'Oc (which also takes in Roussillon) is the most important IGP in France, accounting for ~16% of French wine production and as much as ~92% of French varietal wine (wine with a grape variety on the label). Still today, the entire region remains in a state of flux.

Roussillon ['Red Earth'], or Northern Catalonia, corresponds roughly to the French *département* of Pyrénées-Orientales. For centuries Roussillon belonged to Aragon, with Charles V bestowing upon the capital of Perpignan the title of *Fedelissima* ['Most Faithful City']. Roussillon is rimmed by mountains. This giant amphitheatre with its hot and dry climate and many air currents is especially suited to organic viticulture, and replete with old vines. Yields are low, and output is a small fraction of that of Languedoc.

Broadly speaking, the Languedoc is more reputed for its red wines, and Roussillon for its vin doux naturels (VDNs), notably Rivesaltes, Banyuls, and Maury. In fact, Roussillon is responsible for ~80% of all French VDN production—even though, by volume, more table wine is made. VDNs, including those of Roussillon, are covered in Chapter 24. The Languedoc is also noted for its sparkling Limoux wines and its fortified Muscats, which are covered, respectively, in Chapters 12 and 24.

Sparkling and fortified wines aside, the more notable appellations within the regional Languedoc AOP include Fitou, Corbières-Boutenac, La Clape, Minervois La Livinière, Saint-Chinian, Faugères, Terrasses du Larzac, Pic Saint-Loup, and Picpoul de Pinet. These more traditional appellation wines are prescribed blends of regional varieties, the most prevalent of which are Grenache, Syrah, Mourvèdre, Cinsault, and Carignan for reds and rosés, and, for whites, Bourboulenc, Grenache Blanc, Roussanne, Marsanne, Rolle, Clairette, and Picpoul. International varieties such as Merlot and Chardonnay are also very important, but labelled as IGP.

Cahors

Cahors in the old province of Quercy is the birthplace of John XXII, the *pape* in *Chateauneuf-du-Pape*. The town is surrounded by a U-shaped bend of the River Lot, across which the fortified Pont Valentré, built in the fourteenth century with the help of the devil. Motto in Occitan: *Sèm de Caors, avèm pas paur* ['We're from Cahors, we're not frightened'].

The Black Wine of Cahors enjoyed a splendid reputation in the Middle Ages and into the nineteenth century. The wines were shipped down the Lot and Garonne to be blended with Bordeaux or exported as far afield as England and Russia. Today, Clos Triguedina has revived the historical style by heating harvested grapes overnight in a prune oven. In the late nineteenth century, phylloxera did its worst, and, in 1956, the Great Frost killed off all but one per cent of the vines. The region is still recovering from this disaster, and there remains, in terms of terroir, a great deal of unrealized potential.

Cahors is equidistant from the Atlantic and Mediterranean, with a south-easterly *vent d'autan* [*vent de fous*] and Mediterranean climate in summer, and a sweeping Atlantic climate the rest of the year. Compared to Bordeaux, the winters are colder, but the summers hotter and drier. Spring frosts are a sporadic problem: in 2017 they destroyed some 80% of the crop, and seem to have become more regular in recent years. The heart of the appellation is in fact in the west of the delimited area, a few kilometres to the west of Cahors. The vineyards are planted on three main terraces in the valley of the River Lot, and up on the *causse* or limestone plateau. The causse yields more structured, long-lived wines, while the first and second terraces yield softer, fruitier wines (cf. Chinon, Saint-Emilion).

Cahors is, of course, the ancestral home of the **Malbec** grape, known locally as 'Cot' or 'Auxerrois'. The appellation is for red wine only, with Malbec making up at least 70% of the blend and completed by Merlot and Tannat. Cahors can be reminiscent of Bordeaux, but is darker in colour with more plum, chocolate, and mineral notes, and heavier tannins that can make it austere in its youth. With age, it develops aromas of earth and sousbois with meaty, animally undertones. Other commonly cited descriptors include violet, gentian, ink, and liquorice. On the palate, acidity is high, but body and alcohol are only medium. The best examples are aged in varying proportions of new oak, and improve in bottle for a further 10–15 years. When mature, they pair like a dream with the rich local fare of duck, goose, game, mushrooms, and truffles. Compared to Cahors, Argentine Malbec is softer and riper with a heavier body, higher alcohol, and lower acidity.

Recommended producers of Cahors include Château du Cèdre, Clos Triguedina, Château Lamartine, Château Chambert, Mas del Périé, Domaine de la Bérengeraie, and Domaine Capelanel.

Madiran

Madiran is exceptionally high in procyanidins, and has been most closely linked with the 'French Paradox', the observation that the French suffer a relatively low incidence of coronary heart disease despite enjoying a rich and fatty diet—and nowhere fattier or richer than in Madiran.

The appellation of Madiran, which is coextensive with the appellations of Pacherenc du Vic-Bilh and Pacherenc du Vic-Bilh Sec, lies to the south-west of Cahors, on the left bank of the River Adour. **Madiran** applies to red wines, **Pacherenc du Vic-Bilh** to white wines of varying sweetness, and **Pacherenc du Vic-Bilh Sec** to dry white wines.

'Pacherenc du Vic-Bilh' comes from the Béarnais for 'vines supported on stakes from the old country'. The principal grape varieties for Pacherenc du Vic-Bilh are Petit Manseng (more noble than Gros Manseng) and Petit Courbu. Today, white grape varieties account for a mere 300ha within the delimited area, and the region's reputation rests on red Madiran. This is composed of **Tannat** and smaller proportions of Cabernet Franc [Bouchy], Cabernet Sauvignon, and Fer Servadou [Pinenc], although some of the finer examples are pure Tannat.

Summers are hotter than in Bordeaux. Owing to a Foehn effect, autumns are warm and dry with high diurnal temperature variation, which permits and even encourages late harvests. The terroir is complex. There are, in essence, four parallel north-south ridges with altitudes varying from 180 to 300m: the soils consist of rounded pebbles on the hilltops, mineral-rich calcareous clay on the most favoured steeps, and sand and clay on the inferior slopes.

Madiran is structured, dark, full-bodied, alcoholic, and so tannic that Cabernet Sauvignon is looked upon as a softener. Techniques used to make the wine less astringent and more approachable in its youth include hand picking only the ripest bunches, destemming, gentle pressing, barrel ageing, and micro-oxygenation, first developed in Madiran by Patrick DuCournau. These days, the best Madiran is easily confused with the best Bordeaux, and even the colour can overlap. Leading producers include Château Aydie, Domaine Berthoumieu, and Alain Brumont's Château Montus. When the Montus cuvée La Tyre beat Pétrus in a blind tasting, a journalist quipped, *Avec Montus, Madiran a son Pétrus* ['With Montus, Madiran has its Pétrus']. An ideal pairing for Madiran is duck confit—easy to make, though it takes a long time.

Irouléguy

The bright green Irouléguy at the foot of the Pyrenées in the French Basque Country produces Tannat-dominated wines similar to those of Madiran, along with some white wine and rosé. The appellation is tiny, with no more than 200ha under vine and a score of independent producers. The climate is relatively cool and wet, albeit with long, dry, and warm autumns; and red Irouléguy is fresher, more floral, and more mineral than Madiran. In the nineteenth century, Basque settlers planted Tannat vines in Uruguay, and Tannat is now that country's signature variety (Chapter 30). My favourite Irouléguy producer is Arretxea.

Jurançon

Henry IV of France and Navarre, nicknamed *le vert galant*, was baptized with a drop of Jurançon. Centuries later, novelist Colette (d. 1954) called the wine the *séduction du vert galant*: 'I was a girl when I met this prince; aroused, imperious, treacherous, as all great seducers are.'

Jurançon lies to the south of Madiran, just outside Pau in the Pyrenean foothills. With 1,300mm annual rainfall, humidity is high, but a warm and dry foehn wind extends the ripening season into October and November, with some harvests taking place as late as December and even January. The soils are clay and sand with some limestone at higher altitudes. Many vineyards contain *poudingues* (from the English word 'pudding'), sedimentary rocks of calcareous clay studded with marble-sized pebbles.

The principal varieties are Petit Manseng and Gros Manseng (in Occitan the 'g' is pronounced with a trill), with smaller amounts of Courbu Blanc, Petit Courbu, Camarlet de Lasseube, and Lauzet. Vines are trained high [*conduite en hautain*] to lift the fruit from frost and disease and encourage canopy development. Gros Manseng is normally the principal variety for **Jurançon Sec AOP**, and Petit Manseng for **Jurançon AOP**, which is sweet and sometimes aged in oak. With its thick skin, Petit Manseng is especially suited to drying on the vine [*passerillage*]. It is considered more noble than Gros Manseng, but is lower yielding. Despite the fashion for dry wines, Jurançon is more sought-after than Jurançon Sec and dominates production.

Jurançon is golden in colour, often with a greenish tinge. The nose delivers a medley of tropical fruits such as mango, pineapple, and guava along with flowers and sweet spice and perhaps even beeswax, banana, and coconut. Some of the wines from Domaine Castéra that I tasted displayed prominent truffle. Acidity is very high—higher than Chenin Blanc or even Riesling—but sweetness can vary quite considerably depending on vintage conditions and time of harvest. Sweet Jurançon is more akin to Vouvray than to nearby Sauternes, both in terms of acid structure and aroma profile. At Château Jolys, I tasted a 2001 December harvest that blew me away with notes of caramel, coconut, dried fruits, gingerbread, cloves, and Bourbon vanilla, among others. Dry Jurançon is often mistaken for New World Sauvignon Blanc, but Petit Manseng is less herbaceous. The ageworthy style of dry Jurançon favoured by Charles Hours (pronounced 'Ours' or 'Bear') at Clos Uroulat might easily be mistaken for Savennières.

Top producers in Jurançon include Château Jolys, Clos Lapeyre, Clos Uroulat, Domaine Castéra, Domaine Cauhapé, Domaine Larredya with its biodynamic amphitheatre, and Domaine Guirardel, where Mme Guirardel offered me a fabulous pairing of duck hearts in ginger.

Bergerac

Bergerac lies to the east of Bordeaux, across the Gironde departmental boundary and into the Dordogne. Bergerac is similar and sometimes superior to Bordeaux, but, with its confusing names and appellations, finds it hard to shine in the shadow of its neighbour. The main varieties are the same as in Bordeaux, with Merlot, Malbec, and Semillon leading the pack. In addition to Bergerac AOP, there are 8 sub-regional appellations: Pécharmant for red wines, Côtes de Bergerac and Montravel for red and white wines, and Monbazillac, Saussignac, Rosette, Haut-Montravel, and Côtes de Montravel for sweet and semi-sweet white wines. The ~2,000ha of **Monbazillac** are on the left bank of the River Dordogne, in an area propitious to noble rot. Monbazillac is broadly similar to Sauternes, but often contains more Muscadelle in the blend. It can be more giving in its youth, and with age develops a creamy and nutty character. Saussignac, directly to the west, is similar to Monbazillac, if slightly less luscious.

Corsica

One of the 18 regions of France, the island of Corsica lies to the south-east of mainland France, off the coast of Tuscany and just north of Sardinia. From early antiquity, Greek colonists cultivated the vine in Corsica. In the thirteenth century, control of the island passed from Pisa to Genoa, and then, from 1768, to France. The following year, an Italian noblewoman Maria Letizia Buonaparte gave birth to a boy, Napoleon, in Ajaccio—now the island's capital. In the wake of the Algerian War (1954–1962) many *pied-noirs* resettled in Corsica, contributing to a four-fold increase in vineyard area. In recent decades, initiatives by the European Union have led to a refocussing on quality wine production, with vineyard area falling back to ~7,000ha. This being fairly limited, Corsican wines do not come cheap. But progress in recent years has been phenomenal, and the best examples are worth the outlay.

L'île de Beauté, as the French like to call their favourite holiday place, is very mountainous, and vineyards tend to be planted nearer the coast. The climate is Mediterranean, with hot, dry summers and short, mild winters, although the shifting landscape creates diverse mesoclimates. The sea moderates temperatures, while the mountains can significantly increase diurnal temperature range. The principal threat to the harvest comes from heat and drought. Corsica is essentially granitic, but the Cap Corse peninsula in the far north is rich in schist, Patrimonio just south of Cap Corse is rich in limestone-clay, and Bonifacio in the far south is rich in chalky limestone.

The catch-all Ile de Beauté IGP accounts for more than half of the island's production. The generic Vin de Corse AOP also blankets the island. Subject to stricter rules, five areas can append their names to the Vin de Corse AOP: Coteaux du Cap Corse, Calvi, Sartène, Figari, and Porto Vecchio. Patrimonio and Ajaccio have their own AOPs. Finally, there is an AOP for Muscat du Cap Corse, a vin doux naturel (VDN) made from Muscat Blanc à Petits Grains. Production of Muscat du Cap Corse is small, but the wine can impress with its smoky minerality, high but balanced acidity, and notes of rose petal, orange blossom, litchi, and honey. Rarer still from Cap Corse is Rappu, a red VDN made from the Aleatico grape, which is also behind Elba Aleatico Passito DOCG.

About half of Corsican wine is rosé, a third red, and the remainder white, although, compared to the cooperatives, leading producers tend to make proportionally less rosé. One producer sought to justify his rosé production by telling me, "A Ferrari is not much good without petrol." By far the most important varieties are **Nielluccio** [Sangiovese] and **Sciacarello** [Mammolo] for reds and rosés, and **Vermentino** [Rolle] for whites. Reds and rosés made under Vin de Corse AOP must include at least 50% Nielluccio, Sciacarello, and Grenache. **Patrimonio** reds and rosés are heavily dominated by Nielluccio, which does best on calcareous soils. Sciacarello on the other hand does best on granitic soils, and is the leading variety in **Ajaccio** and the south. Producers are enthusiastic about local varieties, including rarer ones such as Bianco Gentile, Aleatico, Morescola, Morescono, Montanaccia, Carcajolo Nero... One producer I visited was busy grafting Vermentino onto 50-

year-old Grenache vines because "we don't want to drown in the Rhône". Nielluccio is bold and structured with notes of black fruit, tomato leaf, and *maquis* herbs. It is often blended with Sciacarello, which is lighter, with notes of red fruits, almonds, and coffee or pepper. Corsican whites are often 100% Vermentino. They are typically pale in colour, with notes of grapefruit, peach, almond, flowers, fennel, and anise, with balanced acidity and a bitter finish. Depending on terroir, they can be either rich or mineral.

Some favourite producers in Corsica include Pieretti and Clos Nicrosi in Cap Corse, Domaine Arena and Yves Leccia in Patrimonio, and, further south, Jean-Charles Abbatucci, Yves Canarelli, Clos Culombu (try the *Storia di* cuvées), and Domaine Vaccelli (try the *Granit* cuvées). Abbatucci and Canarelli are leading the revival of rarer varieties and, in the case of Canarelli, the limestone terroir of Bonifacio.

12

CHAMPAGNE AND SPARKING WINES

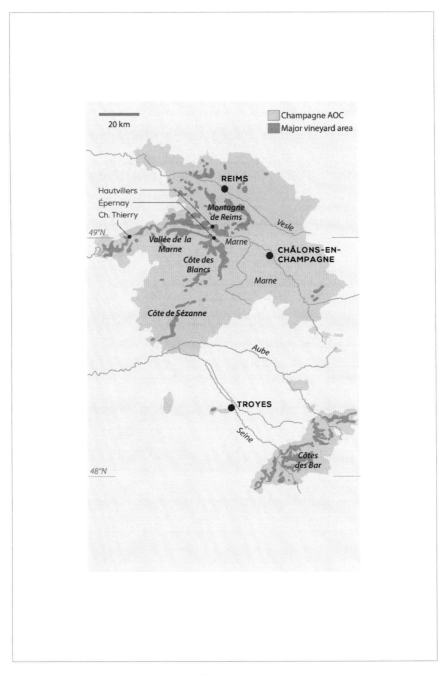

Champagne

*E*arly sparkling wines were produced by the *méthode ancestrale*, with the carbon dioxide gas arising from fermentation in the bottle. The *méthode ancestrale* is still used in certain parts of France such as Gaillac and Limoux; but as the lees are not removed from the bottle, the end product can be cloudy.

Historically in the Champagne, cold weather halted fermentation, which then restarted in the spring. If the wine had been bottled, the carbon dioxide produced by this second fermentation often shattered the bottle. But if the bottle resisted, the result was a sparkling wine not dissimilar to modern champagne. For a long time, the Champenois considered such a wine to be faulty, going so far as to call it *vin du diable*, or 'devil's wine'.

The British, however, acquired a taste for this accidentally sparkling wine and successfully introduced it to the French court at Versailles, then under the regency (1715–23) of Philippe II, duc d'Orléans. The Champenois rose to meet the increasing demand for their *vin du diable*, but struggled to control the process and could not source bottles strong enough to reliably withstand the pressure.

The solutions to these problems came not from Champagne but from across the Channel. (1) In 1662, the English physician and scientist Christopher Merret presented a paper in which he argued, correctly, that any wine could be made sparkling by the addition of sugar prior to bottling. (2) English glassmakers of the seventeenth century turned from wood- to coal-fire ovens, enabling them to make stronger glass and stronger bottles. (3) Finally, the English rediscovered the use of cork stoppers (lost after the fall of the Western Roman Empire), which provided an airtight closure with which to seal in the sparkle.

In 1668, **Dom Pérignon** became cellar master at the Benedictine Abbey at Hautvillers. By improving methods, he perfected the wines that would become sparkling champagne, advocating, among others, aggressive pruning and smaller yields, early-morning harvesting, and the rejection of bruised or broken grapes. However, he regarded sparkling wine as faulty, and recommended Pinot Noir on the grounds that it is less likely to re-ferment.

Until the early nineteenth century, champagne producers did not remove the lees from the bottle. While this preserved all the sparkle, it could make for a cloudy and unpleasant wine. The *veuve* [widow] Cliquot and her cellar master solved the problem by pioneering the process of riddling, which involves progressively migrating the lees into the neck of the bottle and then ejecting it under the pressure of the wine.

The small amount of wine lost through riddling came to be replaced by a variable mixture of sugar and wine called the dosage, which then as today determined the final style of the wine. Throughout most of the nineteenth century, champagne was very sweet. Champagne destined for Russia was sweetest of all, containing as much as 250–300g/l of sugar. At the other end of the spectrum, champagne destined for England contained 'only' 22–66g/l of sugar. Today, the popular style of champagne, *brut*, contains 6–15g/l of sugar, and the sweetest style, *doux*, can contain as little as 50g/l.

In January 1911, in the wake of phylloxera and a succession of poor vintages, riots erupted. Some producers had been making 'champagne' with grapes from outside the region, and the Champenois growers intercepted this fruit in transport and dumped it into the River Marne. To address their grievances, the French government sought to delimit the Champagne region, but the exclusion and then inclusion of the Aube led to further riots that might have descended into civil war had it not been for the outbreak of World War I. The Great War wreaked destruction on buildings and vineyards, and many Champenois took refuge in the *crayères* [chalk cellars] normally used to store and mature their wines.

The Champenois had barely begun to recover from the wounds of war when the lucrative Russian market was lost to the Bolshevik Revolution, and then the US market to Prohibition. The Great Depression also hit sales, as did the advent of World War II. Since the end of World War II, champagne has been in ever increasing demand. This has led to a quadrupling of production to ~300m bottles a year, but it has also led to a great number of imitators throughout France, Europe, and the New World, and, back home, to a controversial expansion or 'revision' of the Champagne delimited area.

The lie of the land

The three main varieties of Champagne are Pinot Noir, Chardonnay, and Pinot Meunier. All three are planted across the appellation, which is the only major single-appellation region in France.

Champagne lies ~85km north-east of Paris at latitude 49–50°N, the northerly extreme of wine making. The climate is marginal with a mean annual temperature of 10°C (vs. 12.5°C in Bordeaux and 14°C in Châteauneuf-du-Pape) and all the problems that come with that, including severe winters, spring frosts, and hail. Most vineyards face between south and east on gently undulating to moderately steep terrain that combines high sun exposure with good drainage. Luckily, the chalk subsoil is able to retain the warmth of the sun—as well as rainfall, which, at 630mm per year, is not all that plentiful.

The marker of the quality of a terroir is not attached to an individual site as in Burgundy, but, rather crudely, to an entire village. On the so-called *Echelle des Crus*, each village within the Champagne demarcated area is attributed a score ranging from 80 to 100%. Villages with a score of 90 to 99% are classified as Premier Cru, and villages with the top score of 100% as Grand Cru. There are as it stands 42 Premier Cru and 17 Grand Cru villages, altogether accounting for just over 30% of the entire demarcated area. Little-known fact: in 2004, the Premier and Grand Cru designations stopped being official and are now merely 'traditional'.

Most of the Cru villages are in just two of the five regional areas or districts, the **Montagne de Reims** to the north of Epernay and the Côte des Blancs to the south. The Montagne de Reims is a forested peak that is mostly given to **Pinot Noir**, which contributes structure and depth of fruit to a blend. The **Côte des Blancs** is an east-facing slope that is mostly given to **Chardonnay**, which contributes fresh-ness and fine fruitiness to a blend. At its heart are the villages of Cramant, Avize, Oger, and Le Mesnil. Compared to Pinot Noir, Chardonnay has the greater ageing potential. Some of the grandest champagnes such as Taittinger's Comtes de Champagne and Ruinart's Dom Ruinart are 100% Chardonnay, so-called *blanc de blancs*. In contrast, almost no one deliberately sets out to make a *blanc de noirs*, that is, a 100% blend of black grapes (Pinot Noir and/or Pinot Meunier).

The Montagne de Reims and the Côte des Blancs are almost contiguous with the **Vallée de la Marne**, which runs west past Hautvillers and then for some 40–50km to a bit beyond Château-Thierry. The Vallée de la Marne is particularly prone to spring frosts and is mostly given to **Pinot Meunier**, which buds late. In a blend, Pinot Meunier contributes notes of flowers and bruised apples, and an early-maturing richness and fruitiness that make for immediate appeal. All the Cru villages in the Vallée de la Marne are concentrated at its chalky, eastern end, nearer to Epernay.

The other two districts, the **Côte de Sézanne** and **Aube** (also known as the Côte des Bar) are effectively detached satellites to the south of the Côte des Blancs. Neither district contains any Grand or Premier Cru villages. Sézanne, which lies north-west of Troyes, is a small area mainly given to Chardonnay. Aube, which lies south-east of Troyes, closer to Chablis than to Reims, and on similar soils of Kimmeridge clay, is, in contrast, mainly given to Pinot Noir. Anecdotally, Aube is also known for its **Rosé de Riceys** (a favourite of Louis XIV) and red Coteaux Champenois.

In all, the Champagne delimited area stands at ~34,300ha spread across ~16,000 growers, 319 villages, and five *départements*. 66% of plantings are in the Marne, and, together, the Marne, Aube, and Aisne account for some 99% of plantings (the other two Champagne *départements* are the Haute-Marne and Seine-et-Marne). Of the three varieties, Pinot Noir is the most commonly planted (38%), although Pinot Meunier (31%) and Chardonnay (31%) are not far behind. For completeness, the other four permitted varieties are Arbane, Petit Meslier, Pinot Blanc, and Pinot Gris.

Plantings are dense at 8,000 vines per hectare. In all Grand Cru and Premier Cru vineyards, pruning must be by the *Taille Chablis* method, favoured for Chardonnay, or the *Cordon de Royat* method, favoured for Pinot Noir. Both methods retain substantial permanent wood, which helps the vine to resist frost. The other pruning method used for Chardonnay and Pinot Noir is the Guyot method. As for Pinot Meunier, it is typically pruned by the *Vallée de la Marne* method, which is similar to Guyot. The harvest base yield is 10,400kg/ha, revisable upwards or downwards depending on vintage conditions, but capped at 15,500kg/ha.

Production

Like many sparkling wines, champagne is produced by the traditional, or classic, method, with a second fermentation in the very bottle in which the wine is to be sold. Champagne grapes require both high acidity and phenolic ripeness, a combination that is much easier to achieve in cool climate Champagne. To preserve acidity, grapes are harvested early at a low must weight. This comes at the expense of sugar content, which is adjusted by the subsequent addition of sugar in the form of *liqueur de tirage* and *liqueur de dosage* (see later), and also, in some cases, by initial chaptalization. In black grapes, it also comes at the expense of colour, which for champagne is of course a benefit.

Harvesting whole bunches by hand minimizes damage to the grapes and, in the press, ensures that the juice can run off quickly along the stalks. The grapes are pressed without delay, traditionally in a Coquard [basket] press although other types of press, notably the Vaslin press and more delicate Wilmes press, are also used. Gentle pressure is applied to minimize the extraction of undesirable colour and tannin. Extraction is limited to a maximum of 102l of must per 160kg of grapes. The first 2l to emerge are discarded, the next 80l are the *cuvée*, and the remaining 20l are the *taille*, which may or may not be included. Anything beyond 102l is the *vin de rebèche*, which cannot be used for champagne. After pressing, the must is clarified, with some solids retained to facilitate the second fermentation. At this stage, the must might also be chaptalized.

Next, the must is fermented into a still wine, normally in stainless steel vats although some houses such as Bollinger and Krug prefer old oak casks. The temperature of the fermentation typically ranges from 18 to 22°C. Too cool a temperature encourages the formation of amylic aromas, which may mask some of the more subtle notes of the finished champagne. Many houses encourage malolactic conversion although some houses such as Lanson and Gosset prefer to forgo it.

Grapes from different plots and parcels are vinified separately. In the spring following the harvest, these *vins clairs* [base wines] are blended along with varying proportions of reserve wine from past vintages. This process of blending, or **assemblage**, aims at balance and complexity, and also at creating a consistent house style. As so much depends on the condition of the vintage, there can be no fixed recipe for the house style, and every release is the product of the skill and judgement of a master blender.

The blended still wine, though full of promise, is not especially pleasant to drink. It is bottled together with the **liqueur de tirage**, a mixture of wine, sugar, and yeast which induces a second, slower fermentation, or *prise de mousse*, in the bottle. This brings alcohol up to around 12% and yields enough carbon dioxide for a bottle pressure of 5–6 atmospheres—equivalent to 5–6 times atmospheric pressure at sea level, or the pressure in a tyre of a double-decker bus!

The bottles are sealed with a crown cap and laid *sur lattes* [horizontally] in a cool cellar. The *prise de mousse* takes place over perhaps four-to-eight weeks after which the wine is left to mature, in some cases for several years, on its lees. During this period of **lees ageing**, the gradual breakdown of yeast cells releases mannoproteins, polysaccharides, and antioxidative enzymes into the wine. This-so-called yeast autolysis results in (1) a fuller body with a more unctuous mouthfeel, (2) reduced bitterness and astringency, (3) complex aromas of biscuit, bread dough, nuts, and acacia, and (4) an enhanced ageing potential. By law, non-vintage wines must sit on the lees for at least 15 months and vintage wines for at least 36 months, although many producers exceed these minima.

Compared to blending and lees ageing, the remaining steps add little to quality. The bottles are agitated to loosen and consolidate the sediment, a process called *poignettage* ['shaking by wrist']. The yeast deposit is then progressively migrated into the neck of the bottle. Traditionally, this process of *remuage*, or **riddling**, is carried out over 8–10 weeks on a *pupitre*, a wooden frame with sixty apertures bored at an angle of 45° on which bottles can be manually turned from horizontal to vertical— each day by a fraction of a turn. Nowadays, riddling is likely to be carried out on a much larger scale and in a much shorter time by a mechanized gyropalette. With riddling complete, the bottles are left in their vertical, upside-down position [*sur pointes*] for a further period of maturation.

Next, the lees are removed. This process of **disgorgement** used to be carried out by hand [*à la volée*, 'on the fly']. Today, it is usually carried out by an automated process that involves freezing the material in the neck of the bottle and ejecting this ice plug under the pressure of the wine. The **dosage**, or *liqueur d'expédition*, is then added. The dosage is a mixture of the base wine and varying amounts of sugar that serves to balance acidity and determine the final style of the wine. By far the most common style is brut with added sugar of 6–15g/l. Other regular styles are extra brut with 0–6g/l and demi-sec with 35–50g/l.

A composite or agglomerated cork with whole cork attached to the base is inserted and held in place by a capsule and wire cage [*muselet*]. However, the wine is not yet ready to be drunk, and a further rest period is required for the dosage to integrate into the wine. During this period, a number of chemical reactions between sugar and amino acids give rise to additional aromas of dried fruit, toast, and vanilla. Some authorities argue that *zero dosage* wines—that is, bone dry wines with no added sugar—are unable to benefit from this so-called Maillard reaction.

For the smallest and largest bottle sizes (half- and quarter-bottles and those beyond jeroboam), the wine is disgorged into a pressure tank, the dosage is added to the tank, and the wine is rebottled—a process called *transversage*.

The above method may be somewhat adapted for different styles of champagne. **Vintage champagne** is not made every year but only in very good to exceptional years. The wines that go into the *assemblage* must all come from the same declared vintage, and the minimum lees ageing is 36 months. Compared to non-vintage champagne, vintage champagne is richer and fuller and more apt to improve with bottle age. A producer might also indulge in a *cuvée de prestige*, normally a vintage champagne made from premium grapes and aged for an even longer period. Pink or rosé champagne, which accounts for some 10% of production, is made by adding 5-20% still red wine (often Bouzy) prior to first fermentation, or, less commonly, by bleeding off some of the juice of a red wine in the making after it has had some limited skin contact (the *saignée* method). The colour using the *saignée* method is more variable, but the champagnes, according to some, have a richer, more vinous character. Champagne labelled as 'recently disgorged' or similar has benefited from prolonged yeast ageing and been released immediately after disgorgement. If consumed soon after release, it can taste especially fresh, fruity, and complex. There is also a trend for single village and even single vineyard expressions, although these are fairly hard to find outside of France.

The Champagne industry

The champagne industry is dominated by about one hundred big houses, the so-called *Grandes Marques*, which are all also *négociants-manipulants* (identified as NM on bottle labels), and account for more than two-thirds of sales and 90% of exports. These big houses own only a small fraction (~13%) of the vineyards, and many are heavily reliant on purchased grapes from growers or *récoltants*.

Some growers instead sell their grapes to a *co-opérative de manipulation* (CM) to produce a champagne and market it under the co-operative's brand. *Récoltants-co-opérateurs* (RC) are growers who 'buy back' the finished champagne from their co-operative to sell it under their own label. Other growers, so-called *récoltants-manipulants* (RM), prefer not to sell their grapes, but to produce something of a boutique champagne. They are gaining in numbers and prestige, with wines that are often more terroir-driven than those of the *Grandes Marques*.

Other entities in the champagne industry are *sociétés de récoltants* (SR), growers who group together to produce a champagne outside the co-operative system; and *négociants-distributeurs* (ND), négocians who buy a finished champagne and market it under their own label. A finished champagne that is marketed under the label of a retailer such as a supermarket group is marked on the label as a *marque auxiliaire* (MA).

In 2019, ~297m bottles of champagne were sold, ~215m by champagne houses and ~83m by growers and co-operatives, for a total of ~5.0bn euros. ~156m bottles (~52.4%) were exported, with the largest export markets being the UK (~27.0m), the US (~25.7m), and Japan (~14.3m)—although the US is the most important market by value. The largest player in the champagne industry is Louis Vuitton Moët Hennessy (LVMH), a luxury goods concern that is listed on the Paris stock market and that operates the brands Moët et Chandon, Veuve Cliquot, Dom Pérignon, Ruinart, Krug, and Champagne Mercier (and also owns the likes of Clos des Lambrays, Cheval Blanc, and Yquem). In 2019, LVMH sold ~65m bottles of champagne, with Veuve Cliquot and Moët et Chandon alone accounting for over 40% of champagne exports to the US. Other important players in the champagne industry include Laurent Perrier, Vranken Pommery Monopole, Pernod Ricard (Mumm, Perrier-Jouët), and Lanson BCC.

Some of my favourite champagne houses include Pol Roger, Bollinger, and Taittinger, which all three remain family-run. Some of my favourite growers include Adrien Renoir, Agrapart, Bérèche et Fils, Chartogne-Taillet, Egly-Ouriet, Étienne Calsac, Francis Boulard, Marc Hébrart, M. Hostomme, Jacques Selosse, Larmandier-Bernier, Marguet, Nicholas Maillart, Pierre Bertrand, Pierre Gimmonet, and Ulysse Collin.

Stronger vintages for champagne include 1996, 2002, 2004, 2008, 2009, 2012, 2013, 2019, and 2020. Especially good are 1996, 2002, 2008, 2012, and 2019.

Next time you pour yourself a glass of champagne, remember that it is essentially a faulty wine from an unpromising place, made great by the genius of man.

Other traditional method sparkling wines

Though most closely associated with Champagne, the traditional method is also used in a large number of other regions in Europe and around the world. Indeed, as we shall see, some French regions have been using the traditional method long before the Champenois came round to it.

France: Alsace

The term *crémant* traditionally referred to a sparkling wine with a lower pressure than that of champagne. In 1994, the Champenois secured the exclusive use of the term *méthode champenoise* on condition that they relinquish the term *crémant* to other French regions. Today, the term is no longer tied to the pressure of a wine but to its provenance, and many modern crémants have a pressure similar to that of champagne. If modern crémants differ from champagne, this is principally in terms of varieties, yields, harvesting, pressing, time on lees, and, of course, regional differences in terroir.

Alsace is the most important producer of crémant in France, with ~30m bottles per year in recent years (~10% of the figure for champagne). Permitted varieties for Crémant d'Alsace are Pinot Blanc, Pinot Gris, Pinot Noir, Riesling, Auxerrois, and Chardonnay. Whereas Chardonnay is not permitted in the still wines of Alsace, Gewurztraminer and Muscat are not permitted in the crémant for being so highly aromatic. In practice, Crémant d'Alsace is often dominated by the relatively neutral Pinot Blanc. Maximum yields are high at 80hl/ha, although this figure can be adjusted according to the vintage. Hand harvesting is compulsory, no more than 100l of juice may be extracted from every

150kg of grapes (a slightly higher extraction ratio than for champagne), and the wine must spend at least nine months on lees.

France: Burgundy

Burgundy produces about one-third less crémant than Alsace. Crémant de Bourgogne can be made in all areas of Burgundy except Beaujolais. Important regional centres are Auxerre and Châtillon-sur-Seine in the north, and Rully further south in the Côte Chalonnaise. Crémants from the north are typically tauter and leaner than those from further south. Permitted varieties are Chardonnay, Aligoté, Pinot Noir, Pinot Blanc, Pinot Gris, Gamay, Melon de Bourgogne, and Sacy. In practice, Crémant de Bourgogne is often dominated by Chardonnay and Aligoté. As in Alsace, hand harvesting is compulsory, no more than 100l of juice may be extracted from every 150kg of grapes, and the wine must spend at least nine months on lees. However, yields are capped at a lower 65hl/ha.

France: Loire

In the Loire, crémant production is centred upon the area of Anjou-Saumur although the Crémant de Loire AOP also extends into Touraine. Producers around Saumur can choose to label their crémant as Crémant de Loire AOP or Saumur Mousseux AOP, although the former is more highly regarded owing to tighter production rules. All the varieties permitted in the still wines of the Loire are also permitted in the crémant, with the exception of the highly aromatic Sauvignon Blanc. Better examples often consist of Chardonnay with varying amounts of Chenin Blanc, Cabernet Franc, and Pinot Noir. Maximum yields are slightly higher than in Burgundy and vary according to the vintage. Other regulations are similar to those in Burgundy and Alsace, except that the wine must spend at least 12 months on lees. Production is around ~20m bottles per year. **Saumur Mousseux**, though not called a crémant, is a fully sparkling wine made by the traditional method. It is mostly produced in poor vintages when the grapes are not sufficiently ripe to make still wines. Chenin Blanc is invariably an important constituent, but Chardonnay, Cabernet Franc, Pinot Noir, and even Sauvignon Blanc may be included in the blend. Maximum yields are lower than for Crémant de Loire, but the wine need spend only nine months on lees. The other sparkling wines of the Loire are Touraine Pétillant and Mousseux, and Vouvray Pétillant and Mousseux, which, on the whole, ages better than Crémant de Loire.

France: Limoux

Much further south, the Languedoc is the home of Blanquette de Limoux AOP and Crémant de Limoux AOP. The climate is considerably warmer with a Mediterranean pattern of hot and dry summers. The best vineyards are on the hills, where cooler conditions conserve acidity. **Blanquette de Limoux** is at least 90% Mauzac, which has a distinct bruised apple character, completed by Chardonnay and Chenin Blanc. **Crémant de Limoux**, in contrast, is up to 90% Chardonnay and Chenin Blanc, completed by up to 40% Pinot Noir and Mauzac, with a maximum 20% Mauzac. For both Crémant de Limoux and Blanquette de Limoux, yields are capped at 50hl/ha. As in Burgundy and Alsace, hand harvesting is compulsory, no more than 100l of juice may be extracted from every 150kg of grapes, and the wine must spend at least nine months on lees. The other Limoux sparkling wine AOP is Limoux Méthode Ancestrale, which is pure Mauzac.

Spain: Cava

Cava (from the *cavas*, or cellars, in which the wine is matured) is the second most important sparkling wine in the world after Champagne, with, in 2021, ~252m bottles produced. ~70% of the production is exported, mostly to five countries: Germany, the US, Belgium, the UK, and Japan. There are ~200 producers (excluding producers of base wines), and the two largest, Cordoníu and Freixenet, account for the bulk of production. Both operate from Sant Sadurni d'Anoia in Penedès, Catalunya.

The *Denominación*, which dates back to Spain's 1986 entry into the EU, includes demarcated areas in several disparate Spanish regions including Catalunya, Aragon, Navarra, Rioja, País Vasco, Valencia, and Extremadura—although the Comtats de Barcelona in Catalunya accounts for more than 95% of production. The best vineyards tend, as in Limoux, to be at relatively high altitudes of up to 800m. Although the total area under vine (~38,000ha) is similar to that of Champagne, production is lower because the vines are bush-trained and more sparsely planted. Yields are now capped at 10,000kg/ha, and only the first pressing, or *cuvée*, can go into making Cava—further reducing effective yields. Minimum lees ageing is nine months rising to 18 months for Reserva, 30 months for Gran Reserva, and 36 months for the single vineyard Paraja Calificado. Alcohol in the base wines must range from 9.5 to 11.5% and pressure must be at least 4atm (although is usually far higher). Today, much of the production is brut, although the historic semiseco style is still holding out. Sweetness levels in ascending order are: brut nature, extra brut, brut, extra seco, seco, semi seco, and dulce. As in Champagne, rosado production stands at ~10%.

The most obvious difference between Cava and Champagne is in grape varieties. For Cava, these are mostly Macabeo [Viura], Xarel-lo, and Parellada. Macabeo lends a delicate aroma, Xarel-lo body and earthy notes (which are absent from Champagne), and Parellada acidity and subtle florality. Chardonnay is increasingly important, especially in top wines in which it might constitute the majority component. For rosado, the traditional black grapes Garnatxa [Grenache] and Trepat are favoured, as is the less traditional Pinot Noir. Other permitted grape varieties are Monastrell [Mourvèdre] and Subirat Parent [Malvasia] for the sweeter styles. Unlike in Champagne, it is uncommon for black grapes to be used in the production of white wines.

In 2019, nine leading producers left the *Denominación*, blowing a big hole in the top Paraja Calificado segment, and now label their wine as Corpinnat [a contraction of the Latin for 'From the heart of the Penedès']. The Cava regulatory body swiftly responded by tightening regulations, with, among others, a new emphasis on zoning and organic farming.

Italy: Franciacorta

Italy's best-known sparkling wines, Prosecco and Asti, are not made by the traditional method, and Franciacorta DOCG, Trento DOC, Oltrepo Pavese Metodo Classico DOCG, and Alta Langa DOCG are the only

Denominazioni that specifically call for it. Franciacorta ['Court of the Franks'], which originated in 1961, is produced from ~3,000ha of vines on undulating moraine hills just south of Lake Iseo in Lombardy. The climate is continental but the lake exercises a subtle moderating effect. Permitted varieties are Chardonnay, which accounts for three-quarters of plantings, Pinot Noir, Pinot Blanc, and the indigenous Erbamat which is being revived. The vines are densely planted and 'big vine' training systems such as pergola are forbidden. Winemaking is similar to champagne. Franciacorta must spend at least 18 months on the lees, rising to 24 months for rosé and blanc de blancs (Satèn), 30 months for vintage *Millesimato*, and 60 months for *Riserva*. The rosé must include 25% Pinot Noir, and, as in Champagne, may be made by blending with still red wine. Total annual production of Franciacorta is ~20m bottles. Little leaves Italy.

Other traditional method sparkling wines in continental Europe

Other notable traditional method sparkling wines in continental Europe are Crémant de Bordeaux AOP, Crémant de Jura AOP, Crémant de Savoie AOP, and Crémant de Die AOP (Southern Rhône). Crémant de Die, mostly made from Clairette, is not to be confused with Clairette de Die Tradition AOP, mostly made from Muscat of Alexandria by the *méthode dioise*. The must is fermented to around 3% alcohol, cooled, and bottled, and then re-ferments in bottle to around 7–8% alcohol. After four months lees ageing, the wine is disgorged by the transfer method. Clairette de Die is in many ways similar to Asti.

Traditional method sparkling wines can also be found in other parts of continental Europe (for example, some top quality Lambrusco or German Sekt), but these regions do not enshrine the traditional method in their regulations.

England

High quality sparkling wines are being made in England using grape varieties and methods of production similar or identical to those in Champagne. The climate, though generally cool and wet, is moderated by the Gulf Stream and gradually warming. The total area under vine stood at 3,800ha in 2020, up from 1,438ha in 2012. Most of the vineyards are in the southern counties of Surrey, Sussex, and Kent, on chalky subsoils that form part of the same shelf that runs through Champagne. The principal varieties are Chardonnay, Pinot Noir, and Pinot Meunier. In 2020, 7.1m bottles of English wine were sold, with direct-to-consumer channels accounting for about half of sales. Still wines are increasingly common and appealing: in 2020, they accounted for 36% of production. English sparkling wines can be difficult to tell apart from Champagne, but tend to be drier and higher in acidity. Top producers include Balfour, Nyetimber, Camel Valley, Chapel Down, Coates and Seely, Denbies, Digby, Hambledon, Hattingley Valley, Ridgeview Estate, and Wiston. In April 2018, Vranken-Pommery became the first of the big Champagne houses to release an English sparkling wine. There is significant vintage variation: 2012 was execrable; 2018 remarkable, and 2020 not too far behind. Very little English sparkling wine is exported, so that it makes an excellent gift from people, like myself, travelling from England.

USA: *California*

Quality bottle-fermented sparkling wines from the New World are often made by a variant of the traditional method called the transfer method. The transfer method is identical to the traditional method up to the riddling stage. Instead of being riddled, the wine is disgorged into a pressurized tank, the lees are filtered out, and a dosage is added. The wine is then rebottled under pressure, circumventing the trouble and expense of the riddling process. Many New World bottle-fermented sparkling wines are Champagne clones made from Chardonnay and Pinot Noir. Unfortunately, many of these clones struggle to achieve the same balance of high acidity and phenolic ripeness as Champagne. Beyond this, there are some idiosyncratic styles such as sparkling Shiraz or Zinfandel.

The largest producers of New World sparkling wine are the USA and Australia. Most US sparkling wine comes from California, which in the past forty years has benefited from considerable investment from a number of larger Champagne and Cava houses. Notable regions include the Anderson Valley in Mendocino County; Carneros at the southern end of Sonoma and Napa; Sonoma itself, especially the Green and Russian River Valleys; and certain more maritime sites in the Central Coast. Despite the cooling influence of the ocean, conditions are not as propitious as in Champagne, with winemakers caught between an early harvest that preserves acidity but risks underripe 'green' aromas, and a later harvest of riper fruit that risks a flabby and overly alcoholic wine. On the other hand, the weather is much more reliable, enabling a vintage wine to be produced nearly every year. The principal varieties are Chardonnay and Pinot Noir; other varieties include Pinot Meunier, Pinot Blanc, and Pinot Gris. Sparkling Zinfandel is an off-dry rosé with a distinct note of 'strawberries and cream'. It is most commonly made by the tank method (see later).

Australia

Like California, Australia has received significant investment from Champagne houses. The principal varieties are Chardonnay and Pinot Noir, and the most notable regions are the Yarra Valley and Tasmania. Tasmanian production remains tiny, but there has been a lot of interest in this coolest of Australian regions, in particular, the subregions of Tamar Valley and Piper's River. Other notable regions include Macedon Ranges, Grampians, Adelaide Hills, Hunter Valley, and Tumbarumba. Australia's equivalent of California's Central Valley is the Big Rivers zone, which is the source of vast quantities of basic bubbly. With much more reliable weather than Champagne, the blending focus in Australia is a lot more horizontal (across vineyards and sub-regions, and even across regions) than vertical (across vintages). Sparkling Shiraz is a unique piece of Australiana with roots in nineteenth century Victoria. The best examples of this deep red, semi-sweet wine are made by the traditional method, mostly from Shiraz but also from Merlot or Carbernet Sauvignon. They are high in alcohol (14%) and tannins, and may have spent time in oak prior to the second fermentation. Sparkling Shiraz is, I am told, the ideal accompaniment to a barbecued Sunday brunch.

New Zealand

In New Zealand, traditional method sparkling wine production is concentrated in Marlborough and carried out on a very small scale. The important exception is Montana, which produces most of New Zealand's sparkling wine. Montana's top *cuvée*, Lindauer Grandeur, is traditional method, as is the Deutz Marlborough Cuvée and the Cloudy Bay Pelorus. Other notable regions are Central Otago, Gisborne, and Hawke's Bay.

South America

South America has received investment from some bigger Champagne and Cava houses. Most of the production, which remains small, is consumed within South America itself. Argentina is currently the biggest producer of sparkling wine in South America, with Mendoza accounting for the bulk of Argentine output. Sites with great potential such as the Limarí Valley in Chile and Rio Grande del Sul in Brazil are yet to be fully exploited.

South Africa

Simonsig released the first South African traditional method sparkling wine in 1971. Production of traditional method sparkling wine ('Méthode Cap Classique', or MCC), mostly from Chardonnay and Pinot Noir, remains on a small scale. Top producers include Simonsig, Boschendal, Graham Beck, JC le Roux, Pongrácz, Villera, Haute Cabrière, The House of Krone, and Colmant.

Other sparkling wines

Italy: Prosecco

The autolytic character and long ageing associated with the traditional method is well suited to Chardonnay and Pinot Noir, but not, for instance, to the Prosecco grape Glera. The other major method of making sparkling wine is the **tank method** [*cuve close*, Charmat], used, among others, for Prosecco, most Lambrusco, and most Sekt. Sugar and yeast are added to the base wine in a large pressurized tank, which may be fitted with rousing paddles to increase yeast contact. Once the second fermentation is complete, the wine is cooled, clarified by centrifugation and filtration, and enriched with a dosage. The tank method is cheap and consistent, and preserves freshness and varietal character. On the other hand, it requires a large upfront investment and a skilled operator to prevent any loss of pressure—and, of course, lacks the traditional method's character and cachet.

The extensive Prosecco DOC, established in 2009, covers over 30,000ha in Veneto and Friuli-Venezia Giulia, where the cool continental climate is ideally suited to the late-ripening Glera grape. Glera may be completed by up to 15% of Glera Lunga, Verdiso, Perera, Bianchetta Trevigiana, Chardonnay, Pinot Blanc, Pinot Gris, and Pinot Noir. The appellations are like Russian dolls. Nested within Prosecco DOC are the Treviso and Trieste *menzioni speciali*, and nested within the Treviso special mention are the Conegliano and Valdobbiadene DOCG and the Asolo DOCG. Nested within Conegliano and Valdobbiadene DOCG are the Conegliano Valdobbiadene Prosecco Superiore Rive DOCG (from one of 43 specific communes or vineyard areas) and the Valdobbiadene Superiore di Cartizze DOCG (from the 107ha hill of Cartizze). Those DOCG wines that are re-fermented in bottle, with the sediment remaining in the bottle [*col fondo*], are labelled as *Sui Leviti* [On the Lees].

The bulk of Prosecco production is *spumante* [fully sparkling] and the rest is *frizzante* [lightly sparkling] or still. Prosecco DOC stipulates six levels of sweetness, although the drier styles predominate, especially on the export market. Since 2020, Prosecco DOC (but not yet the DOCGs) allows for a dry rosé *spumante* to be made from Glera completed by 10-15% Pinot Noir. In 2021, production of Prosecco DOC for the first time surpassed 600m bottles, including ~70m bottles of the new rosé. The US and the UK accounted for over half of exports by value.

Prosecco ought to be drunk young. It is light, fresh, and aromatic with alcohol of ~11% and a signature slightly bitter finish. It is the main ingredient of the Bellini cocktail, the other ingredient being puréed white peaches.

Italy: Asti

Once upon a time, Prosecco was almost indistinguishable from Asti. Asti DOCG (formerly Asti Spumante) is made from Muscat Blanc à Petits Grains in south-eastern Piedmont, just south of Asti. The method of vinification is the **Asti method**, or single tank fermentation. The must is transferred into large tanks and chilled to almost 0°C to inhibit fermentation—effectively enabling Asti to be made on demand. The tanks are sealed and pressurized and the temperature is raised to 16–18°C for a single fermentation to 7–7.5% alcohol and ~5atm. The wine is then cooled to 0°C to arrest fermentation and membrane filtered to remove the yeasts and yeast nutrients. Asti is fresh and intensely fruity and floral with dominant aromas of peach and musk and enough acidity to balance the 3–5% residual sugar. It should not be confused with **Moscato d'Asti DOCG**, which is made from the same grape in the same production zone, but is *frizzante*, sweeter, and even lower in alcohol.

Italy: Lambrusco

Lambrusco today is mostly a red (bright purple) *frizzante*. The major component is the eponymous Lambrusco, a black variety that has been cultivated since Etruscan times and that encompasses a ragbag of genetically unrelated varieties. In the 1970s and 80s, when the pink and white styles were more common, it was the biggest import wine in the US. Lambrusco is made in four areas of Emilia-Romagna and one area of Lombardy. The climate is Mediterranean, the soils are fertile, and the yields are often too high. Most Lambrusco is made in co-operatives by the tank method and is bottled as IGT Emilia. Of the Lambrusco DOCs, **Lambrusco di Sorbara** around Modena is the most highly regarded, with the finest examples made by the traditional method. Lambrusco is dry or off-dry, with high acidity and a dominant note of sour cherries.

Germany: Sekt

Most Sekt is made from inexpensive base wine sourced from outside Germany—mainly Italy, France, and Spain. The remainder is Deutscher Sekt (Sekt made only from German grapes) and Sekt b.A.

(Sekt made only from grapes from one of the 13 German quality wine regions). Sekt is generally made by the tank method and sold under the label of a large and inexpensive brand. A small amount is made by the traditional method, mostly from Riesling, Chardonnay, or one of the Pinot varieties. Premium Sekt, or **Winzersekt** ['Winegrower's Sekt'], is usually made by a grower from his or her own vineyards, and bears the vineyard and vintage on the label. Sekt is big business in Germany, where annual per capita consumption of sparkling wine is still 3.2l.

Printed in Great Britain
by Amazon

85996118R00144